Wall~papers of France
1800~1850

Odile Nouvel

Wall~papers of France
1800~1850

A Contribution to the Study
of the Decorative Arts

with an Introduction
by Jean-Pierre Seguin

translated by Margaret Timmers

A. Zwemmer Ltd.

The exhibition 'Three Centuries of Wall-papers' was organized at the Musée des Arts Décoratifs, Paris, in 1967 by Yolande Amic, curator at the museum, with the valuable collaboration of Jean-Pierre Seguin, head curator of the Cabinet des Estampes at the Bibliothèque Nationale, Paris, and with the help of Yvonne Brunhammer and Françoise Guerin, also curators at the Musée des Arts Décoratifs. On that occasion, the history of French wall-paper was reconsidered in its entirety, and it is on the basis of that work that it has been possible to assemble this book.

First published in Great Britain 1981
by A. Zwemmer Ltd,
26 Litchfield Street, London WC 2

ISBN 0-302-00547-1

Copyright © 1981 Office du Livre
English translation copyright © 1981
Office du Livre
German translation by
Christine Schaer-Leuthardt

Printed and bound in West Germany

Table de matières

Table of contents

Inhaltsverzeichnis

Avant-propos

Cet ouvrage présente une sorte d'abrégé de la grammaire décorative du papier peint entre 1800 et 1850.

Le parti retenu est une sélection de 600 documents les plus représentatifs de l'évolution d'une technique spécifique, à partir des collections publiques françaises: le Musée des Arts Décoratifs à Paris, le Musée de l'Impression sur Etoffes de Mulhouse, et la Bibliothèque Forney à Paris. Seule la collection du Musée de l'Impression sur Etoffes est constituée d'un ensemble homogène: pour cette période, ses documents proviennent tous de la Manufacture Zuber; dans la mesure où celle-ci a conservé la quasi-totalité de ses archives, les échantillons qui en proviennent peuvent être datés avec précision et sont des points de repère essentiels. Les collections publiques sont d'origines diverses: dons, notamment de fabricants ou de dessinateurs, ou achats. Ces échantillons gardent souvent le secret le plus total sur les dessinateurs qui les ont conçus ou les manufactures qui les ont produits. De plus, ces collections publiques, conservées en des lieux prestigieux, ne font état que des modèles jugés les plus séduisants, les plus parfaits; tous les petits papiers, modestes, les dessinateurs anonymes, les manufactures éphémères furent vraisemblablement plus nombreux que les lauréats des Expositions, et contribuèrent pour une part non négligeable à diffuser les styles et procédés techniques successifs lancés par les ténors. (C'est pour cette raison que seuls 11 bois, marbres, caissons, cannages, balustrades et corniches ont pu être présentés ici.) Or, nous n'en avons pas trace. Ce mystère explique les incertitudes d'attribution et de datations auxquelles se heurte le chercheur pour la majorité des documents du XIXe siècle. Cette lacune est d'autant plus lourde de conséquences, que le papier peint a toujours été considéré par les érudits comme un domaine d'imitation, une sous-catégorie des arts dits «mineurs».

Odile Nouvel
Conservateur
au Musée des Arts Décoratifs, Paris

Preface

This work attempts to summarize the decorative elements found in wall-paper between 1800 and 1850. The choice made is a selection of 600 examples taken from French public collections – the Musée des Arts Décoratifs in Paris, the Musée de l'Impression sur Etoffes in Mulhouse, and the Bibliothèque Forney in Paris – that best represent the evolution of specific techniques. Only the Musée de l'Impression sur Etoffes has a collection made up of a homogeneous group: for this period, all its documents come from the Zuber Factory. Since the latter has preserved its archives almost intact, the samples from it can be dated precisely and are essential points of reference. The French public collections have been assembled from various sources: gifts, particularly from manufacturers or designers, or purchases. These samples often reveal absolutely nothing about the designers who conceived them or the manufacturers who produced them. Furthermore, the public collections in famous museums only take account of those specimens judged to be the most fascinating or the most perfect. All the little, modest wall-papers, produced by ephemeral factories, were probably more numerous than these acclaimed exhibits and contributed in no small way to the spreading of styles and successive technical processes pioneered by the show-pieces. That is why only eleven examples of wood, marbling, coffering, canework, balustrade and cornice patterns could be shown here. Of others we now have no trace. This explains the uncertainties of attribution and dating that confront researchers into most of the documents of the nineteenth century. The consequences of these missing links are as grave as the fact that wall-paper has always been considered by the erudite as one of the imitative arts, a sub-category called 'minor'.

Odile Nouvel
Curator,
Musée des Arts Décoratifs, Paris

Vorwort

Dieses Werk möchte eine Art Abriß über die Entwicklung der Dekorformen bei den Papiertapeten der Zeit zwischen 1800 und 1850 geben.

Dazu haben verschiedene französische öffentliche Sammlungen eine Auswahl von 600 der für die Entwicklung und den Wandel einer ganz spezifischen Technik repräsentativsten Dokumente zur Verfügung gestellt: das Musée des Arts Décoratifs in Paris, das Musée de l'Impression sur Etoffes (Museum für Stoffdruckkunst) in Mülhausen und die Bibliothèque Forney in Paris. Nur die Sammlung aus dem Museum für Stoffdruckkunst ist einheitlich: Die Muster aus der genannten Epoche stammen alle aus der Zuberschen Manufaktur; da fast alle ihre Archive erhalten geblieben sind, können die daraus stammenden Dokumente exakt datiert werden und erlauben die Datierung anderer Stücke unbekannter Entstehungszeit. Die öffentlichen Sammlungen haben verschiedene Provenienzen: Gaben, vor allem von Fabrikanten und Entwerfern, und Käufe. Die Dokumente schweigen sich oft über ihre Entwerfer und Manufakturen aus. Außerdem sind diese Sammlungen an sehr berühmten Orten ausgestellt und zeigen nur die schönsten und vollkommensten Stücke. Alle unscheinbaren Tapeten, die anonymen Entwerfer und die vergessenen Manufakturen waren jedoch viel größer an Zahl als die Preisgekrönten der Ausstellungen und halfen in großem Umfang mit, die von den Berühmten lancierten Moden und technischen Neuerungen zu verbreiten. (Deshalb können an dieser Stelle auch nur elf Imitationen von Holz, Marmor, Kassetten, Flechtwerk, Balustraden und Simsen gezeigt werden.) Da wir nichts von diesen »Kleinen« wissen, versteht man die Schwierigkeit, Zeugen des 19. Jahrhunderts zu datieren und jemandem zuzuschreiben. Dieser Mangel ist um so schwerwiegender, als die Papiertapeten von der Wissenschaft immer als Imitation abgetan und in eine Unterkategorie der »minderen« Künste abgedrängt wurden.

Odile Nouvel
Conservateur
am Musée des Arts Décoratifs, Paris

Introduction

par Jean-Pierre Seguin

Inspecteur Général des Bibliothèques

Au moment où va commencer l'ère industrielle, le papier peint atteint à un degré de perfection qui ne sera jamais surpassé. Sur des feuilles d'une qualité extraordinaire, s'impriment des parfaites imitations d'étoffes et des décors souvent dûs à d'excellents artistes, auxquels les couleurs à la détrempe ou des hachures d'étoffes confèrent relief et chatoiement dans la lumière. De surcroît, toutes ces tentures, y compris celles fabriquées à bas prix pour les pièces non nobles et les intérieurs de placards, sont d'une solidité remarquable. Lorsque se produisent ces chefs d'œuvre, tous les éléments de leur confection: papier, colorants, hachures d'étoffes, bois et procédés d'impression font appel seulement à la main de l'homme.

Cependant, dans la seconde moitié du XVIIIe siècle, dans le temps où l'on voit ce merveilleux aboutissement de tâtonnements qui ont duré pendant plusieurs siècles, se poursuit aussi une double gestation infiniment plus rapide, qui bientôt va tout changer. La «mécanique», qui commence à intervenir dans l'impression des étoffes, va bientôt servir aussi à la fabrication en continu et en grandes quantités des papiers de tenture, et Réveillon, en rompant délibérément avec la tradition des petits ateliers artisanaux, monte une manufacture où l'organisation de la production est poussée au point d'être prête à répondre aux exigences de l'industrie.

On comprendrait mal ce que la période qui va de 1800 à 1850 va apporter de nouveau á l'histoire du papier peint si l'on ignorait ce que celle-ci fut auparavant et à quels problèmes, aujourd'hui non perçus, furent confrontés ses promoteurs.

Le papier peint avant le XIXe siècle

Dans le dernier tiers du XIVe siècle, la technique de la gravure sur bois, déjà employée antérieurement pour la décoration d'etoffes, sert aussi à des impressions sur papier. A la fin du XVe siècle, en Allemagne, on sait également utiliser celle qui consiste à saupoudrer de hachures de laines des feuilles préalablement imprimées avec des mordants propres à fixer ces étoffes. Comme l'on savait d'autre part contrecoller ces feuilles de manière à obtenir des surfaces relativement importantes, il n'est pas impossible que dès cette époque des bois comme celui connu sous le nom de «bois Protat» (vers 1380, 60 × 23 cm) aient servi à fabriquer des sortes de tentures analogues aux tapisseries ou aux cuirs ornés qui servaient par exemple à garnir les devants d'autel.

Cependant, il fut longtemps encore tout à fait impossible de se servir de papiers imprimés ou peints pour revêtir des murs, car l'imperfection et la fragilité de ces papiers et l'état des revêtements muraux, leur humidité,

Introduction

by Jean-Pierre Seguin

Inspector-general for the French Libraries

Just as the industrial era was about to begin, wall-papers achieved a degree of perfection which was never surpassed. Perfect imitations of fabrics and patterns that were often the work of excellent artists were printed on papers of outstanding quality, to which distemper colours or the application of powdered textiles gave effects of relief and sheen in the light. In addition, all these wall-papers, including those made cheaply for non-stately rooms and for the interiors of wall-cupboards, had a remarkable solidity. When these works of art were being produced, all the elements in their make-up – paper, colourings, powdered textiles, wood and means of printing – required only the hand of man to form them.

However, during the second half of the eighteenth century, the period which saw the marvellous culmination of experiments that had been under way for several centuries, an infinitely swifter process of production was beginning, one that was soon to change everything. The 'machine', which began to intervene in the printing of textiles, was soon to be used for the continuous large-scale production of wall-paper, and the firm of Réveillon, deliberately breaking with the tradition of small workshops of craftsmen, set up a factory geared to meet the demands of industry.

It is hard to understand the new developments that came about in the history of wallpaper from 1800 to 1850 if one is ignorant of what preceded them and of the problems, not appreciated to-day, which faced their promoters.

Wall-papers before the Nineteenth Century

In the last third of the fourteenth century, the technique of wood-engraving, already used previously for the decoration of textiles, was also employed for printing on paper. By the end of the fifteenth century in Germany, the process of dusting chopped wool onto sheets of paper previously impressed with adhesives that would fix the material was also known. As the technique of joining these papers together so as to build up fairly large surfaces was known too, it is not impossible that from this time onwards wood-blocks, such as those termed *bois Protat* (about 1380, 60 × 23 cm), were employed to print kinds of wall-paper similar to the tapestries or decorated leather used to adorn altar-fronts, for example.

However, for a long time it remained quite impossible to use printed or painted papers to cover walls, because of the imperfection and fragility of the papers, the state of the wall-facings, their dampness, and the presence of insects and rodents, all of which militated com-

Einleitung

von Jean-Pierre Seguin

Inspecteur Général der Bibliotheken

Kurz vor Beginn des Industriezeitalters hat das als Tapeten verwendete Buntpapier einen Grad der Vollkommenheit erreicht, der seither nicht mehr übertroffen worden ist. Auf Papier von hervorragender Qualität werden perfekte Stoffimitationen aufgedruckt und Dekors, die oft namhaften Künstlern zu verdanken sind. Tiefenwirkung und Glanzlichter werden durch Leimfarben und Wollstaub erzielt. Überdies sind diese, wie auch die im billigeren Verfahren hergestellten und für weniger vornehme Räume und zur Auskleidung von Schränken bestimmten Tapeten von bemerkenswerter Solidität. Die Fertigung dieser Kunstwerke geschieht ausschließlich in Handarbeit, wozu auch das Herstellen des Papiers, der Farben, des Wollstaubes, der Druckplatten und natürlich der Druck selbst gehören.

Doch während der zweiten Hälfte des 18. Jahrhunderts, als das jahrhundertelange beharrliche Suchen zum Ziele führt, bereiten sich sehr rasch zwei verschiedene Entwicklungen vor, die der bisherigen Tradition große Veränderungen bringen werden. Zum einen wird die Mechanisierung, die beim Stoffdruck immer mehr Einzug hält, nun auch bei der serienmäßigen Herstellung großer Mengen von Papiertapeten benutzt werden; zum andern hat Réveillon mit der Tradition der kleinen Handwerksbuden gebrochen, indem er eine allen Erfordernissen der Industrie genügende Manufaktur gründete.

Wüßte man nicht, mit welchen heute vergessenen Problemen die früheren Förderer der Tapeten zu kämpfen hatten, so könnte man nur schwer die Bedeutung der Zeitspanne von 1800 bis 1850 ermessen, die sie in der Geschichte der Buntpapiere einnimmt.

Papiertapeten der Zeit vor dem 19. Jahrhundert

Schon im letzten Drittel des 14. Jahrhunderts wird Papier mit Holzschnittplatten bedruckt, im gleichen Verfahren, das man schon früher für Stoffe angewandt hatte. In Deutschland werden zu Ende des 15. Jahrhunderts auch Papiere, die vorher mit einem speziellen Bindemittel bedruckt worden sind, mit Wollstaub bestreut. Da man diese Papierbogen zu relativ großen Flächen zusammenzusetzen wußte, ist es möglich, daß schon seit dieser Zeit Druckplatten in der Art des »Bois Protat« (um 1380, 60 × 23 cm) zur Herstellung einer Art Tapeten verwendet wurden, die den zum Beispiel als Antependien dienenden Tapisserien und geprägten Ledertapeten ähnlich waren.

Doch war es lange Zeit absolut unmöglich, diese bedruckten oder gemalten Buntpapiere als Mauerverkleidung zu gebrauchen, da sie einerseits noch sehr unvollkommen und wenig reißfest waren und andererseits die Mauern ihrer Rauhheit und Feuchtigkeit wegen nicht verkleidet werden konnten; außer-

la présence d'insectes et de rongeurs s'y opposaient absolument. Enfin, on n'avait pas encore mis au point le procédé permettant de raccorder entre eux les dessins de manière à constituer des décors pouvant couvrir une surface de haut en bas.

Cette continuité des dessins apparaît dès le XVIe siècle et d'abord grâce aux «dominos» produits par les imagiers et les cartiers: feuilles ornées alors le plus souvent de petits motifs répétitifs imprimés en noir et coloriés au pochoir. Accolées, ces feuilles, pouvaient servir à garnir et à décorer des petites surfaces moins exposées que les murs, comme des intérieurs de meubles.

A la même époque, en Europe et en Angleterre, d'autres impressions reproduisant de grands motifs servent au même usage. Un exemple en est donné par des bandes de tapisserie de papier décoré de dessins répétés qui ornent les poutres d'un plafond du Christ's College à Cambridge, élevé en 1509. Les feuilles accolées qui forment cette frise comportent des motifs sur le verso blanc de feuillets d'un livre imprimé par Hugh Goes, qui s'était établi à York la même année.

Il a fallu attendre la seconde moitié du XVIIe siècle pour que les progrès conjugués de l'impression et du raccordement des motifs permettent de passer d'usages partiels, qui pratiquement n'étaient jamais tentés sur des murs, à la réalisation de véritables décors d'intérieurs; les essais poursuivis parallèlement pour le perfectionnement des papiers à hachures d'étoffes, dit «tontisses» n'y réussirent pas non plus avant cette époque. Certes, dès après 1560 environ, des Anglais et des Hollandais parviennent à produire des décors réalisés de cette manière qui, parfois posés sur les murs, donnent l'illusion de matériaux plus «riches». Vers 1620, en France, le Rouennais le François sait imiter sur toile et sur papier les «tapisseries en paysage et en histoire»; on n'a pas retrouvé de témoignages de son ingéniosité, mais les spécimens connus de ses émules français ou étrangers sont loin d'atteindre à la qualité technique et à l'éclat qui eussent déterminé les amateurs éventuels, forcément fortunés, à abandonner à leur profit des matériaux plus éprouvés: bois, cuir ou étoffes véritables.

La situation commence à évoluer rapidement à partir du dernier tiers du XVIIe siècle, grâce au développement des techniques dans les divers domaines concernés, grâce aussi à l'ingéniosité d'artistes-artisans tels que Jean-Michel Papillon à Paris. Graveur en bois formé dans l'atelier de son père et dessinateur, celui-ci sait tirer le meilleur parti des progrès de la dominoterie et des «tontisses», comme de la révélation des tentures en papier importées d'Extrême-Orient. En outre, il se passionne pour la gravure en camaïeu ou «clair obscur», qui permet de se servir de bois gravés pour imprimer les couleurs, et de remplacer ainsi le pochoir traditionnel. Papillon n'est pas un inventeur à proprement parler, et c'est indûment qu'il s'attribue par exemple la «découverte» du dessin à raccords, mais il sait le parfaire. En outre, il est l'un des premiers à comprendre que la fortune du papier peint dépend aussi, et d'une manière contraignante, des techniques de la pose et du collage. Il apprend en procédant lui-même à ce travail, à user, comme surfaces adhérentes, de toiles tendues par des châssis qui évitent les irrégularités des surfaces et protègent de l'humidité des murs.

pletely against wall-papers. Finally, the process of joining together patterns to cover a surface from top to bottom had not yet been perfected.

This continuity of designs appeared from the sixteenth century onwards, at first thanks to the 'dominotier' papers made by the makers of popular prints and cards: these papers were most frequently decorated with small diaper patterns printed in black and coloured by stencil. Joined together, they could be used to decorate small surfaces that were less exposed than walls, such as the insides of furniture.

At the same time, in Europe and in England, other prints using large-scale motifs were employed for the same purpose. One such example is provided by the fragments of a block-printed wall-paper, decorated with a repeat design, that adorned the beams of a ceiling in the Master's Lodge, Christ's College, Cambridge (completed in 1509). The fragments which make up this design are printed on the back of documents issued in the first year of Henry VIII's reign and bear the initial 'h' and a bird like a goose, probably a rebus on the name of Hugo Goes, who established himself in York in the same year.

It was necessary to wait until the second half of the seventeenth century before progress in both the printing and joining-up of patterns allowed a change-over to be made from partial usage, practically never attempted on walls, to the carrying-out of true interior decorations. The parallel efforts to perfect flock papers (tontisses) was just as unsuccessful before this period. Certainly, after about 1560, the English and Dutch succeeded in producing designs executed in this manner, which were sometimes used as wall-paper and gave the illusion of 'richer' materials. About 1620, in France, Le François of Rouen is said to have known methods of imitating 'tapestries with landscapes and histories' on cloth and paper. No products of this ingenuity have been found, but the known examples produced by his French or foreign rivals are far from achieving the technical quality and brilliance that would have induced potential patrons, necessarily rich, to abandon with advantage traditional materials: wood, leather or real textiles.

The situation began to develop rapidly after the second third of the seventeenth century, thanks to the advancement of techniques in the various fields concerned and also to the ingenuity of artist-craftsmen such as Jean-Michel Papillon of Paris. A wood-engraver, trained in his father's studio, and a designer, he knew how to turn to best account the progress in 'dominotier' and flock papers, as well as the eye-opening discovery of wall-papers imported from the Far East. In addition, he was passionately fond of chiaroscuro prints that enabled colours to be printed by wood-engraving, thus replacing the traditional stencil method. Papillon was not, strictly speaking, an inventor, and it was wrong for him to credit himself with, for example, the 'discovery' of the linking-up of designs, although he certainly did perfect the process. Over and above this, he was one of the first to understand that the fortunes of wall-paper also depended on techniques of hanging and pasting to a very great extent. By carrying out such work himself, he learned to use cloths stretched on frames as adhesive surfaces, thus avoiding irregularities in wall surfaces and providing a protection against the dampness of walls.

dem verbot nagendes und kriechendes Ungeziefer die Bespannung der Wände mit Papier. Dazu kannte man das Prinzip der Rapportzeichnung noch nicht und konnte demzufolge keine fortlaufenden Bahnen bilden.

Fortlaufende Zeichnungen erscheinen seit dem 16. Jahrhundert, und zwar zuerst dank der Dominos oder Dominotierpapiere, die von Bildermachern und Spielkartenzeichnern hergestellt wurden und aus kleinen, sich wiederholenden Motiven bestanden. Diese wurden schwarz auf die Bögen gedruckt und mit der Schablone oder Patrone koloriert. Zusammengeklebt konnten diese Bögen sehr wohl zur Bespannung kleinerer, nicht exponierter Flächen gebraucht werden, wie etwa zum Ausschlagen eines Schrankes.

Zur gleichen Zeit benutzt man in Europa und England Drucke mit großen Motiven zum selben Zweck. Deckenbalken des 1509 in Cambridge erbauten Christ's College wurden zum Beispiel mit einem Fries aus aneinandergefügten Blättern mit wiederholten Motiven bedeckt, diese »Tapete« war so nichts weniger als aus der weißen Rückseite der Blätter eines Buches gemacht, das der im selben Jahr in York ansässig gewordene Hugh Goes gedruckt hatte.

Aber erst in der zweiten Hälfte des 17. Jahrhunderts gelang es, die Drucktechnik und die Rapportzeichnungen so zu vervollkommnen, daß die Papiertapeten als »Innendekoration« verwendet werden konnten; vor diesem Zeitpunkt hatte man sie kaum jemals auf Mauern aufgezogen. Gleichzeitig bemühte man sich auch, die »Tontisses« genannten Velourtapeten, das heißt Buntpapiere mit aufgeklebtem Wollstaub, zu verbessern. Zwar war es Engländern und Holländern schon seit ungefähr 1560 gelungen, Tapeten, die sogar manchmal auf Mauerwerk aufgezogen wurden, in dieser Technik zu fabrizieren und auf diese Art wertvolleres Material vorzutäuschen. In Frankreich gelingt es um 1620 Le François aus Rouen, auf Leinwand und Papier »Tapisserien mit geschichtlichen und Landschaftsmotiven« zu imitieren, also Bildtapeten herzustellen. Leider sind alle Zeugnisse seines Schaffens verloren gegangen; aber seine französischen und ausländischen Nacheiferer haben ihre Technik auf keinen so hohen Stand gebracht, daß die dafür in Frage kommende Kundschaft deswegen auf Altbewährtes wie Holz, Leder oder Stoffe verzichtet hätte.

Diese Situation ändert sich im letzten Drittel des 17. Jahrhunderts sehr schnell dank der in den einschlägigen Gebieten weiterentwickelten Arbeitsmethoden und dank auch dem Erfindergeist gewisser Kunsthandwerker, wie etwa Jean-Michel Papillon in Paris. Dieser bei seinem Vater ausgebildete Holzstecher und Entwerfer weiß aus den Fortschritten der Dominotierpapiere und der Tontisses Vorteil zu ziehen, ebenso aus den papierenen Wandbespannungen, die aus dem Fernen Osten importiert wurden. Er begeistert sich auch für Drucke im Camaieu oder Clair-obscur, die es erlauben, mit der gestochenen Holzplatte Farben zu drucken, so daß die Schablone entbehrlich wird. Papillon ist nicht ein eigentlicher Erfinder, und er schreibt sich zu Unrecht die Entdeckung der Rapportzeichnung zu, die er aber doch sehr verbessert hat. Er ist auch einer der Ersten, einzusehen, daß der Aufschwung der Buntpapiere wesentlich von ihrer Eignung, geklebt und aufgezogen zu werden, abhängt. Während der Arbeit lernt er, durch in Rahmen gespanntes Tuch einen glat-

Cette curiosité et ce goût pour l'invention et la nouveauté ne sont pas le monopole de Papillon, ni la seule raison de son succès. En effet, c'est en 1686 que la fabrication des toiles peintes ou «indiennes» introduite en France à fin du XVIᵉ siècle, est interdite en France. Du coup, des graveurs qui taillaient les «moules» nécessaires à leur impression viennent mettre au profit d'imprimeurs sur papier leur expérience en matière de décoration.

Ils trouvent en particulier aussitôt leur place chez les «dominotiers», fabricants de papiers, d'images et de cartes, qui se servaient, pour leurs impressions, de bois très semblables aux leurs, pour la taille comme pour le style. C'est à leur apport qu'il faut attribuer pour une part la prolifération de feuilles comportant de grands dessins juxtaposables et par là propres à constituer de véritables tentures. «Sur la fin du XVIIᵉ siècle», écrit Savary des Bruslons, «on pousse les papiers de tenture à un tel point de perfectionnement à l'agrément qu'outre les grands envois qui s'en font pour les pays étrangers et pour les principales villes du royaume, il n'est point de maison à Paris, pour magnifique qu'elle soit, qui n'en ait en quelque endroit, soit garderobes, soit lieu encore plus secret qui n'en soit tapissé et assez agréablement orné».

Cette constatation marque aussi les limites du succès des «dominos», qui servent surtout aux gens de la campagne et au petit peuple des villes. Aux autres s'adressent les productions de Papillon et de ses émules, mais aussi les papiers d'Extrême-Orient. Ceux-ci sont jusqu'au milieu du XVIIIᵉ siècle préférés par les gens fortunés à des tontisses encore un peu pauvres et aux papiers «peints» imprimés à l'encre grasse et donc sans relief ni chatoiement. La faute en revient, en France, à Papillon, cette fois pris gravement en défaut. En effet, celui-ci, ayant eu entre les mains des papiers imprimés par les Anglais au moyen de couleurs à la détrempe, ne vit pas quel parti il en pouvait tirer, les jugeant trop peu solides à l'usage.

C'est d'Angleterre qu'allait venir, au milieu du siècle, l'impulsion décisive, grâce à la fabrication de papiers décorés inspirés de ceux d'Extrême-Orient, au perfectionnement de la pratique du «flockage», et à l'obtention d'une qualité de peintures à la détrempe rendant celles-ci épaisses, solides et lumineuses.

Importées en France, ces productions et surtout les papiers «veloutés», connus chez nous sous le nom de «papiers bleus d'Angleterre» connaissent un énorme succès et pour la première fois déterminent les gens de la bonne société et jusqu'à ceux de la Cour à se servir de ces revêtements jusque dans les pièces «nobles».

Ici, Jean-Baptiste Réveillon prend la relève de Papillon. Comme lui, il a en qualité d'apprenti commencé par poser des papiers, notamment ceux venus d'Angleterre, mais son esprit d'entreprise et son génie inventif lui ont permis en peu d'années, en des circonstances il est vrai plus favorables, d'atteindre à un degré de novation et de réussite que Papillon n'avait pas connus. Devenu fabricant, Réveillon, produira lui-même ses papiers, en rouleaux faits de feuilles préalablement assemblées; il perfectionnera les techniques d'impression, il emploiera des couleurs indestructibles; il les superposera jusqu'à obtenir les nuances les plus délicates; il fera appel aux meilleurs artistes des divers domaines des arts décoratifs: peintres de fleurs et de pay-

This curiosity and taste for invention and novelty were not the prerogative of Papillon, nor the only reason for his success. Indeed, when the manufacture of printed calicos, called *indiennes* (introduced into France at the end of the sixteenth century), was forbidden in France in 1686, the engravers who had cut the blocks for printing them suddenly gave the benefit of their experience in the matter of decoration to the printers on paper.

In particular they immediately found themselves at home with the 'dominotiers' who, in the manufacture of their papers, popular prints and cards, used wood-blocks for printing that were similar, in size as well as style, to those used by the textile printers. It is in part to their contribution that we must attribute the proliferation of papers bearing large, juxtaposed designs, which could properly be called wall-papers. 'At the end of the seventeenth century', wrote Savary des Bruslons, 'wall-papers have reached such a peak of perfection and charm that, besides the large consignments sent to foreign countries and to the prinicpal cities of the kingdom, there is no house in Paris, however magnificent, that does not have some spot, be it a dressing room or some more secret place, which is not papered and thereby rather pleasantly decorated'.

This acceptance also marked the limits of the success of the 'dominotier' papers, which were used above all by people in the country and small towns. The others favoured the products of Papillon and his rivals, and also the wall-papers from the Far East. Until the middle of the eighteenth century, the well-to-do preferred the latter to flock papers which were still of rather poor quality, and to 'painted' papers printed with oily inks that made them flat and lustreless. In France the deficiency was Papillon's fault; this time he was badly caught napping. Indeed, even though he had had in his hands papers printed by the English in distemper colours, he failed to see how they could be employed to advantage, judging them not solid enough to use.

Thanks to the manufacture of decorated papers inspired by the Far East, it was England, in the middle of the century, which gave the decisive drive so necessary to perfect the flocking technique and to achieve a quality of distemper-printing in which the colours appeared thick, solid and luminous.

Imported into France, these products, especially the 'velvet' papers known by the name *papiers bleus d'Angleterre* ('blue papers from England'), had an enormous success and for the first time persuaded people in high society, and those at Court, to use these hangings, even in state rooms.

At this point, Jean Baptiste Réveillon took over from Papillon. Like the latter, Réveillon had, in his capacity as apprentice, started out by hanging wall-papers, in particular English ones; however, his spirit of enterprise and his inventive genius enabled him, in a few years, and in admittedly favourable circumstances, to achieve a degree of innovation and success which Papillon had never known. Having become a manufacturer, Réveillon produced his own papers, made up in rolls of previously assembled sheets; he perfected techniques of printing and used fast colours, which he superposed to achieve the most subtle shades. He commissioned the best artists in various fields of the decorative arts: flower and landscape painters, designers in woodwork, specialists working on the Oberkampf-de-

ten Grund herzustellen und das Papier daraufzukleben; diese Methode hat den Vorteil, die Tapete von den Unregelmäßigkeiten des Mauerwerkes und seiner Feuchtigkeit zu isolieren.

Diese Neugierde und die Vorliebe für Erfindungen und Neuheiten sind allerdings nicht nur Papillon eigen, auch sind sie nicht die einzige Ursache seines Erfolges. Als 1686 die Herstellung des Ende 16. Jahrhundert in Frankreich aufgekommenen Kattuns, der »Indienne«-Drucke, verboten wird, kommen die Holzstecher für die Kattunmodel zum Zug, indem sie ihre Erfahrung in den Papierdruckern verkaufen. Sie treten insbesondere in den Dienst der Dominotierer, die Papierhersteller, Zeichner und Spielkartenfabrikanten in einem waren und fast dieselben Druckplatten wie ihre neuen Gehilfen benutzten, was Größe und Art anbelangt. Ihnen muß man auch die Herstellung großer Bögen mit zusammensetzbaren Bildern zuschreiben, aus denen große Wanddekorationen entstanden. Darüber schreibt Savary de Bruslons: »Gegen Ende des 17. Jahrhunderts werden die Papiertapeten so perfektioniert, daß man nicht nur große Mengen ins Ausland und in die bedeutendsten Städte des Königreiches exportieren kann; es ist auch in Paris kein noch so vornehmes Haus, das nicht irgendwo, sei es in Garderoben oder noch geheimeren Orten, mit hübschen Papiertapeten geschmückte Wände hätte.«

Diese Feststellung bezeichnet die Grenze des Erfolgs der Dominotierpapiere, die vor allem vom Landvolk und den städtischen Kleinbürgertum geschätzt wurden. Für die andern Leute sind eher die Werke Papillons und seiner Konkurrenten bestimmt oder auch die Tapeten aus dem Fernen Osten. Bis Mitte des 18. Jahrhunderts werden diese von den wohlhabenden Leuten den noch etwas ärmlichen Tontisses oder den mit ölhaltigen Farben bedruckten, relief- und glanzlosen Buntpapieren vorgezogen. Diesmal ist der Fehler allein bei Papillon zu suchen. Als er einmal englische, mit Leimfarben bedruckte Papiertapeten zu sehen bekam, erkannte er den Nutzen nicht, den er daraus hätte ziehen können, denn er fand sie für den Gebrauch zuwenig widerstandsfähig.

Aus England kam Mitte des Jahrhunderts der entscheidende Impuls, dank der Fabrikation fernöstlich inspirierter Dekortapeten, dank der Vervollkommnung des »Flocking« und dank besserer Leimfarben, die ihrer Qualität wegen dick, solide und leuchtend waren.

Diese Tapeten werden nach Frankreich importiert und haben einen großen Erfolg, besonders die sammetartigen, die man auch unter dem Namen »Papiers bleus d'Angleterre« kannte. Erst jetzt lassen sich auch die vornehmen Leute, ja, sogar der Hof, davon überzeugen und schmücken auch die »guten« Räume mit Papiertapeten.

In dieser Zeit wird Papillon von Jean-Baptiste Réveillon abgelöst. Wie Papillon hatte auch Réveillon als Lehrling angefangen, Tapeten — besonders englische — aufzuziehen, aber innerhalb weniger Jahre hat er dank seinem Erfindergeist und seinem Handelssinn einen so hohen Stand an Bekanntheit und Erfolg erreicht, wie ihn Papillon, wohl auch widriger Umstände wegen, nie gekannt hat. Réveillon wird Fabrikant und stellt seine eigenen Tapetenpapiere her, und zwar in Rollen aus vorher zusammengeklebten Papierbögen. Er perfektioniert auch die Drucktechniken und benutzt unverwüstliche Farben, die er bis zum Errei-

sages, décorateurs de boiseries, spécialistes travaillant pour les toiles d'Oberkampf ou les tapisseries des Gobelins. Il développera les techniques de pose de manière à ce que les tentures en papier s'intègrent parfaitement dans l'architecture intérieure des hôtels particuliers et des châteaux, originellement conçue pour d'autres matériaux. Enfin, il saura monter une véritable entreprise pré-industrielle dans laquelle un personnel nombreux et diversifié se partagera des tâches précises en fonction de ses compétences et de la nature des produits. Car à la folie Titon, siège de sa manufacture, l'on produit et l'on vend aussi bien des papiers à bas prix, avec une seule couleur, que des tentures à la détrempe pouvant comporter jusqu'à 80 passages de planches d'impression différentes et rivalisant avec les peintures à la main les plus sophistiquées, ou des «tontisses» imitant à la perfection les velours, damas ou satins des étoffes les plus fines, ou même les tapisseries des Gobelins.

Souvent et dans tous les genres, une réussite aussi éclatante que celle de Réveillon et de ses émules précède des changements radicaux. En matière de papiers peints, ceux-ci allaient survenir dès après la retraite de Réveillon, qui lui-même les avait préparés. Pour que l'on pût atteindre son objectif: la présence de papiers peints sur tous les murs, dans toutes les habitations, il fallait que la science et l'industrie naissantes permettent d'obtenir la quantité de production suffisante. Et pour ce faire, il fallait aussi changer la qualité d'une production qui, afin d'être vulgarisée, devait cesser de prétendre au chef d'œuvre, d'emploi forcément limité, pour tendre à l'utile et à l'économique.

La période 1800–1850

En 1795 déjà, moins d'un demi-siècle après que le papier peint ait commencé à pouvoir être utilisé couramment en guise de tenture, Houel écrivait dans le *Journal des inventions:* «pour le coup d'œil, la propreté, la fraîcheur et l'élégance, ces papiers sont préférables aux riches étoffes d'autrefois; ils ne laissent aucun accès aux insectes, et quand ils sont vernis, conservent long-temps toute la vivacité et l'agrément de leurs couleurs; enfin, ils peuvent être changés trèsfacilement et, en nous mettant à la portée de renouveler ainsi nos asiles, en les nettoyant plus souvent, en les rendant plus gais et plus agréables, les papiers peints contribuent à répandre l'intérêt sur notre existence et méritent d'être regardés comme un object d'industrie de première nécessité».

Les préoccupations exprimées dans ce texte vont être celles de la plus grande partie de la clientèle des papiers peints au XIXᵉ siècle. Si l'on produit encore des chefs d'œuvre et notamment de vastes «panoramas», c'est avant tout, comme en matière de haute couture, pour maintenir une frange de prestige indispensable à la promotion du genre, et à l'invention de formes nouvelles. Mais le rapporteur de l'exposition de 1819 met les fabricants en garde contre la généralisation de cette formule. Il leur rappelle qu'ils ne sauraient rivaliser sérieusement avec la peinture et, surtout, qu'il est vain de chercher à faire durer très longtemps des tentures qui, le voudraient-ils, ne sauraient avoir la robustesse des matériaux

signed cottons or the Gobelin tapestries, and he developed techniques of hanging in such a way that the wall-papers integrated perfectly with the interior architecture of individual large houses and châteaux, which were originally designed with other materials in mind. Finally Réveillon set up a real pre-industrial enterprise, in which a large and varied staff shared out precise tasks according to their own skills and the nature of the product. For at the Folie-Titon, centre of the factory, cheap papers printed with a single colour were sold, as well as distemper-prints that required up to 80 impressions from different plates and rivalled the most sophisticated painting by hand, as well as flock papers that imitated perfectly the finest quality velvets, damasks, satins and even Gobelin tapestries.

Often, in every genre, a success as brilliant as that of Réveillon and his rivals precedes radical changes. In the field of wall-paper, these were to occur after the retirement of Réveillon, who had prepared the way for them. In order to achieve his objective – the presence of wall-paper on all walls and in every dwelling – science and nascent industrialism had to find the means to produce a sufficient quantity of wall-paper. To do this it was also necessary to alter the quality of the product in order to popularize it, and to stop aiming at masterpieces, of necessarily limited use, in order to produce useful objects at a lower price.

The Period 1800 to 1850

By 1795, less than half a century after wall-paper had begun to be readily usable as hangings, Houel wrote in the *Journal des Inventions:* 'for the view, the cleanliness, the freshness and the elegance, these papers are preferable to the rich materials of the past; they do not allow any access to insects, and when they are varnished, they retain all the vivacity and charm of their colours for a long time. Finally, they can be changed very frequently, and by making us thus inclined to renovate our homes – cleaning them more often and making them gayer and more attractive – wall-papers add to our interest in life, and deserve to be regarded as a manufactured object of prime necessity'.

The sentiments expressed in this text were to be those of the majority of wall-paper customers in the nineteenth century. If masterpieces were still being produced, notably vast 'panoramas', it was above all, as in the world of high fashion, in order to maintain the element of prestige necessary to promote the genre and to encourage new forms. But the reporter at the 1819 exhibition put manufacturers on their guard against the generalization of this formula. He reminded them that they would never be able seriously to rival painting, and, above all, that it was vain to try to endow wall-papers with great durability, since they would never have the robustness of the materials they imitated. Nor should manufacturers forget that henceforth the greatest demand would come not from the wealthy classes but

chen der feinsten Nuancen übereinandergedruckt. Die besten Vertreter der dekorativen Künste stehen ihm zur Verfügung: Blumen- und Landschaftsmaler, Boiserie-Künstler, Spezialisten der Stoffdruckateliers von Oberkampf oder der Gobelins sind ihm gerade gut genug. Er verbessert die Methoden zum Anbringen der Papiere so, daß die Tapeten perfekt in die ursprünglich für andere Materialien konzipierten Interieurs der vornehmen Häuser und Schlösser passen. Schließlich errichtet er ein wahres vor-industrielles Unternehmen, in dem viele verschiedene Handwerker ihren ganz spezifischen Arbeitsbereich haben.

Denn in seiner Manufaktur von la Folie-Titon fertigt und verkauft man ebensowohl billige, einfarbige Tapeten wie auch solche mit komplizierten Mustern, die bis zu 80 Passagen der Druckplatte für die Farbgebung erfordern und es mit den schönsten Gemälden aufnehmen können, wie auch Tontisses, die Samt, Damast, Satin oder sogar echte Gobelins vollkommen imitieren.

Diese Art von Erfolg, wie er Réveillon und seinen Nacheiferern beschieden war, zieht oft – und dies in jeder Beziehung – beachtliche Veränderungen nach sich. Bevor sich Réveillon aus dem Geschäftsleben zurückzog, hatte er eine weitreichende Entwicklung im Papiertapeten-Sektor schon vorbereitet. Sein Ziel, alles Mauerwerk in jedem Haus mit Papiertapeten zu bekleiden, konnte nur mit Hilfe der Wissenschaft und der beginnenden Industrialisierung erreicht werden, die eine genügend große Produktion möglich machten. Dies wiederum bedingte eine Veränderung der Qualität, sollten doch die Tapeten jedermann zugänglich und deshalb billiger und einfacher sein, statt sich als Kunstwerke auszugeben.

Die Zeit von 1800 bis 1850

Schon 1795, ein halbes Jahrhundert nachdem die Papiertapeten endlich als gängige Wandverkleidung benutzt werden konnten, schrieb Houel in dem *Journal des inventions:* »Durch ihren Anblick, ihre Sauberkeit, Frische und Eleganz sind diese Papiere den früheren, schweren Stoffen vorzuziehen. Sie können nicht durch Insekten zerstört werden, und gefirnißt behalten ihre Farben sehr lange Glanz und Frische; auch können die Tapeten leicht ausgewechselt werden, so daß man sein Heim öfters umdekorieren und besser reinhalten und es dadurch fröhlich und angenehm gestalten kann. Diese Papiertapeten sind von größtem Interesse und verdienen es, als ein unentbehrliches Industrieprodukt angesehen zu werden.«

Die Überlegungen in diesem Text geben die Ansicht des größten Teils der Papiertapeten-Kundschaft des 19. Jahrhunderts wieder. Man stellt zwar noch Kunstwerke, besonders riesige Bildtapeten – Panoramen – her, doch nur, um ein gewisses, der Branche und der Erfindung neuer Formen nötiges Prestige aufrecht zu erhalten, ähnlich wie heute in der Haute Couture. Doch der Berichterstatter der Ausstellung von 1819 rät den Verfechtern dieser Theorie zur Vorsicht. Er weist darauf hin, daß die Tapetenhersteller kaum ernstlich mit der Malerei rivalisieren könnten und es müßig sei, Papiertapeten, die ja doch nicht die Robustheit von Gemälden haben, Langlebigkeit um jeden Preis zu verleihen. Die Fabrikanten sollten auch nicht vergessen, daß jetzt, jedenfalls

qu'ils imitent. Les fabricants ne doivent pas oublier non plus que, désormais, l'essentiel de la demande commence à provenir non plus des classes riches, mais de gens qui accèdent à l'aisance et même des milieux populaires, au moins dans les villes, Cette clientèle nouvelle est forcée de se contenter de papiers à bas prix et veut pouvoir les renouveler sans beaucoup de dépense.

Tout au long de la période 1800–1850, et maintenant encore, les fabricants de papiers peints vont donc poursuivre simultanément quatre objectifs, assez contradictoires: accroître et diversifier la production, promouvoir (ou simuler) la qualité, rechercher une certaine durée et, dans le même temps, produire en des quantités et à des prix tels que les changements souhaités ou rendus nécessaires, soient possibles.

Pour satisfaire à ces exigences, les fabricants participent à la fièvre d'innovation qui touche jusqu'aux métiers les plus attachés à la tradition. En matière de papier, d'abord, Zuber perfectionne la technique introduite par Réveillon et produit des lés de 9 m de longueur faits de feuilles accolées dans le sens de leur largeur. Ce procédé est encore le plus habituel vers 1830, mais à cette époque déjà commence la fabrication de papier en continu, brevetée par Louis Robert en 1799 et d'abord utilisée par les Anglais. Quelques années plus tard, il devient possible de substituer du papier mécanique à celui fabriqué à la main. Ces changements permettent à la fois d'augmenter la production et de se servir de cylindres pour l'impression.

Ce dernier point est essentiel. A la fin du siècle précédent déjà, le recours aux cylindres gravés était pratiqué pour les étoffes. Son extension aux papiers se fait progressivement, de 1830 environ à 1850, d'abord grâce à la gravure en taille douce, puis à celle en relief. Successivement, Zuber, puis Leroy, entre autres, s'y emploient, butant longtemps sur des difficultés d'encrage, dues à l'épaisseur des couleurs à la détrempe, et c'est seulement vers 1840 que Leroy, à la suite encore des Anglais, utilise un drap sans fin plongé dans la cuve alimentaire à couleurs, qui répartit celles-ci sur les cylindres d'une manière égale. Entre temps, vers 1830, Zuber, mettant à profit une autre technique anglaise pour l'impression sur étoffes, commence à produire mécaniquement des rayures de couleurs variées, grâce à un système de canaux parallèles percés aux endroits où chaque couleur doit être produite.

Grâce aux recherches comme celles de Chevreul, et aux progrès de l'industrie, ces couleurs sont de plus sophistiquées dans leurs nuances, brillantes et solides. Les fabricants se livrent au début du siècle à de rudes concurrences pour l'obtention du vert-pré, du vert foncé du vert-fleur, du vert de Schweinfurth, du jaune minéral, obtenu avec de l'oxyde de plomb, du vert de chrome, du bleu superfin, du bleu minéral, du cramoisi lustré, de la laque rouge, de rehauts ou reflets de bronze, d'argent et d'or, etc. Ils rivalisent dans l'invention de procédés permettant de fixer et de consolider les couleurs; ils savent se servir de vernis incolores et inodores éloignant les insectes et dès 1839, ils se vantent de pouvoir vendre des papiers «lavables», obtenus en broyant les couleurs à l'huile.

Ces progrès conditionnent le développement et la structuration des fabriques et vont se traduire progressivement au cours du demi-siècle par un quasi monopole de Paris (ex-

from people coming into easier circumstances, and even from the ordinary populace, at least in the cities. This new clientele had of necessity to make do with cheap papers, and they would want to renew them without great expense.

For the whole of the period 1800 to 1850, and even to-day, manufacturers of wall-papers were to pursue four somewhat contradictory objectives simultaneously: to increase and diversify production, to promote (or stimulate) quality, to improve durability, and, at the same time, to produce in quantities and at prices that made it possible to bring about the hoped-for or necessary changes.

To satisfy these demands, manufacturers joined the frenzy of innovation that was affecting even the most traditional crafts. In the matter of paper, to begin with, Zuber perfected the technique introduced by Réveillon and produced strips of paper 9 metres in length, made by joining the sheets together across their breadth. This was still the most usual process until about 1830, but by then the production of continuous paper had begun. This process was patented by Louis Robert in 1799 and first used by the English. A few years later, it became possible to substitute machine-made paper for that made by hand. These changes helped to increase production and made it possible to use cylinders for printing.

This last point was essential. By the end of the preceding century, it had become practicable to use engraved cylinders for the printing of textiles. Its extension to the printing of papers was made progressively from about 1830 to 1850, first thanks to metal engraving, then to relief-printing. Among others, Zuber, then Leroy, used it successively, struggling for a long time over the difficulties of inking, due to the thickness of distemper colours; it was only in 1840 that Leroy, again following the lead of the English, used a roller-cloth dipped in a feed-tank of colours to distribute the latter equally. Meanwhile, in about 1830, Zuber, taking advantage of another English technique for printing textiles, began to produce stripes of colours mechanically, thanks to a system of sinking parallel grooves in the cylinders at the places where each colour was to occur.

Owing to research by people like Chevreul, and to industrial progress, colours became increasingly subtle, brilliant and solid. At the beginning of the nineteenth century, manufacturers engaged in stiff competition to obtain grass-green, dark green, leaf-green, Schweinfurth green, mineral yellow (made from lead oxide), chrome green, superfine blue, mineral blue, lustrous crimson, lacquer red, and highlights or reflections of bronze, silver, gold, etc. They rivalled each other in the invention of processes to fix or strengthen colours. They were able to make use of colourless, odourless varnishes that kept insects at bay, and from 1839, they boasted of their ability to sell 'washable' papers, achieved by grinding their colours in oil.

This progress conditioned the development and the organization of factories and during the course of the next half-century resulted in the near monopoly of Paris (Mulhouse being an exception) and in an expansion of large businesses at the expense of the workshops of craftsmen. These factories, for which Réveillon provided the prototype, employed workmen, designers, chemists and mechanics. They made their own papers and colours; they had a network of representatives and

in den Städten, das Gros der Kundschaft nicht mehr aus der Oberschicht, sondern aus der Mittel-, ja, sogar Proletarierklasse stammt. Diese neue Käuferschicht sieht sich genötigt, billigen Produkten den Vorzug zu geben, zumal sie sie auch ab und an ohne zu viele Kosten auswechseln will.

Während der ganzen Zeitspanne von 1800 bis 1850, und noch heutzutage, verfolgen die Fabrikanten vier ziemlich widersrüchliche Ziele: Anheben und Erweitern der Produktion, Verbessern der Qualität, Erreichen einer gewissen Solidität und gleichzeitig Produktion zu niederen Preisen, so daß der »Tapetenwechsel« kein finanzielles Problem bringt.

Die Fabrikanten wetteifern um die Erfüllung dieser Forderungen, sogar die am meisten der Tradition verpflichteten Berufszweige geraten in dieses Fieber. Auf dem Gebiet der Papierfabrikation ist es Zuber, der die von Réveillon eingeführte Technik verbessert und zuerst neun Meter lange Bahnen aus der Breite nach zusammengeklebten Bögen herstellt. Bis 1830 bleibt dies die gebräuchlichste Methode, aber schon zur Zeit Zubers beginnt man, Papierrollen herzustellen, ein Verfahren, das Louis Robert 1799 brevetieren ließ und das zuerst von den Engländern angewendet wurde. Ein paar Jahre später weiß man das handgeschöpfte Papier durch maschinell hergestelltes zu ersetzen. Diese Entwicklung erlaubt eine größere Produktion und ein Bedrucken mittels Walzen.

Dieser letzte Punkt ist von großer Bedeutung. Schon zu Ende des vorhergehenden Jahrhunderts benutzte man den gravierten Zylinder zum Bedrucken von Stoffen. Die Verwendung des Zylinders auch beim Papierdruck verbreitet sich von 1830 bis etwa 1850 nach und nach, zunächst dank des Kupferstichzylinders, dann des reliefierten. Zuerst von Zuber, dann von Leroy und andern angewendet, bereitet diese Technik aber immer Schwierigkeiten mit der dickflüssigen Leimfarbe, und erst gegen 1840 benutzt Leroy – vor ihm schon die Engländer – ein Endlostuch, das die Farben gleichmäßig vom Farbkasten auf die Walze überträgt. In der Zwischenzeit, um 1830, macht sich Zuber eine andere englische Stoffdrucktechnik zu eigen, um mechanisch verschiedenfarbige Streifen zu drucken, dies mittels eines Systems parallel laufender Kanäle, die, dort wo der Streifen gewünscht wurde, durchbohrt waren.

Verschiedene Forscharbeiten, wie diejenigen von Chevreul, und Fortschritte in der Industrie erlauben die Herstellung immer nuancierterer, glänzenderer und widerstandsfähigerer Farben. Zu Anfang des Jahrhunderts kämpften die Fabrikanten geradezu darum, die schönsten Farben zu haben, wie Wiesengrün, Dunkelgrün, Lichtgrün, Schweinfurther Grün, Mineralgelb aus chromsaurem Bleioxyd, Chromgrün, Superfeines Blau, Mineralblau, glänzendes Karmesinrot, roter Lack, Glanzlichter aus Bronze, Gold und Silber usw. Sie rivalisieren in ihren Erfindungen zum Fixieren und Härten der Farben, sie entdecken den farb- und geruchlosen Lack, der dazu noch das Ungeziefer fernhält, und ab 1839 rühmen sie sich ihrer »abwaschbaren« Tapeten, deren Farben mit Öl gerieben wurden.

Diese Fortschritte bedingen eine Entwicklung und Neuorganisation der Fabriken, und während des nächsten halben Jahrhunderts hat Paris – abgesehen von Mülhausen – das beinahe ausschließliche Monopol der Tapetenherstellung; große Unternehmen entste-

ception faite pour Mulhouse), et par la généralisation des grandes entreprises, aux dépens des ateliers artisanaux. Ces manufactures, dont Réveillon avait fourni le prototype, disposent à la fois d'ouvriers, de dessinateurs, de chimistes et de mécaniciens. Elles fabriquent leurs papiers et leurs couleurs. Elles ont un réseau de démarcheurs et de correspondants; elles exportent dans les divers pays d'Europe et dans les deux Amériques.

En 1849, pour la première fois, le rapport du jury de l'Exposition évoque dans le détail, à propos de Zuber, le matériel et le fonctionnement d'une véritable usine de papiers peints. Zuber «possède une machine à vapeur et une turbine représentant ensemble la force de 62 chevaux, employées à faire mouvoir 44 machines différentes, les unes propres à fabriquer du papier, les autres destinées à l'imprimer, à le gauffrer, à le satiner, etc. Il possède encore un moulin à broyer l'outremer et les autres couleurs; de plus, 50 tables pour l'impression à la main. Si l'on ajoute que 500 ouvriers, dont le salaire varie de 1 à 3 francs par jour, sont occupés dans cette fabrique, on ne sera pas surpris d'apprendre que l'exploitation d'une matière première aussi coûteuse que le chiffon puisse produire chaque année pour plus d'un million de marchandises et que Monsieur Zuber paie à ses ouvriers 250000 francs de main d'œuvre». Ajoutons qu'à cette époque déjà, les papiers produits à la machine sont vendus à la moitié du prix pratiqué pour les impressions à la main.

Cependant, ce sont encore les productions de haut de gamme, maintenues parce qu'elles satisfont les goûts et la vanité des riches, anciens et surtout nouveaux, et parce qu'elles assurent aux papiers français une prééminence favorisant l'exportation, qui sont les plus révélatrices des modes de l'époque, qu'elles suivent étroitement.

Au début du siècle, Jacquemart et Bénard par exemple, abandonnent les corbeilles fleuries, les charmilles et les arabesques de Réveillon et s'ingénient à rendre parfaitement l'aspect des plus belles étoffes, la variété et la finesse de leurs dessins les plus sophistiqués, leurs plus brillantes couleurs, les brochés de toute espèce, les veloutés, les satinés, damassés et brodés à l'aiguille, etc. Plusieurs fabricants se disputent l'honneur d'avoir inventé le moyen de produire une imitation parfaite du linon baptiste et, plus tard, le parisien Baudouin se vante de pouvoir imprimer une tenture bleue recouverte d'un tulle d'argent drapé dont les dégradations de nuances sont obtenues d'un seul coup de planche à l'aide de blancs de couleurs variables, tandis que Zuber s'enorgueillit de la réussite de ses tentures irisées.

Ainsi naissent une infinité de modèles de draperies tenues par des embrasses, chargées de passementeries et de festons, bordées de frises, séparées par des piques, ou par des éléments d'architecture, le style général et les détails allant du genre sévère et un peu guindé de l'Empire à une étouffante prolifération de trophées, d'attributs, de figures ailées et de toutes sortes de décorations surabondantes pendant la Restauration et jusque vers 1840, ajoutant encore à la pesanteur du mobilier d'alors. Les couleurs à la détrempe s'allient aux tontisses pour multiplier les effets, parachever l'illusion jusqu'à donner celle du relief, souligner la richesse par des reflets d'argent ou d'or parachevant le bariolage de couleurs souvent agressives.

correspondents, and they exported to various European countries and the two Americas.

In 1849, for the first time, the report of the jury of the exhibition described in detail, apropos of Zuber, the stock-in-trade and the workings of a real wall-paper factory. Zuber 'possesses a steam-engine and a turbine representing together 62 horse-power, used to operate 44 different machines, some intended to make paper, others to print, emboss or satin it, etc. He also has a mill to grind lapis lazuli [for ultramarine blue] and other colours and 50 tables for hand-printing too. If one adds that 500 workers, whose salary varies from 1 to 3 francs a day, are employed in this factory, one will not be surprised to learn that the exploitation of a raw material as expensive as ragpaper can produce every year more than a million pieces of merchandise, and that Monsieur Zuber pays his workmen 250000 francs for their man-power.' Let us add, in conclusion, that by this period, machine-made papers were already being sold for half the price of those printed by hand.

However, it was still the products in the upper range, maintained because they satisfied the tastes and vanity of the rich (particularly the nouveaux riches) and also because they ensured to French wall-papers a pre-eminence that gave them an advantage in the export market, that reveal most clearly contemporary fashions, which they followed very closely.

At the beginning of the century Jacquemart and Bénard, for example, abandoning the flowered basket-work, arbours and arabesques of Réveillon, contrived to convey perfectly the appearance of the most beautiful fabrics, their variety and delicacy of design and their brilliant colours: brocades of all kinds, velvets, satins, damasks, embroideries, etc. Several manufacturers contended for the honour of having invented the method of producing a perfect imitation of 'baptiste' lawn. Later, the Parisian Baudouin boasted of being able to produce a blue paper covered with draped silver tulle, in which the gradations of shade were achieved by a single application of the printing block with the aid of various shades of white; Zuber, meanwhile, prided himself on the success of his *irisé* wall-papers.

Thus, an infinite number of designs with draperies came into being: draperies held by loops, embellished with trimmings and festoons, edged with friezes, separated by stitching, or by architectural elements. The general style and the details moved from the severe and slightly restrained Empire manner to an overwhelming proliferation of trophies, symbols, winged figures and all kinds of superabundant decorations, which were in favour during the period of the French Restoration and up to 1840. All this added to the general heaviness of interior furnishings. Distemper colours united with flocking to increase the effect and complete the illusion of relief, underlining the richness with reflections of silver or gold, which often produced a medley of very aggressive colours.

Tableaux, used for panels, over-doors, chimney-screens, draught-screens, etc. were also in fashion. The large, floral compositions of Malaine looked like survivors from the past. Mythological or genre scenes were preferred: representations of the months, seasons, countrysides, animals, shipwrecks, etc., created by specialist artists, such as Charvet, Fragonard the Younger, Blondel, Laffitte,

hen, sehr zum Schaden der kleinen Handwerksbetriebe. Die von Réveillon »erfundenen« Manufakturen beschäftigen Arbeiter, Entwerfer, Chemiker und Mechaniker und stellen ihre eigenen Papiere und Farben her. Außerdem verfügen sie über ein Netz von Vertretern und Korrespondenten und exportieren in die europäischen Länder sowie nach Nord- und Südamerika.

1849 wird erstmals im Detail auf eine Papiertapetenfabrik mit ihren Materialbeständen und ihrer Tätigkeit eingegangen, beleuchtet doch im Ausstellungsbericht die Jury eingehend Zubers Werk: Zuber »besitzt eine Dampfmaschine und eine Turbine mit der Kraft von 62 PS, die 44 verschiedene Maschinen antreiben, von denen die einen zur Papierherstellung dienen, die andern das Papier bedrucken, gaufrieren und satinieren usw. Er besitzt auch ein Mahlwerk, um Ultramarin und andere Farben zu reiben, außerdem 50 Tische für den Handdruck. Wenn man weiß, daß in dieser Fabrik 500 Arbeiter mit Tageslöhnen von 1 bis 3 Fr. beschäftigt sind, erstaunt es nicht, daß die Ausbeutung eines so teuren Rohstoffes wie Hadernpapier jedes Jahr mehr als eine Million Rollen Ware ergibt und Herr Zuber seinen Arbeitern für 250000 Fr. Löhne auszahlt!« Zum Schlusse sei beigefügt, daß schon zu jener Zeit die maschinell gedruckten Tapeten halb so teuer wie die handgedruckten waren.

Es ist aber nach wie vor die Herstellung wertvoller Tapeten, die die Überlegenheit der französischen Produkte gewährleistet und den Export fördert; diese Tapeten befriedigen Geschmack und Eitelkeit eines vor allem neureichen Publikums und, was von Bedeutung ist, sie geben das Bild der damaligen Moden sehr genau wieder.

Anfang des Jahrhunderts verlassen zum Beispiel Jacquemart & Bénard die Pfade Réveillons und damit die Blumenkörbe, Laubengänge und Arabesken, um sich der perfekten Imitation der schönsten Stoffe mit der Verschiedenheit und Feinheit ihrer aufwendigsten Dessins zu widmen. Sie imitieren die leuchtendsten Farben, alle Arten Brochierungen, Sammet, Satins, Damaste, Nadelspitzen und anderes mehr. Mehrere Fabrikanten machten sich die Erfindung der perfekten Nachahmung von Leinenbatist strittig; später rühmt sich der Pariser Baudouin, die Imitation eines blauen Tuches mit einer silbernen Tülldraperie mit einer einzigen Druckplatte herstellen zu können, dies mit Hilfe verschiedener Weißschattierungen, während Zuber stolz auf seine Iristapeten ist.

So entstehen ungeahnte Mengen von mit Kordeln gerafften, mit Tressen und Festons überladenen und mit Friesen bordierten Draperien, die durch Lanzen oder Architekturelemente getrennt werden. Der allgemeingültige Stil und die Details reichen vom strengen und etwas steifen Empire bis zur erstickenden Vielfalt von Trophäen, Attributen, geflügelten Figuren und allerlei pompösen Dekors während der Restauration und bis 1840, was das an sich schon schwere Mobiliar der Epoche noch mehr belastet. Leimfarben und Tontisse werden gemeinsam zum Erzielen vielfältiger Effekte eingesetzt, täuschen Reliefs vor und unterstreichen mit Gold und Silber die ohnehin oft agressiven Farben.

Für Panneaus, Kaminschirme, Paravents und Supraporten benutzt man mit Vorliebe bildliche Darstellungen. Nur selten noch sieht man Malaines große Blumenbilder, es werden ihnen mythologische oder Genreszenen vor-

La mode est aussi aux tableaux, utilisés pour les panneaux, les dessus de porte, les devants de cheminée, les paravents, etc. Les grandes compositions florales d'un Malaine apparaissent comme des survivances du passé. On leur préfère des scènes mythologiques, ou de genre: représentation des mois et des saisons, paysages, animaux, naufrages, etc., composées par des artistes spécialisés: Charvet, Fragonard fils, Blondel, Laffitte, Mader, Mongin, Deltil, Chenavard. Ces compositions, dont l'origine remonte au siècle précédent et en particulier à John Baptist Jackson, prennent de l'extension au fur et à mesure que le papier intervient comme unique élément de décor de tous les murs d'une pièce; elles trouvent leur expression la plus parfaite dans l'éclosion du genre des papiers «panoramiques», traités en grisaille, en camaieu ou en couleurs, à l'origine desquels furent Joseph Dufour et Jean Zuber. Grâce à leur initiative, exploitée par de nombreux émules, le papier peint se substitue à la peinture et à la tapisserie murales dans plusieurs dizaines de milliers d'intérieurs et dans le monde entier. Elles y font rêver de mythologie, d'histoire, de nature, de la découverte du Nouveau monde, des aventures de Télémaque, de Paul et Virginie, de Renaud et Armide.

Quoi qu'en dise Balzac, qui se moque en 1834 du «décor démodé, défroque de misère» des tentures panoramiques dans la pension Vauquier, leur vogue est grande encore dans les années 1840 et bien au delà. Cependant, il est vrai qu'à cette époque les papiers peints changent, sous la double influence du développement de l'industrie, qui a pour conséquence la démocratisation de l'emploi, et du changement de styles.

L'accroissement de la production incite les fabricants à s'intéresser davantage à une fabrication de qualité moyenne propre à satisfaire les goûts du plus grand nombre de clients. Le dessinateur et graveur Victor Poterlet, par exemple, réalise pour plusieurs fabriques d'innombrables dessins courants au rapport et les albums de dessins «industriels» de Chavant servent un peu partout de répertoires. C'est vers 1840 aussi que l'on sait comment fabriquer et poser des décors complets en fonction de la surface et de la dimension des pièces à recouvrir. Enfin, les papiers à dessin courant au rapport reçoivent de nouveaux décors: combinaisons de fleurs et de feuillages avec des rayures et des ferronneries, volutes, fleurs, cartouches avec scènes de styles Renaissance, rocaille ou baroque, et ornements gothiques, etc.

Ainsi s'achève cette période de l'histoire du papier peint, époque de transition où l'on commence à passer des chefs d'œuvre de Réveillon à des productions en série, où l'usage de tentures en papier, presque nouveau et très partiel au début du siècle, se généralise dans toutes les pièces des habitations et dans toutes les classes sociales, la paysannerie exceptée.

Les progrès des techniques sous-tendent et conditionnent ces changements, qu'ils vont précipiter. 1850 est l'année où dans les ateliers des fabriques, la machine tient autant de place que le travail à la main, et produit davantage. Très peu de temps après, elle va intervenir dans tous les postes de travail, au moins pour la production, immensément accrue, des papiers courants. Une véritable revolution va s'en suivre, en conjonction avec les bouleversements qu'introduit l'éclosion de l'ère industrielle.

Mader, Mongin, Deltil, Chenavard, etc. These compositions, whose origins can be traced back to a preceding century, and in particular to John Baptist Jackson, grew in popularity as, little by little, paper became the sole decorative element on all the walls of a room. Their most perfect expression can be found in the burgeoning genre of 'panoramic' papers – executed in grisaille, monochrome or colours – the originators of which were Joseph Dufour and Jean Zuber. Thanks to their initiative, which was exploited by numerous imitators, wall-paper was substituted for painting or tapestries in tens of thousands of interiors throughout the world. Wall-papers evoked dreams of mythology, history, nature, the discovery of the New World, the adventures of Télémaque, Paul and Virginie, and Renaud and Armide.

Although Balzac mocked the panoramic wall-papers in the pension Vauquier in 1834, calling them *décor démodé, défroque de misère* ('old-fashioned cast-offs'), they still enjoyed a great vogue in the 1840's and even after that. But it is true that in the last decade of the century, the nature of wall-papers changed, due to the double influence of changing styles and industrial development, with its subsequent democratization of usage.

Increased production prompted manufacturers to take a greater interest in making medium-quality papers, which would satisfy the tastes of the majority of their clients. The designer and engraver Victor Poterlet, for example, produced innumerable repeat designs for several factories, and Chavant's albums of 'industrial' designs were used as pattern-books everywhere. It was also around 1840, that the technique of manufacturing and installing complete décors, adapted to the scale and dimensions of the rooms to be decorated was discovered. Finally, papers with continuous repeats were endowed with some new types of decoration: combinations of flowers and foliage with stripes and iron-work, acanthus scrolls, flowers, cartouches with various scenes in the Renaissance, Rococo or Baroque styles, Gothic architecture and ornament, etc.

And so this period of wall-paper history came to a close, a transition period in which the masterpieces of Réveillon were superseded by works of serial production and in which the novel, and far from widespread, idea of using paper for wall-hangings became more generally accepted and employed in all the rooms of a house by all social classes, except for peasants.

Technical advances coincided with and conditioned the changes they were to precipitate. By 1850 the machine held an equal place with hand-craftsmanship in manufacturing workshops, yet produced more. Only a short time later, machines had a part in all the stages of work, at least in the enormously increased production of everyday wall-papers. A veritable revolution was to follow, paralleling the upheavals that marked the start of the industrial era.

gezogen, wie die Darstellung der Monate oder Jahreszeiten, Landschaften, Tiere, Schiffbruchszenen usw. Charvet, Fragonard d. J., Blondel, Laffitte, Mader, Mongin, Deltil, Chenavard und andere mehr sind hierin Spezialisten. Diese Bilder, deren Ursprung auf das vorhergehende Jahrhundert und besonders auf John Baptist Jackson zurückgeht, nehmen immer größere Ausmaße an, je mehr die Papiertapeten als einziges Dekorationselement eines Raumes gebraucht wird. Ihre Blüte erfahren sie mit dem Aufkommen der großen Bildtapeten in Grisaille, Camaieu oder in Farben, deren Ursprünge bei Joseph Dufour und Jean Zuber zu suchen sind. Dank diesen Männern und ihren Nacheiferern verdrängen die Papiertapeten die Wandmalereien und Tapisserien in mehreren zehntausend Häusern und auf der ganzen Welt. Sie erwecken Träume von Mythologie, Geschichte und Natur, von der Entdeckung der Neuen Welt, von den Abenteuern des Telemachos, von Paul und Virginie, von Renaud und Armida.

Was auch Balzac darüber sagen mag, der sich 1834 über die Bildtapeten der Pension Vauquier mokiert und sie als »altmodischen Dekor und armseligen Plunder« abtut, sind sie bis weit nach 1840 sehr beliebt. Aber von 1840 bis 1850 ändern sich die Tapeten gleichwohl, einerseits des Einflusses der Industrialisierung wegen, die sie jedem zugänglich macht, andererseits wegen des Stilwechsels.

Durch die Vergrößerung der Produktion werden die Fabrikanten gezwungen, das Augenmerk vermehrt auf die Herstellung einer qualitativ mittelmäßigen Tapete zu richten, die dem Geschmack einer größtmöglichen Kundschaft genügt. Der Entwerfer und Graveur Victor Poterlet – um ein Beispiel zu nennen – zeichnet für mehrere Fabriken unzählige Rapportdekors, und Chavants Album »industrieller« Entwürfe wird vielfach benutzt. Gegen 1840 beherrscht man die Technik der Herstellung und des Aufziehens ganzer Dekors, die den Flächen und der Größe der zu dekorierenden Raumes gerecht werden. Die gebräuchlichsten Rapportdekors werden nun durch verschiedene neue Elemente bereichert: Blumen- und Blattornamente werden mit Streifen oder »Schmiedeeisen« kombiniert, Akanthusranken, Blumen, Kartuschen mit verschiedenen Szenen im Renaissance-, Barock- oder Rocaille-Stil, gotische Architekturelemente und Ornamente sowie anderes mehr kommen hinzu.

So geht diese Epoche der Papiertapete zu Ende. Es ist eine Übergangszeit, in der die Kunstwerke Réveillons durch Serienproduktionen ersetzt werden und die am Anfang des Jahrhunderts fast neuartigen und nur teilweise verwendeten Buntpapiere in immer mehr Räumen und in allen sozialen Schichten, ausgenommen bei den Bauern, Einzug halten. Die Fortschritte der Technik veranlassen diese rasche Veränderung. 1850 nimmt die maschinelle Herstellung den gleichen Rang ein wie die Handarbeit und ist dazu noch produktiver. Wenig später benutzt man, was die ungeheuer angewachsene Produktion der gängigen Tapeten anbelangt, in allen Arbeitsbereichen Maschinen. Daraus erwächst, zusammen mit der Neuerung des Industriezeitalters, eine wahre Revolution.

Fabrication des papiers peints

Manufacturing Wall-papers

Die Herstellung der Papiertapeten

L'ensemble des techniques d'impression du papier peint dans la première moitié du XIXᵉ siècle répond à un impératif permanent dans ce métier: tenter d'illusionner le spectateur par la séduction du matériau, ses épaisseurs, ses brillances qui couvrent les murs à l'intérieur desquels il vit; établir un décalage entre la perception visuelle et la réalité de la surface murale, entre l'effet suggéré et la matière brute. Toute l'histoire de ce métier tourne autour des lois de la perception. La noblesse des papiers peints s'enracine dans ce défi et a exigé de ses artisans un génie inventif, des fantaisies techniques, particulièrement importants de 1800 à 1850.

Le but des fabricants n'a pas été d'abuser l'œil, ni de faire passer leurs papiers pour des tissus, des bois, ou des marbres, en trompant sur la marchandise. Leur objectif était plutôt d'imiter, c'est-à-dire d'obtenir des effets équivalents à ceux des soieries, des cabochons ou des stucs où la lumière se joue. Ces recherches d'analogies dans les sensations visuelles se sont traduites par une relecture originale et neuve des volumes ou des surfaces qui servaient de source d'inspiration. A cet égard la démarche du fabricant de papiers peints du début du XIXᵉ siècle est comparable à celle du lithographe ou photographe qui lui étaient contemporains[1]. Or l'un et l'autre de ces deux modes d'expression ont acquis un statut d'art noble et créateur, tandis que le papier peint est resté affecté d'une appréciation péjorative qui le classe dans une sous-catégorie des arts dits «mineurs»; c'est peut-être là le résultat d'un abus de langage qui trouverait sa source dans le terme original «papier de tenture», remplacé peu à peu par le vocable «papier peint». La première dénomination correspond à la période du XVIIIᵉ siècle où les papiers étaient en effet conçus pour remplacer à moindre prix les tentures textiles. Mais très vite les papiers peints s'étendent à toutes sortes de types décoratifs, jusqu'aux plus prestigieux et se démarquent de la seule notion de remplacement à bon marché. Il n'en reste pas moins que l'utilisation ambiguë du mot «tenture» pour qualifier un papier semble avoir entraîné, à tort, le jugement négatif de «sous-produit», ou «d'imitation» au sens péjoratif du terme, et a oblitéré l'aspect novateur et indépendant du papier peint[2].

Le papier peint reprend les grandes catégories décoratives de l'époque: dessins à motifs répétitifs, bordures, panneaux décoratifs ou «intermédiaires», rosaces de plafond etc . . . De même qu'il n'innove pas dans la hiérarchie décorative de l'ornement: somptuosité des stucs à poudre d'or, modestie des petits géométriques, chaleur des veloutés, fraîcheur des bouquets de fleurs, ou encore rigueur officielle des ors et bleus royalistes, ordre des écossais, clinquant des gauffrés, etc . . . Les bordures tiennent une place particulière, si l'on en juge par le raffinement du graphisme, le nombre important des couleurs, la richesse des techniques utilisées, notamment velou-

All the printing techniques of wall-paper during the first half of the nineteenth century responded to a permanent requirement of the craft: an attempt to give the onlooker the illusion of an attractive material, rich and brilliant, with which to cover the interior walls of his home and to bridge the gap between the visual impression suggested and the reality of the wall surface, between the intended effect and the raw material. The whole history of this craft turned around the laws of perception. The grandeur of wall-papers was rooted in this challenge, requiring of its craftsmen inventive genius and imaginative techniques, particularly during the crucial years 1800 to 1850.

The aim of the manufacturers was not to deceive the eye, nor to pass the wall-papers off as fabrics, woods or marbles by cheating on the nature of the merchandise. Their object was rather to imitate, that is to say, to achieve effects equivalent to those of light playing on silks, ornamental brass nails or stucco. This research into the analogies of visual effects resulted in a new and original re-interpretation of the volumes and surfaces that acted as a source of inspiration. In this respect the approach of the wall-paper manufacturer at the beginning of the nineteenth century was comparable to that of the lithographer or photographer who was his contemporary.[1] Both lithography and photography have acquired the status of important and creative art, while wall-paper has remained affected by pejorative appraisal that classifies it as a sub-category of the so-called 'minor' arts. Perhaps this is the result of an abuse of language that sprang from the original term *papier de tenture* ('paper hangings'), which was gradually replaced by the words *papier peint* (literally 'painted paper' or 'wall-paper'). The first appellation applies to the eighteenth-century period, when wall-papers were in fact designed as a low-cost replacements for textile hangings. But wall-papers rapidly branched into all sorts of decorative forms, even the most ambitious, and thus freed themselves of the taint of being merely cheap replacements. It was probably the ambiguous use of the descriptive term *tenture* ('hanging') to designate a paper wall-covering which incorrectly brought with it the negative view that wall-papers were 'sub-products' or 'imitations', in the pejorative sense of the word, and which obliterated the innovative and independent nature of the genre.[2]

Wall-paper mirrored the main decorative categories of the period: diaper patterns, borders, decorative or 'intermediary' panels, ceiling-roses, etc. In the same way, it made no changes in the decorative hierarchy of ornament: the sumptuousness of gold-dusted stucco, modesty of small geometrics, warmth of velvet, freshness of bouquets of flowers, or even the official severity of the Royalist blues and golds, the orderliness of plaids and the gaudiness of embossing, etc. Borders held a special place, if one is to judge by the delicacy of the drawing, the considerable number of

Alle in der ersten Hälfte des 19. Jahrhunderts beim Druck von Papiertapeten verwendeten Techniken entsprechen einer in diesem Handwerk stets gültigen Forderung: Es gilt, den Betrachter mit reizvollen, dichten und glänzenden Verkleidungen seiner vier Wände zu bezaubern und eine Verschiebung zwischen visueller Wahrnehmung und Realität der glatten Wand, zwischen dem gewollten Effekt und dem einfachen Material zu erreichen. Die ganze Geschichte der Papiertapetenherstellung dreht sich um die Gesetze der Wahrnehmung. Die Noblesse der Buntpapiere wurzelt in dieser Herausforderung und hat den Herstellern zwischen 1800 und 1850 viel Erfindergeist und große technische Vorstellungskraft abverlangt.

Die Fabrikanten wollten jedoch nie das Auge täuschen, indem sie ihre Ware als Stoff, Holz oder Marmor ausgaben. Ihr Ziel war vielmehr das Erreichen derselben Effekte auf Papier wie auf Seidenstoffen, auf einem Cabochon oder auf Stuck, auf denen das Licht spielt. Auf der Suche nach Übereinstimmung im visuellen Empfinden sah man plötzlich Volumen und Flächen, die als Quelle der Inspiration dienten, in ihrer Ursprünglichkeit und aus neuer Sicht. Die Bemühungen des Tapetenherstellers aus dem Anfang des 19. Jahrhunderts liegen hier auf gleicher Ebene wie die der Lithographen oder Photographen, die seine Zeitgenossen waren[1]. Doch während Lithographie und Photographie in die hohe Schule der Kunst und Kreativität aufgenommen wurden, blieb der Papiertapete nur ein kümmerliches Dasein als eine Untergruppe der »minderen« Künste. Dies ist – zumindest in Frankreich – vielleicht das Ergebnis eines Sprach-Irrtums, dessen Quelle im ursprünglichen Terminus *papier de tenture* (Papier-Wandbehang) zu suchen ist, der nach und nach durch die Bezeichnung *papier peint* (Papiertapeten, wörtlich: bemaltes Papier) abgelöst wurde. Die erste Benennung stammt aus der Zeit des 18. Jahrhunderts, in der diese Papiere wirklich als billigere Alternative zu den textilen Wandbespannungen gewählt wurden. Doch innerhalb kurzer Zeit wurden mit Papiertapeten vielerlei Art Dekorationen, auch sehr prächtige, hergestellt, was sie von der »billigen Alternative« abhob. Doch hat wohl die Benutzung des zwiespältigen Begriffes *tenture* (Wandbehang, Wandbespannung) zur Bezeichnung eines Papieres fälschlicherweise den Beigeschmack von »Nebenprodukt« oder »Imitation« im negativen Sinne nach sich gezogen und die bahnbrechenden Merkmale der Selbständigkeit der Papiertapete verwischt.[2]

Die Papiertapete nimmt die wichtigsten Kategorien der Dekorationskunst ihrer Zeit auf: repetierte Motive, Bordüren, Panneaus mit Mustern oder bildlichen Darstellungen, Deckenrosetten usw. Sie bleibt auch der dekorativen Rangordnung treu mit dem goldverzierten, prächtigen Stuck, den bescheiden kleinen, geometrischen Mustern, dem warmen Samt, den frischen Blumensträußen, oder

tages et dorures plus fréquents qu'ailleurs. Elles constituent comme un autre «lieu décoratif», dont la beauté invite l'œil à circuler pour délimiter un espace.

Le problème majeur dans l'art du papier peint est de savoir jouer avec la lumière; deux moyens s'offrent aux fabricants: la couleur et la brillance. La multiplicité des brevets d'invention déposés au cours du XIXe siècle démontre les limites de l'impression à la planche, en même temps que l'évolution des goûts. Parfaitement adaptée pour le rendu des plages de couleurs bien délimitées et successives, la planche traditionnelle permet de déposer une matière colorée épaisse, mate; les «jaspures (sortes de minuscules trainées au milieu des à-plats) et les bourrelets le long des contours accrochent le regard et donnent à une bonne impression ce caractère imprévu qui charme le regard.

Dans certains cas, la couleur brute a semblé insuffisante aux fabricants. Aussi ont-ils très rapidement mis au point le procédé du veloutage, dans lequel le papier a un rôle de support d'un matériau différent. Outre qu'elle a permis aux artisans de jouer sur l'opposition des brillants et des mats, suivant que les plages étaient veloutées ou non, cette technique a ouvert la voie à toutes sortes d'autres adjonctions au papier: feuilles et poudres d'or ou d'argent, fibres végétales, poils d'animaux, poudre de grès, mica, etc . . . Le rôle du papier en tant que support est ici fondamental puisque lui seul permet à de grandes surfaces murales d'être couvertes de matériaux fantaisistes et inhabituels, répondant à la recherche permanente chez les fabricants de l'étrange et de l'irréel. L'harmonisation de plusieurs effets, apparemment contradictoires sont ici réunis dans une démarche créatrice.

La couleur brute étant inadéquate aux jeux de lumière, les fabricants ont élaboré plusieurs procédés permettant d'obtenir différents degrés de brillance: satinage, lissage, vernissage. Ces recherches correspondent à un besoin de raffinement et permettent d'évoquer les matières lisses et précieuses, telles que la soie, la moire, la nacre, la laque, etc . . . Ces effets introduisent la notion de reflet, qui modifie la sensation de profondeur, «éloigne» les fonds jusqu'à créer une sensation d'irréalité.

Dans l'impression à la planche, le motif décoratif est conçu comme un module, au sein duquel le couple graphisme – couleur est indissociablement lié. Or, une technique, l'«Irisé» ou le «Fondu», qui consiste à faire éclater ce binôme, donne à la couleur son indépendance par rapport aux motifs. Ainsi la notion, jusqu'ici essentielle, du rapport du dessin, devient fluctuante. C'est là que réside toute la difficulté d'exécution des irisés: seule l'expérience et la sensibilité de l'imprimeur pouvait assurer la réussite d'un lé. De fait, les audaces vont grandissant dans la réalisation des irisés d'abord limitée aux seuls fonds, qui s'étend à l'impression, elle-même subdivisée en plusieurs vagues de fondus. Ainsi l'on obtient des effets de relief ou de clair-obscur très trompeurs, par une véritable réinterprétation du dessin, où le fond et le motif sont inextricablement liés dans l'effet final.

La taille-douce également introduit la notion d'intensité progressive de la couleur. Mais alors que les irisés conservent le principe des à-plats de couleurs, dans la taille-douce, les minuscules creux gravés dans le cylindre déposent des particules de couleurs fraction-

colours, the wealth of techniques employed, notably flocking and gilding which were more prevalent in borders than elsewhere. They seemed to form a separate decorative area, which with its beauty, invited the eye to travel around its confines.

The major problem in the art of wall-paper is understanding how to play with light; there are two ways in which a manufacturer can achieve this: by colour and by brilliancy. The great number of inventions patented during the course of the nineteenth century showed both the limits of block-printing, and the development of changing tastes. The block-print, perfectly adapted for rendering large areas of well-defined and successively printed colours, made it possible to lay down thick, matt colouring matter; 'marbling' (miniature trails drawn through flat tints) and padding along the contour lines caught the eye and endowed a good print with a certain unexpectedness that makes it so delightful to look at.

In certain cases, colour as a raw material had seemed inadequate to the manufacturers. Therefore, they had very rapidly developed the flocking process, in which papers played a supportive role for other materials. Apart from the fact that this process allowed the craftsmen to play on the contrast of glossy and matt tones, according to whether areas were to be flocked or not, this technique opened the way to all sorts of other additions to the paper: gold and silver leaf and dust, vegetable fibres, animal hair, powdered sandstone, mica, etc. The role of paper as a supporting material was a fundamental point, since it alone allowed large mural surfaces to be covered with exotic and unusual materials that met the manufacturers' continual quest for strange and unreal effects. Several apparently contradictory effects could be brought together and fused in a creative form.

Raw colour being inadequate to show the play of light, manufacturers evolved several processes that made it possible to achieve varying degrees of brilliance: satining, smoothing and varnishing. This research corresponded to a need for subtlety and made it possible to evoke shiny, precious materials such as silk, moiré, mother of pearl, lacquer, etc. These effects introduced the idea of reflection, which altered the sense of depth, removing the background into the distance to create a feeling of unreality.

In block-printing, the decorative motif was designed as the module in which the twin elements of drawing and colour were indissolubly linked. A technique known as irisé or fondu split this link and gave colour its independence in relation to patterns. Thus the idea of the repeat design, which had been essential up to this point, now became variable. Here lay all the difficulties of executing irisé paper: only the experience and sensitivity of the printer could assure the success of a strip of it. In fact, there was increasing boldness in the execution of irisé papers, at first confined to the background only, then spreading to the impression, which was broken up into several waves of blended colours. Very deceptive effects of relief or chiaroscuro were obtained by a genuine re-interpretation of design, the background and the pattern becoming inextricably linked in the final effect.

In the same way, metal engraving introduced the idea of progressive intensity of colour. But while irisé papers maintained the principle of flat-toned colours, in metal engrav-

aber mit dem streng offiziellen, royalistischen Gold und Blau, mit den ordentlichen Schottenmustern und den schillernden Gaufrierungen usw. Die Bordüren nehmen kraft ihrer eleganten Zeichnungen, der Anzahl der verwendeten Farben, des Aufwandes der angewandten Techniken einen besonderen Platz ein. Auch kommen hier Veloutage und Vergoldung häufiger vor als anderswo. Die Bordüren stellen beinahe eine andere Dekorationsart dar, deren Schönheit das Auge in andere Dimensionen entrückt.

Das größte Problem der Papierdruckkunst ist das Wissen um das Spiel zwischen Licht und Schatten. Um diese Wirkungen zu erhalten, gibt es zwei Wege, nämlich Farbe und Glanz. Die Vielfalt der im 19. Jahrhundert ausgestellten Patente deckt nicht nur die Grenzen des Handdruckes auf, sondern auch die Entwicklung der Geschmacksrichtungen. Der Handdruck eignet sich hervorragend für große, gut abgegrenzte und nacheinander gedruckte Farbflächen, man kann mit der Druckplatte dickflüssige, stumpfe Farben auftragen; die kleinen Sprenkel in den Farbflächen und die Wülstchen an ihren Rändern halten den Blick fest und geben einem guten Druck seinen ganz speziellen, gefälligen Charakter.

In einigen Fällen scheint aber die bloße Farbe ungenügend. So wurde sehr früh das Veloutieren erfunden, bei dem das Papier Träger eines andern Materials wird. Nicht nur erlaubte diese Technik das Spiel mit matten und glänzenden Flächen, je nachdem, welche Teile man veloutierte oder frei ließ; man begann auch, das Papier mit allerlei andern Materialien zu bekleben: mit Blattgold und -silber, Gold- und Silberstaub, Pflanzenfasern, Tierhaaren, Sandsteinpulver, Glimmer usw. Die Rolle des Papiers als Träger ist hier wesentlich, weil man nur dank dem Papier große Wandflächen mit extravaganten und ungewöhnlichen Materialien schmücken kann, was ganz der unermüdlichen Suche der Hersteller nach Merkwürdigem und Unwirklichem entgegenkommt. Das Zusammenspiel verschiedener gegensätzlicher Effekte wird hier zum schöpferischen Unterfangen.

Da die bloße Farbe für das Spiel von Licht und Schatten ungeeignet war, haben die Fabrikanten mehrere Verfahren erarbeitet, die es ermöglichten, verschiedene Glanzabstufungen zu erreichen: Satinieren, Glätten, Firnissen. Die Forschungen entsprachen einem Bedürfnis nach Verfeinerung und erlaubten, glatte, kostbare Materialien wie Seide, Moiré, Perlmutt oder Lack in Erinnerung zu rufen. Diese Behandlung des Papiers erzeugt den Eindruck von Reflexen, was die Tiefenwirkung ändert und den Fond bis zur Vermittlung eines Eindruckes von Unwirklichkeit wegzurücken scheint.

Beim Handdruck verschmelzen Zeichnung und Farbgebung zur Einheit des als Modul aufgefaßten Motivs. Die Technik des Irisdruckes aber löst diese Einheit auf. Zeichnung und Farben werden als getrennte Größen angesehen. Der bis anhin wichtige Begriff einer klaren Rapportzeichnung wird verwischt. Dies macht die Herstellung der Iristapeten so schwierig, nur die Erfahrung und das Fingerspitzengefühl des Druckers entscheiden über die glückliche Vollendung einer Bahn. Man bemüht sich um immer erstaunlichere Effekte; war der Irisdruck erst nur auf die Fondfarben beschränkt, so irisiert man nun auch das gedruckte Motiv, das selbst noch unterteilt wird. Die Wirkung ist verblüffend: Grund und Motiv sind untrennbar

nées et d'intensité variable. Ce procédé est entièrement fondé sur le pressentiment de la loi des contrastes simultanés des couleurs, selon laquelle l'œil, en s'éloignant lira non pas une série de petits «picots», mais une «tache» globale. Outre la grande vitesse de l'impression, l'intérêt de cette nouvelle technique réside dans la subtilité que l'on peut donner aux intensités de couleurs et par conséquent aux effets de clair-obscur, de relief, d'éloigné-rapproché sans que l'œil n'«accroche» sur des contours précis.

ing the tiny grooves engraved in the cylinder deposited particles of fragmented colour of variable intensity. This process was based entirely on the principles of the law of simultaneous contrasts of colour, according to which the eye, at a distance, would blur the colours into a whole, rather than reading them as a series of small dots. Apart from the speed of printing, the interest of this new technique lay in the subtlety that could be given to depths of colour and consequently to effects of chiaroscuro, relief and interplay in depth, which could be achieved without the eye fixing on precise outlines.

miteinander verschmolzen und erzeugen täuschende Relief- und Clair-obscur-Effekte.

Durch den Kupferstich entsteht der Begriff der verschiedenen Farbintensitäten. Die Iristapeten bewahren ihrerseits das Prinzip der uniformen Farbflächen, was die Intensität betrifft, während die in den winzigen Vertiefungen des Druckzylinders enthaltenen Farbpartikel in kleinste Einheiten zerteilte Farbflächen von unterschiedlicher Intensität abgeben. Dieses Vorgehen ist auf der Gesetzmäßigkeit der simultanen Farbkontraste begründet, nach der das Auge in großer Entfernung statt einer Unzahl Punkte nur noch einen Flecken wahrnimmt. Außerdem ist die Kupferstichtechnik nicht nur sehr rationell, sie vermittelt durch ihre Fähigkeit, Farbintensität zu graduieren, einen besseren Eindruck von Hell-Dunkel-, Relief- oder Nah-Fern-Wirkung, ohne daß der Blick an scharfen Konturen hängen bleibt.

Rôle du Dessinateur

L'importance du dessinateur au début du XIXe siècle est fondamental dans le succès et le prestige d'une manufacture: il est intégré à un établissement[3], conçoit les nouveaux dessins et se tient informé de l'évolution des goûts, il donne toutes les instructions au graveur pour l'exécution de la planche jusque dans ses moindres détails et surveille la qualité de l'impression des papiers peints[4]. Il est généralement spécialisé dans la composition des dessins et bordures, et ne réalise que très rarement des décors panoramiques[5]. Ce dessinateur «industriel» se distingue de l'artiste non seulement par le type de travail qu'il effectue, mais aussi par un anonymat quasi-total[6]: vivant dans les secrets d'une manufacture, faisant l'objet de concurrences acharnées, tout vedettariat lui est interdit. En cela il participe à l'ambiguité de tout papier peint qui, même très beau, ayant fait l'objet des soins les plus attentifs, destiné aux pièces les plus somptueuses, reste un objet décoratif modeste, anonyme.

Role of the Designer

At the beginning of the nineteenth century, the importance of the designer was fundamental to the success and prestige of a factory: he was integrated into the business,[3] conceived new designs, kept himself abreast of changing tastes, gave all the instructions to the engraver of the printing block, down to the smallest detail, and inspected the quality of printing of the wall-papers.[4] The designer generally specialized in the composition of patterns and borders and only rarely undertook panoramic decorations.[5] This 'industrial' designer was distinguished from the artist not only by the kind of work he undertook, but also by his almost total anonymity:[6] living with the secrets of the factory, the object of unending rivalries, he himself was denied any claim to fame. In this, the designer shared the same ambiguity of status that characterized all wall-paper: although very beautiful, the object of the most careful attention, destined for the most magnificent rooms, yet it remained a modest and anonymous object of decoration.

Die Rolle des Entwerfers

Der Einfluß des Entwerfers im 19. Jahrhundert ist ausschlaggebend für Erfolg und Ansehen einer Manufaktur. Er gehört sozusagen zum Inventar[3], denkt neue Dessins aus und ist stets auf dem Laufenden, was die Entwicklung des Publikumsgeschmackes betrifft. Außerdem gibt er dem Graveur umfassende und detaillierte Angaben über die Ausführung der Druckplatte und überwacht die Qualität des Tapetendruckes[4]. Meistens ist der Entwerfer Spezialist für Rapportzeichnungen und Bordüren, nur selten wird er für die Ausführung von Bildtapeten herangezogen[5]. Dieser »Industriezeichner« unterscheidet sich vom Künstler nicht nur durch die Art seiner Arbeit, sondern auch durch eine fast vollständige Anonymität[6]: An seine Manufaktur gebunden und als Gegenstand einer unerbittlichen Konkurrenz ist ihm jedes In-Erscheinung-Treten versagt. Hiermit hat er Anteil am zwiespältigen Charakter der Papiertapete, die, wenngleich von großer Schönheit und unter den sorgfältigsten Bedingungen gearbeitet, den vornehmsten Räumlichkeiten zur Zierde bestimmt, doch nur bescheidene, namenlose Dekoration bleibt.

Les Manufactures

De toutes les manufactures actives durant la première moitié du XIXe siècle, aucune ne semble avoir existé avant la Révolution: Jacquemart et Bénard, associés de Réveillon, à la Folie-Titon, prennent sa succession après 1789, la Manufacture Hartmann Risler, qui deviendra Zuber, à Rixheim, naît en 1797, Dufour apparait dans les archives en 1804 à Mâcon, mais existait vraisemblablement peu avant, Dauptain est cité comme marchand à Paris en 1784 et devient fabricant par la suite, Marguerie est fondé en 1832, ainsi que Riottot, Délicourt en 1838 et Isidore Leroy en 1842, tous à Paris. Leurs fortunes sont variables: Zuber et Leroy sont les seules manufactures à traverser le XIXe siècle sans rencontrer d'obstacles majeurs à leur développement. Jacquemart et Bénard au contraire disparaissent en 1840. A l'exception de Zuber, les manufactures les plus prestigieuses du XIXe siècle ont une origine commune: les ateliers de Dufour. Celui-ci en effet s'associe à son gendre, Amable Leroy

The Factories

Of all the factories active during the first half of the nineteenth century, none seems to have existed before the French Revolution: Jacquemart and Bénard, partners with Réveillon at the Folie-Titon, took over from him in 1789; the Hartmann Risler (later Zuber) Factory at Rixheim originated in 1797; Dufour appeared in the Mâcon archives in 1804, but probably existed a little before; Dauptain was listed as a trader in Paris in 1784 and subsequently became a manufacturer; Marguerie, like Riottot, was founded in 1832; Délicourt in 1838 and Isidore Leroy in 1842, all in Paris. Their fortunes were variable: Zuber and Leroy were the only factories to go through the nineteenth century without encountering any major obstacles to their development. Jacquemart and Bénard, by contrast, disappeared in 1840. With the exception of Zuber, the most important nineteenth-century factories all had a common origin – the workshops of Dufour.

Die Manufakturen

Von all den in der ersten Hälfte des 19. Jahrhunderts tätigen Manufakturen scheint keine vor der Revolution bestanden zu haben. Jacquemart und Bénard, die Partner Réveillons in der Manufaktur Folie-Titon, übernehmen diese nach 1789; die Manufaktur Hartmann Risler in Rixheim, die später von Zuber übernommen wird, entsteht 1797; Dufour tritt in den Archiven von Mâcon 1804 in Erscheinung, bestand aber offensichtlich schon wenig früher; Dauptain ist in Paris 1784 als Händler bekannt und wird später Fabrikant; die Manufakturen Marguerie und Riottat werden 1832, Délicourt 1838 und Isidore Leroy in Paris gegründet. Nicht alle haben Glück: Zuber und Leroy sind die beiden einzigen Manufakturen, die heil und ohne große Hindernisse für ihre Entwicklung durch das 19. Jahrhundert kommen. Hingegen verschwinden Jacquemart et Bénard 1840. Mit Ausnahme von Zuber haben alle namhaften Manufakturen des 19. Jahrhunderts eine gemeinsame Wurzel, nämlich die

en 1821 et lui abandonne toute l'activité de l'établissement aux environs de 1828–1830; l'affaire est définitivement cédée à Lapeyre en 1836, passe à Kob en 1859, puis à Desfossé en 1865. D'autre part, Xavier Mader s'est formé et a dirigé les dessinateurs et graveurs de Dufour jusqu'en 1823, date à laquelle il fonda sa propre manufacture. Sa veuve vend les ateliers à Desfossé en 1851. Enfin, Délicourt débute comme commis chez Dufour et suit les Mader en 1823, avant de lancer sa propre affaire en 1838.

La reprise d'une manufacture de papiers peints signifie non seulement l'acquisition du stock de planches, mais également la propriété de tous les secrets de fabrication, et par conséquent, les moyens de poursuivre une production de qualité. Ainsi se sont créées de véritables lignées de manufactures de premier ordre. Un point réunit toutes ces entreprises qu'elles soient héritières de traditions prestigieuses ou nouvellement créées, c'est leur acharnement à inventer de nouveaux procédés techniques, consistant essentiellement à améliorer la qualité des papiers peints, sans qu'interviennent encore les impératifs de productivité[7].

Les Motifs

Comme dans les autres domaines de l'art décoratif, le règne végétal, ramages, bouquets, guirlandes, verdures, charmilles, constitue la base de la grammaire décorative du papier peint. Les fleurs et feuillages sont utilisés soit comme thème principal, soit en accompagnement, mais sont toujours traités avec soin. Les bordures florales occupent une place particulièrement importante: on y trouve en moyenne un grand nombre de couleurs, des veloutages et repiquages fréquents, des irisés[8]. Les verdures représentent un marché moins important que les papiers à fleurs polychromes: le papier peint à cette période recherche volontiers les couleurs vives, souvent très pures et contrastées, et souvent très surprenantes dans notre conception actuelle des harmonies. Leurs tonalités s'adoucissent vers 1830 dans une relecture plus tempérée de la nature. Durant le Premier Empire le rendu des reliefs et des ombres est généralement obtenu par de petites hachures en dents de scie, de teintes plus ou moins sombres, tandis qu'à partir de 1840, on observe des plages concentriques de teintes dégradées à contours linéaires.

Les draperies tiennent une place à part dans le contexte de l'imitation. Elles font leur apparition dans les bordures, au tout début du XIXᵉ siècle, stylisées, géométrisées et sont fabriquées jusqu'en 1840–1850, nécessitant en moyenne 10 à 15 couleurs (les cas extrêmes vont de 7 à 26 couleurs). Les grandes draperies, jouant le rôle de panneaux intermédiaires non répétitifs (Nᵒˢ 542 à 550), connaissent une vogue limitée dans le temps, entre 1808 et 1825 environ; généralement 11 à 27 couleurs d'impression permettent de rendre les retombées d'un plissé. Les dentelles, moires, capitons, satins, etc . . . sont réalisés à peu de frais entre 1825 et 1840: 2 à 4 couleurs; mais ils vont jusqu'à 21 couleurs entre 1840 et 1850. Le veloutage n'est jamais utilisé dans les documents qui subsistent dans les collections actuelles, et pour les bordures, ils sont très rares, contrairement aux autres types de mo-

Dufour went into partnership with his son-in-law, Amable Leroy, in 1821 and left all the running of the factory to him from about 1828–30; the business was eventually made over to Lapeyre in 1836, passed to Kob in 1859, then to Desfossé in 1865. Moreover, Xavier Mader was trained at Dufour and managed Dufour's designers and engravers until 1823, the date at which he founded his own factory. His widow sold the studios to Desfossé in 1851. Finally, Délicourt began as a clerk at Dufour's and followed the Maders in 1823, before setting up his own business in 1838.

The taking-over of a wall-paper factory meant not only acquiring the stock of printing-blocks but also all the secrets of manufacture and consequently the means to achieve a product of quality. Thus a real stock of first-rate factories was created. Whether they had inherited famous traditions or were newly formed, these enterprises all had one thing in common – their desperate eagerness to invent new technical processes, essentially in order to improve the quality of wall-papers, for requirements of productivity were not yet their prime concern.[7]

The Designs

As in other fields of the decorative arts, the vegetable kingdom – floral designs, bouquets, garlands, foliage, bowers – formed the basis of the decorative vocabulary of wall-paper. Flowers and foliage were used either as the principal theme or as accompaniment, but always treated with care. Floral borders played a particularly important role: they were normally made up of a great many colours, frequently flocked, over-printed or irisé.[8] The market for foliage designs was less important than that for polychrome floral papers. Wall-papers at this period tended to take on bright colours, often pure and surprisingly contrasted according to our current ideas of harmony. Tonalities softened by about 1830, in a more restrained re-interpretation of nature. During the First Empire (1804–15), the rendering of relief and shadow was generally achieved by small areas of serrated flocking in more or less sombre colours, whereas the period after 1840 saw the appearance of concentric areas of colour shading off in linear contours.

Draperies played a separate part in the context of imitative wall-papers. Stylized and geometric examples appeared in borders at the very beginning of the nineteenth century and were manufactured up to 1840–50, requiring on average 10 to 15 colours (the extremes ranged from 7 to 26 colours). Large draperies, used as intermediary, non-repetitive panels (Nᵒˢ 542–50), enjoyed a limited vogue between about 1808 and 1825; printing from 11 to 27 colours made it possible to reproduce the effects of hanging folds. Lace, moirés, cappadine, satins, etc. were produced at little cost in 2 or 4 colours between 1825 and 1840, but they had up to 21 colours between 1840 and 1850. Flocking was never used in the examples of drapery-work extant in current collections and was rarely found in borders, unlike other types of design. Manufacturers executed sumptuous trompes-l'œil draperies and fabrics, without using the method that would have best created the illusion, that of flocking. There is no doubt that they would

Dufourschen Ateliers. Dufour verbindet sich 1821 mit seinem Schwiegersohn Amable Leroy und überläßt ihm das Unternehmen um 1828–1830, 1836 wird es von Lapeyre übernommen, um 1859 an Kob und 1865 an Desfossé überzugehen. Andererseits wurde Xavier Mader bei Dufour ausgebildet und hat dann die Entwerfer und Stecher von Dufour bis 1823 angeleitet, in diesem Jahr hat er seine eigene Manufaktur gegründet. Seine Witwe verkauft alles an Desfossé im Jahre 1851. Délicourt seinerseits tritt als Gehilfe bei Dufour ein und wird 1823 von Mader »übernommen«, bevor 1838 seine eigene Firma gründet.

Eine Papiertapeten-Manufaktur übernehmen, heißt nicht nur Erwerben sämtlicher Druckplatten, sondern auch Kennenlernen aller Fabrikationsgeheimnisse. Deshalb war es möglich, die Produktion qualitativ stets auf dem Höchststand zu halten. So entstanden wahre Geschlechter bester Manufakturen. Eines ist allen diesen Manufakturen, ob alteingesessen oder neugegründet, gemeinsam: die Bemühungen um technische Neuerungen zum Erhalt bester Tapetenqualität, ohne daß die Forderungen nach Produktivität eine Rolle gespielt hätten[7].

Die Motive

Wie in anderen Gebieten der Dekorationskunst bilden auch bei den Papiertapeten allerlei Pflanzenmotive den Grundstock der Muster, so zum Beispiel Zweige, Baumgruppen, Girlanden, Blattwerk und Lauben. Blüten und Blätter kommen entweder als Hauptthema oder als begleitende Verzierung vor, sind aber immer mit großer Sorgfalt ausgeführt. Bordüren mit Blumenmustern nehmen einen wichtigen Platz ein, findet man doch auf ihnen meistens große Farbenvielfalt, oft sind sie auch veloutiert, repiquiert oder irisiert[8]. (Bei der Repiquage werden veloutierte Teile des Musters mit einem Überdruck versehen). Tapeten mit reinem Blattwerk sind etwas weniger gut verkäuflich als solche mit bunten Blumenmustern: Die damalige Zeit liebte kräftige, oft klare und kontrastreiche Farben, die uns heute in ihrer Zusammenstellung überraschen. Gegen 1830 sieht man die Natur mit andern Augen, die Farben werden weicher. Während des Premier Empire werden Relief und Schatten meist durch Sägezahnschraffierung in mehr oder weniger dunkler Farbe gebildet, nach 1840 erreicht man diese Wirkung durch konzentrisch degradierte Farbflecken mit linearen Konturen.

Eine Besonderheit unter den Imitationen bilden die Drapierungen. Zu Anfang des 19. Jahrhunderts erscheinen sie erstmals stilisiert und geometrisch auf Bordüren und werden bis etwa 1840–1850 hergestellt, wobei man im Durchschnitt 10 bis 15 Farben benutzt (in extremen Fällen 7 bis 26 Farben). Große Draperien als Einsatzstücke ohne Wiederholung des Motivs (Nr. 542 bis 550) werden etwa von 1808 bis 1825 in begrenztem Maße geschätzt. Meistens braucht man 11 bis 27 Farben, um einen Faltenwurf zu reproduzieren. Spitzen, Moirés, Polsterungen, Satins usw. sind zwischen 1825 und 1840 weniger aufwendig, sie benötigen nur etwa zwei bis vier Farben, haben aber bis zu 21 Farben zwischen 1840 und 1850. Keines der uns verbliebenen Dokumente dieser Art ist veloutiert, und die Bordüren sind es sehr selten, im Gegensatz

tifs. Les fabricants ont réalisé des trompe l'œil somptueux de draperies et tissus, sans utiliser le moyen qui aurait le mieux permis d'abuser l'œil, à savoir la poudre de laine. Qu'ils aient voulu imiter des étoffes plus délicates que les velours, tels que satins, soieries et guipures, ne fait aucun doute; il est surprenant qu'ils soient allés jusqu'à éliminer la possibilité qui leur était techniquement familière d'utiliser le papier comme support d'un matériau textile. Sans doute peut-on y voir la preuve de l'une des caractéristiques de ce métier: il ne s'agissait pas tant d'imiter servilement que de recréer un produit nouveau, agréable à l'œil à partir d'un matériau différent, et de lui assurer le succès en lui donnant des caractères distincts de sa source d'inspiration directe: techniques différentes, sensations visuelles inhabituelles, prix généralement inférieur.

Dans ce même contexte d'indépendance dans l'imitation de matériaux différents du papier, les fabricants se sont très tôt intéressés au décor en stuc qui apparait dans les bordures à la fin du XVIIIe siècle, tandis que l'on trouve les fleurs dites «d'ornement», c'est-à-dire figées dans une représentation sculpturale à partir de 1825. Dans l'un et l'autre cas, le nombre des couleurs est assez réduit (1 à 5 pour les dessins répétitifs, 2 à 12 pour les bordures). Les veloutages et repiquages, les rehauts de poudres dorées ou argentées sont fréquents dans les bordures.

Les autres documents inspirés de la pierre sculptée, dans le style gothique ou rocaille, créés entre 1820 et 1845, témoignent des mêmes tendances: nombre relativement réduit de couleurs, veloutages fréquents des bordures.

Enfin, les cabochons, plumes et bois font une apparition ponctuelle entre 1835 et 1845. Outre les engouements de la mode, cette période correspond au moment où les fabricants recherchent d'autres nouveautés dans le domaine des matériaux réels ou de fantaisie, collés ou reproduits sur le papier[9].

Les motifs à figures se divisent en deux catégories: les sculptures hiératiques et les personnages illustrant un épisode d'un récit en vogue et présentés généralement en médaillons. Les premiers, inspirés de reliefs antiques de pierre et plus rarement de bronze, sont une constante dans le répertoire des fabricants de papiers peints. Les personnages sont drapés dans la dignité sévère des grisailles rigoureusement dégradées du noir au blanc. Les bronzes reproduisent ce même échelonnement, du bleu-vert pâle au noir, avec toutefois un reflet de poudre dorée.

Les figures en médaillons (Nos 556 à 559), comme montées en scène pour évoquer l'épisode d'une fable ou d'un roman, apparaissent vers 1835. Elles sont polychromes et nécessitent entre 20 et 40 couleurs d'impression. La représentation des figures dans les dessins et bordures à motifs répétitifs constituent une sorte de défi au principe même du raccord. La richesse de l'iconographie relève autant du devant de cheminée que du dessus de porte.

Entre 1800 et 1850, le papier peint atteint sa majorité, c'est-à-dire qu'il prend son autonomie technique et occupe une place spécifique dans l'évolution de la grammaire décorative. Il témoigne de la relation privilégiée que nourrit l'homme à l'égard des murs qui le protègent.

have liked to imitate materials more delicate than velvets, such as satins, silks, guipures; it is surprising that they should have practically eliminated the possibility of using a method that was technically familiar to them – paper as a support for textiles. Here lies the proof of one characteristic of the craft: it was concerned not so much with servile imitation as with the creation of a new, visually attractive product from a different material, which achieved its success by possessing characteristics distinct from its source of inspiration: different techniques, unusual visual effects and a generally lower price.

In this same context of independence in the matter of imitating materials other than paper, manufacturers very soon took an interest in stucco decoration; this appeared in borders at the end of the eighteenth century, while so-called 'ornamental' flowers, which were set in a sculptural background, were found after 1825. In both cases, the number of colours was relatively low (1 to 5 for repeat designs, 2 to 12 for borders). Flocking, over-printing and highlights of gold and silver dust were prevalent in the borders.

The other specimens inspired by sculpted stone and created between 1820 and 1845 in the Gothic or Rococo style, show the same tendencies: a somewhat lower number of colours, with flocking prevalent in the borders.

Finally, ornamental brass-nails, feathers and wood appeared on cue with fashion between 1835 and 1845. In addition to following crazes of fashion, this period corresponded to the manufacturers' search for further novelties in the field of real or imaginary materials, which were applied to or reproduced on paper.[9]

Figure designs were divided into two categories: hieratic sculptures and characters illustrating an episode from a narrative currently in vogue, the latter generally presented in medallions. The former, inspired by antique reliefs in stone and, more rarely, bronze, were a constant theme in the wall-paper manufacturers' repertoire. The figures were draped and executed in the severe dignity of grisaille, rigorously shaded from black to white. The bronzes reproduced this same gradation, shaded in their case from pale greenish-blue to black, always with a reflection of gold dust.

Figures in medallions (Nos 556–59), which looked as though they had been put on stage to evoke an episode from a fable or fictional tale, appeared about 1835. They were in polychrome and required between twenty and forty colours for printing. The portrayal of figures in designs and borders with repetitive motifs constituted a sort of challenge to the very principle of repeats. These richly iconographic designs were used to enhance chimney-screens as well as over-doors.

Between 1800 and 1850, wall-paper came of age: it achieved its technical autonomy and won a specific place in the evolution of the grammar of decoration. It was evidence of the privileged relationship that man fosters with regard to the walls that protect him.

zu Bordüren mit andern Motiven. Die Fabrikanten haben verblüffende Imitationen von Draperien und Geweben hergestellt, ohne aber das Material zu verwenden, das das Auge am besten getäuscht hätte, nämlich den Wollstaub. Zweifellos wollten sie feinere Stoffe als Sammet imitieren, wie zum Beispiel Satin, Seide oder Guipure, indessen ist es erstaunlich, daß sie die ihnen geläufige Technik, das Papier als Träger eines anderen, textilen Materials zu verwenden, nicht ausgenützt haben. Sicher beweist dies eine Eigenheit des Berufsstandes, es ging ja nicht in erster Linie darum, getreulich nachzuahmen, als vielmehr ein gefälliges neues Produkt aus einem anderen Material zu schaffen und ihm den Erfolg zu sichern, indem man ihm den Charakter des nachgeahmten Materials gab; mit andern Techniken erreichte man ungewöhnliche Wirkungen zu – meist – niedererem Preis.

In diesem Zusammenhang, andere Materialien beliebig auf Papier nachahmen zu können, gehört auch die Imitation des Stucks. Schon zu Ende des 18. Jahrhunderts erscheinen die ersten Stuckbordüren, während man nach 1825 Blumen wie in Bildhauerarbeit findet. In beiden Fällen beschränkt man sich auf wenige Farben, eine bis fünf bei wiederholten Motiven, zwei bis zwölf für die Bordüren, die oft veloutiert, repiquiert oder mit Gold- oder Silberstaub verziert sind.

Die andern von der Bildhauerkunst inspirierten Dokumente, entweder im gotischen oder im Rocaillestil, treten zwischen 1820 und 1845 auf. Sie haben häufig dieselben Merkmale wie die obgenannten: relativ wenig verschiedene Farben und veloutierte Bordüren.

Cabochons, Federn und Hölzer erscheinen zeitlich begrenzt zwischen 1835 und 1845. Diese Zeitspanne kennt exzentrische Moden und entspricht der Epoche, in der die Fabrikanten nach Neuheiten auf dem Gebiet echter oder nachgeahmter Werkstoffe suchen, um diese auf dem Papier zu imitieren oder aufzukleben[9].

Die figürlichen Darstellungen gehören zwei verschiedenen Kategorien an: Skulpturen mit religiösen Motiven und Darstellungen bekannter und beliebter Romanfiguren, diese meistens in Medaillons. Die ersten, meist antiken Stein- oder – seltener – Bronzereliefs nachempfunden, gehören zum eisernen Bestand der Tapetenfabrikanten. Die steinernen Figuren sind als Grisaillen in strenger, peinlich genau von Schwarz bis Weiß reichender Abtönung dargestellt, die Bronzen haben dieselbe Farbabstufung, aber von sehr hellem Blaugrün bis Schwarz, allenfalls durch etwas Goldstaub aufgelockert.

Gegen 1835 findet man Medaillons (Nr. 556 bis 559) mit Szenen aus Fabel und Roman. In ihrer Buntheit benötigen sie 20 bis 40 Farben. Die Darstellung der Figuren in den Dessins und den Bordüren mit wiederholten Motiven sind eine Art Herausforderung an das Prinzip des nahtlosen Zusammenfügens der Bahnen. Die Pracht der Motive machte auch vor Kaminschirmen und Supraporten nicht halt.

Zwischen 1800 und 1850 wird die Papiertapete mündig, ihre Technik wird selbständig, und sie nimmt endlich den ihr gebührenden Platz in der Entwicklung der Dekorationsmöglichkeiten ein. Die Papiertapete ist der Beweis für den Wunsch des Menschen, seine vier Wände in ein behagliches Heim zu verwandeln.

Les Techniques

Toute sorte de papier peut être utilisé pour la fabrication des papiers peints. Cependant les impressions les meilleures se font sur papier chiffon au début du XIXe siècle.

Jusqu'en 1850, les feuilles étaient fabriquées à la cuve, pièce par pièce. A la fin du XVIIIe siècle, les fabricants imaginèrent de coller ces feuilles les unes aux autres pour constituer un rouleau de 10 mètres de long environ. Le raccord de chacune de ces feuilles à la suivante se nomme «rabouture».

Fonçage Après que le rouleau de papier ait été constitué, intervient l'opération de fonçage, qui consiste à étendre une couleur de fond uniformément sur toute la surface du papier. Pour cela trois ouvriers se succèdent: le premier utilise une brosse rectangulaire très allongée, la trempe dans la couleur et la passe rapidement dans le sens longitudinal du rouleau de papier préalablement étendu sur une table longue de 10 mètres. Le second se sert d'une brosse identique avec laquelle il égalise la couleur dans le sens transversal. Enfin le troisième travaille avec une brosse ronde qu'il fait tourner légèrement dans le sens circulaire sur toute la surface du papier. Ces trois brossages qui se succèdent très rapidement avant que la couleur n'ait eu le temps de sécher, ont pour effet de donner au fond une uniformité sans accrocs.

The Techniques

All kinds of paper can be used for the manufacture of wall-papers; however, at the beginning of the nineteenth century, the best prints were made on rag-paper. Until 1850, the sheets of paper were made in vats, piece by piece. At the end of the eighteenth century, the manufacturers contrived to paste these sheets to one another to make up a roll about 10 metres in length. The joining of each sheet to the following one was called *rabouture* ('joining end to end').

Laying the Ground. After the roll of paper was made up, came the operation of grounding, which consisted of spreading a ground colour uniformly over the whole surface of the paper. For that operation, three workmen followed one another: the first used a very elongated rectangular brush, which he dipped in the colour and passed rapidly along the length of the roll of paper that had previously been spread out on a table 10-metres long. The second used an identical brush to spread the colour evenly across the width of the roll. Finally, the third worked with a round brush that he turned lightly in circles over the whole surface of the paper. These three brushing movements, which followed each other very rapidly before the colour had time to dry, had the effect of providing a uniform ground with no breaks.

Die Techniken

Zur Herstellung von Papiertapeten eignet sich jede Art von Papier. Doch die schönsten Drucke entstehen anfangs 19. Jahrhundert auf Hadernpapier, also aus Lumpen hergestelltem Papier.

Bis 1850 wurden die einzelnen Bögen von Hand aus der Bütte geschöpft. Ende 18. Jahrhundert begannen die Fabrikanten, die Bögen zu etwa 10 m langen Rollen zusammenzukleben. Die Nahtstellen zwischen den einzelnen Bögen nannte man *rabouture* (Ende an Ende fügen).

Grundieren Ist die Papierrolle hergestellt, wird sie anschließend grundiert. Dabei wird die Fondfarbe regelmäßig über das ganze Tapetenpapier verteilt. Drei Arbeiter sind bei diesem Vorgang beschäftigt. Der erste benützt eine rechteckige, sehr lange Bürste, die er nach Eintauchen in den Farbkasten rasch in der Längsrichtung über das Papier führt, welches auf einem 10 m langen Tisch ausgebreitet ist. Der zweite Arbeiter egalisiert die Farbe mit einer ebensolchen Bürste, aber in Querrichtung. Der dritte schließlich fährt mit einer Rundbürste kreisförmig über das Papier. Diese drei Arbeitsgänge müssen in schneller Folge vor sich gehen, bevor die Farbe zu trocknen beginnt; nur so wird ein gleichmäßiger Grund gewährleistet.

Deux brosses de fonçage et une planche d'impression. Collection Musée des Arts Décoratifs, Paris

Two brushes for laying the ground and a printing block. Musée des Arts Décoratifs, Paris

Zwei Bürsten zum Grundieren und ein Druckstock. Paris, Musée des Arts Décoratifs

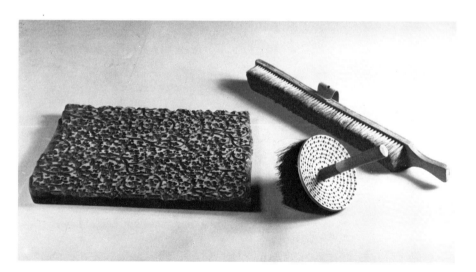

Lissage Dans certains cas, les pièces ainsi foncées, puis séchées, peuvent être lissées ou satinées. Pour le lissage le papier est posé à l'envers, c'est-à-dire la couleur au contact de la table. L'ouvrier y roule une sorte de galet de cuivre arrondi, et donne ainsi au papier un aspect parfaitement uni (le papier fabriqué à la cuve présente toujours à l'état brut des vergures ou des irrégularités), tout en préservant la matité de la couleur.

Satinage Le satinage au contraire a pour but de faire briller la couleur de fond. Dans ce cas le papier, posé à l'endroit, est talqué avant que l'ouvrier n'y passe énergiquement une brosse à poils courts et durs.

Smoothing. In certain cases, the sheets coloured in the manner described above and then dried could be smoothed or satined. For smoothing, the paper was placed the wrong way up, that is to say with the colour face down on the table. The workman rolled a sort of rounded copper roller over it, giving the paper a perfectly smooth appearance (paper made in a vat always shows wire marks or irregularities in its raw state), while preserving the matt colouring.

Satining. By contrast, the aim of satining was to make the ground colour shine. In this case the paper, placed the right way up, was sprinkled with talc before the workman passed a brush with short, hard bristles over it.

Glätten In gewissen Fällen werden die grundierten und getrockneten Tapeten geglättet oder satiniert. Zum Glätten wird das Papier mit der Farbseite nach unten auf den Tisch gelegt. Der Arbeiter fährt mit einer Art an den Kanten abgerundetem Zylinder aus Kupfer darüber, was dem Papier absolute Glätte verleiht (unbehandeltes handgeschöpftes Papier hat immer Wasserstreifen oder Unregelmäßigkeiten) und die Mattheit der Farbe nicht beeinträchtigt.

Satinieren Beim Satinieren wird der Grundfarbe Glanz verliehen. In diesem Fall wird das Papier mit der Farbseite nach oben hingelegt, mit Talkpuder bestreut und mit einer kurz- und harthaarigen Bürste kräftig gebürstet.

*Atelier d'impression à la planche
au XIXᵉ siècle*

*Nineteenth-century workshop
for block-printing*

Handdruck-Werkstatt des 19. Jahrhunderts

Impression a la planche L'impression proprement dite des pièces se fait à l'aide de planches de bois gravées. Elles sont constituées de trois épaisseurs de bois collées à contrefil; la dernière d'entre elles, en bois de fruitier, porte la gravure en relief du dessin à imprimer; elle est exécutée par le graveur, appelé aussi «metteur sur bois». A chaque couleur correspond une planche, de sorte qu'un dessin de 7 couleurs par exemple nécessite 7 planches complémentaires. Chacune de ces planches porte la gravure d'une hauteur de dessin (dit aussi «rapport»), de sorte que l'imprimeur la déplace successivement sur toute la longueur du rouleau de papier. Afin que les raccords d'un coup de planche à l'autre ne soient pas visibles, l'imprimeur se sert de picots de repère, sorte de petites pointes en laiton, plantées sur les côtés de la planche.

La gravure des planches se fait habituellement par évidement du bois. Les graveurs ont aussi utilisé des profilés de laiton plantés dans le bois, qui reproduisent le cerné des dessins les plus compliqués. Enfin les planches dites «chapaudées» ont été inventées: les profilés de laiton n'y contournent pas les masses de bois, mais sont remplies de feutre, de tontisse ou de vieux chapeaux (d'où leur nom).

La table à imprimer le papier peint est constituée d'un plateau de chêne massif, sur lequel s'articule un long levier destiné à donner une pression régulière à la planche posée sur le papier. A droite se trouve le baquet à couleur, sorte de grande cuvette carrée, au fond de laquelle ont été placés successivement de l'eau, une peau de veau et un drap. C'est sur ce dernier que l'apprenti étend la couleur. Ce système particulièrement souple permet à la planche de prendre une égale quantité de couleur sur toute sa surface.

Block-printing or Printing With Engraved Wood-blocks. The blocks were made of three thicknesses of wood glued together against the grain; the last of them, in fruit-tree wood, had the relief engraving of the design to be printed. This was executed by the engraver, also known as the *metteur sur bois* ('wood-engraver'). Each colour corresponded to a different block, for example, a design of 7 colours required seven complementary blocks. Each of these blocks bore an engraving that was the same height as the design (also termed the 'repeat'). The printer moved the block successively along the whole length of the roll of paper. In order that the joins between one block print and the next should not be visible, he used register marks, little brass points, placed on the sides of the block.

Blocks were usually engraved by gouging the design out of the wood. The engravers also used brass sections embedded in the wood, which reproduced the outlines of the most complicated designs. Finally, blocks called *chapeaudées* were invented: in these, the brass sections did not encircle wood masses, but were filled with felt, flock or old hat material (whence their name from the French *chapeau*, meaning 'hat').

The table for printing wall-paper was made up of a shelf of solid oak, on which was hinged a long lever, designed to give even pressure to the block placed on the paper. On the right was the bucket of colour, a sort of large square vat, at the bottom of which water, calf skin and a cloth were placed in turn. The apprentice spread the colour on top of the cloth. This particularly flexible system allowed the block to receive an equal quantity of colour on its surface.

The printer thrust his block into the vat of

Handdruck Der Druck der Papiere geschieht mittels gravierter Holzplatten. Diese Druckmodel bestehen aus drei über Hirn zusammengeklebten Schichten. Dem Holzstecher obliegt es nun, in die oberste Schicht aus Obstbaumholz das zu druckende Motiv einzugravieren. Für jede Farbe benötigt man ein Model, so daß zum Beispiel für einen siebenfarbigen Druck sieben verschiedene Model notwendig sind. Jedes Model trägt einen sogenannten Rapport, d. h. das zu wiederholende Motiv. Der Drucker muß nun mit dem Model die ganze Papierrolle bedrucken, und zwar so, daß man die Nahtstellen zwischen den einzelnen Drucken nicht sieht. Dazu sind auf den Seiten des Models kleine Messingstifte, die Paßmarken oder Picots, eingelassen.

Gewöhnlich wird das Muster als Relief in das Holz graviert. Die Holzstecher bedienen sich aber auch in das Holz eingefügter Messingbänder, um komplizierte, feine Dessins zu bilden. Später setzt man die Messingstreifen etwas überhöht und füllt den Raum mit Filz, Wollstaub oder in Stücken geschnittenen alten Hüten.

Die Platte des Drucktisches ist aus massivem Eichenholz und hat einen beweglichen Hebel, um damit die Druckform fest und gleichmäßig auf das Papier zu pressen. Rechts vom Tisch steht der große, viereckige Farbkasten, auch Chassis genannt; dahinein kommt erst Wasser, darauf ein Kalbsleder und zuletzt ein Filztuch, auf das ein Lehrling die Farbe aufstreicht. Diese geschmeidige Oberfläche erlaubt ein sehr gleichmäßiges Einfärben der ganzen Druckplatte.

Der Drucker schlägt das Model leicht in den Farbkasten, um es gründlich einzufärben, und drückt es anschließend auf das teilweise auf dem Tisch ausgerollte Papier; dabei achtet er

L'imprimeur frappe sa planche dans le bac à couleur pour bien l'imbiber, et la reporte sur le papier, partiellement déroulé sur la table, en se guidant à l'aide des picots de repère. Il pose sur la planche un morceau de bois appelé chevalet, ou tasseau, sur lequel vient appuyer le levier auquel l'imprimeur donne une forte pression, avec l'aide de l'apprenti. Après avoir retiré le levier, le tasseau et la planche, en la soulevant à la verticale (ce qui provoque les «jaspures» de la couleur, dues à l'«arraché» de la planche), le papier est avancé, et l'opération est ainsi répétée autant de fois qu'il est nécessaire sur toute la longueur du rouleau.

Dans le cas où en certains endroits, la planche aurait déposé une quantité insuffisante de couleur, l'imprimeur corrige ce petit défaut par pinceautage à la main. Les opérations suivantes sont facultatives, et répondent aux exigences de la sophistication dans l'effet terminal.

Veloutés Les papiers tontisses ou veloutés sont obtenus par adjonction de poudre de laine sur la surface du papier. Pour cela l'imprimeur déroule son papier sur une table de longueur habituelle; mais son plateau est remplacé par une sorte de grande caisse dont le fond est constitué d'une peau de veau très tendue. A l'aide d'une planche gravée reproduisant la couleur à velouter, l'imprimeur dépose non pas de la couleur, mais de la colle. Avant que celle-ci ne sèche, l'apprenti répand la poudre de laine colorée sur toute la surface du papier à l'aide d'un tamis. Puis, après avoir fermé le couvercle de la longue caisse, il se glisse sous la table, et avec deux baguettes, il frappe vigoureusememnt le fond en peau de sorte que la poudre de laine s'incruste dans la colle fraîche et constitue un velours dense. Lorsque tout le rouleau a été ainsi saupoudré, on le laisse sécher à la verticale, en ayant soin de recueillir la poudre qui n'a pas été retenue par la colle. Par la suite l'imprimeur ombre ce velouté en surimprimant des teintes plus claires ou plus sombres suivant la méthode habituelle. Cette opération se nomme le repiquage.

Dorés La dorure s'obtient par adjonction au papier soit de feuille d'or ou d'argent, soit de poudre dorée (généralement de laiton) ou argentée. Dans ce cas l'ouvrier imprime de la colle, de la même manière que pour le veloutage, et y dépose des feuilles d'or ou de la poudre.

Les couleurs utilisées Les couleurs utilisées étaient soit terreuses soit végétales. Toutes sont mélangées à des colles animales, dans des proportions précises qui permettent de les imprimer sans qu'elles écaillent au séchage.

L'ordre d'impression des couleurs était généralement celui-ci: d'abord la nuance moyenne d'une couleur, puis les foncés, enfin les clairs et le blanc.

Impression à l'auge Pour améliorer l'exécution des rayures, Jean Zuber mit au point en 1843 l'utilisation de l'auge. Cet appareil est constitué d'un godet, généralement en laiton massif, allongé, de forme triangulaire, divisé en compartiments (voir ill.). Sa base, la partie la plus effilée du triangle est fendue d'ouvertures dont la dimension correspond à la largeur des rayures que l'on veut obtenir. Cet appareil est posé sur une longue table, base fen-

colour to saturate it well, carried it over to the paper partially unrolled on the table and guided it with the help of the register marks. On the block he put a piece of wood called a bridge, or a batten, on which the lever could lean; the printer, with the help of an apprentice, applied strong pressure to the latter. Having withdrawn the lever, bridge and block, by lifting them up to the vertical (the movement that brings about the 'marbling' of colour, caused by the 'uprooting' of the block), the printer moved the paper forward and repeated the operation as many times as necessary along its whole length.

If the block had not deposited a sufficient quantity of colour in certain places, the printer corrected this small defect with touching-up by hand.

The following operations were optional and met sophisticated requirements in their final effects.

Flocks. Flocked or velveted papers were achieved by adding powdered wool to the surface of the paper. For this the printer unrolled his paper onto a table of the usual length; but his shelf was replaced by a sort of large case, the bottom of which was made up of a very taut calf skin. With the help of an engraved block reproducing the colour to be flocked, the printer deposited glue not colour. Before the latter dried, an apprentice spread coloured powdered wool over the whole surface of the paper with the help of a sifter. Then, having closed the lid of the long case, he slid under the table and, with two rods, vigorously beat the skin bottom in such a way that the powdered wool settled in the fresh glue and formed a dense 'velvet'. When all the roll had been dredged thus, it was left to dry vertically, care being taken to collect the powder that had not adhered to the glue.

Finally the printer shaded this flock by overprinting with lighter or darker shades in the normal way. The operation was called *repiquage*.

Gilding. Gilding was achieved by adding either gold or silver leaf, or gold (generally of brass) or silver dust to the paper. In this case the workman printed some glue, in the same way as for flocking, and deposited gold leaf or powder on it.

The Colours Used. The colours used were either earth or vegetable ones. All were mixed with animal glues in the precise proportions that allowed them to be printed without flaking as they dried.

The order of printing the colours was generally this: first the medium shades of a colour, then the dark ones, finally the light ones and white.

Trough Printing. To improve the process for making stripes, in 1843 Jean Zuber began to use the 'trough'. This apparatus consisted of an elongated, triangular-shaped colour-pan, generally of solid brass, which was divided into compartments (see Fig.). Its base, which was the sharpest part of the triangle, was split by openings, the dimensions of which corresponded to the width of the required stripes. The apparatus was placed on a long table, the split base towards the bottom. Once the trough was filled with colours, the printer gradually unrolled the paper beneath the openings, from which stripes of colour were deposited.

darauf, daß die Paßmarken genau übereinstimmen. Zwischen Model und Hebel kommt ein »Bock« genanntes Brett. Mit Hilfe des Lehrjungen drückt der Arbeiter nun den Hebel mit aller Kraft nach unten. Nach Entfernen des Hebels und des Bocks wird die Druckplatte senkrecht abgehoben, was in der Farbe kleine Sprenkel gibt. Dann wird das Papier weitergeführt und der Vorgang so oft wiederholt, bis die ganze Papierrolle bedruckt ist.

Ist an einer Stelle der Druck mangelhaft, so wird er vom Drucker mit dem Pinsel ausgebessert.

Die folgenden Vorgänge sind fakultativ und werden nur zum Erzielen bestimmter reizvoller Effekte verwendet.

Veloutieren Die Tontisses oder Velourtapeten entstehen durch Aufstreuen von Wollstaub auf das Papier. Dazu entrollt der Drucker das Papier auf einem speziellen Tisch der üblichen Länge, dessen Platte durch eine Art langen Kasten ersetzt wurde; seine Unterseite besteht aus einem stark gespannten Kalbsleder. Mit dem Druckmodel für die zu veloutierenden Teile wird nun statt Farbe zäher Leim auf das Papier gedruckt. Bevor dieser antrocknet, wird vom Gehilfen farbiger Wollstaub durch ein Sieb auf das ganze Papier gestreut. Dann wird der Kasten verschlossen, der Junge kriecht unter den Tisch und schlägt dort mit zwei Stöcken heftig gegen das Leder, wobei sich der Wollstaub gut mit dem frischen Leim verbindet und einen dichten »Sammet« bildet. Nachdem die ganze Rolle so eingestäubt worden ist, hängt man sie zum Trocknen auf. Der nicht angeklebte Wollstaub wird wieder fein säuberlich eingesammelt.

Nach dem vollständigen Trocknen des Papiers schattiert der Drucker die Veloutage, indem er veloutierte Teile mit der üblichen Methode heller oder dunkler überdruckt. Diesen Vorgang nennt man Repiquage.

Vergolden Beim Vergolden wird Blattgold oder -silber oder aber Staub verwendet, wobei der »Goldstaub« im allgemeinen Messingstaub ist. Wie bei der Veloutage werden die gewünschten Partien mit Leim gedruckt und mit Gold oder Silber in Blatt- oder Staubform belegt.

Die Farben Die verwendeten Farben sind entweder mineralischer oder pflanzlicher Herkunft. Allen werden tierische Leime beigefügt, und zwar in genau bekannten Proportionen, die das Abspringen der Farben nach dem Trocknen verhindern.

Meistens druckte man zuerst die mittleren Farbnuancen, dann die dunklen und endlich die hellen Farben sowie das Weiß.

Drucken von Streifen mit dem Streifenzieher oder Gaudet 1843 gelang es Jean Zuber, einen Apparat zum Drucken von Streifen zu entwickeln. Er besteht aus einem langen, sich nach unten verjüngenden Farbtrog aus Messing, der in verschiedene Fächer aufgeteilt und unten mit Schlitzen zur Abgabe der Farbe versehen ist. Die Fächer können je nach gewünschter Streifenbreite verstellt werden. Der Gaudet wird quer über dem Drucktisch gelagert. Sind die Fächer mit Farbe gefüllt, zieht man das Papier unter dem Gaudet durch – die Streifen entstehen. Die Fächeraufteilung erlaubt ein gleichzeitiges Drucken von verschiedenfarbigen Streifen. Im Gegensatz zum Handdruck mit dem Model, wo man immer die

Auge. Collection du Musée des Arts Décoratifs, Paris

A 'trough'. Musée des Arts Décoratifs, Paris

Streifenzieher oder Gaudet. Paris, Musée des Arts Décoratifs

due vers le bas. Une fois l'auge remplie de couleurs, et au-fur-et-à-mesure que l'imprimeur déroule le papier sous elle, les ouvertures y déposent un filet de couleur. Le compartimentage de l'auge permet d'imprimer plusieurs rayures de couleurs différentes à la fois. Ce procédé présente l'avantage de pouvoir rapidement exécuter des rayures parfaitement régulières, tandis qu'à la planche elles laissaient toujours deviner des «décrochements» à la limite de la planche et étaient exécutées très lentement. De plus si l'imprimeur donne à l'auge un mouvement de va et vient doux et régulier dans le sens transversal du papier, l'on obtient non des rayures, mais des ondulations.

Impression en taille-douce C'est également Jean Zuber qui fit breveter le procédé de l'impression en taille-douce, en 1826. Le principe de la taille-douce consiste à déposer la couleur sur le papier à l'aide de cylindres et non plus de planches. Ces cylindres, généralement en laiton massif, sont gravés en creux; c'est à-dire que de petites cavités sont creusées dans la masse métallique, les unes à côté des autres. Plus le creux est profond, plus la quantité de couleur qui y sera recueillie sera grande, plus l'intensité de l'impression sera grande. Par ce moyen l'on obtient une impression plus ou moins dense des teintes, et les ombrés ou dégradés d'une même nuance se font à l'aide d'un seul cylindre. Comme pour l'impression à la planche, il y a autant de cylindres que de couleurs. Chaque cylindre plonge partiellement dans un bac à couleur, vient frotter contre une râcle qui enlève le surplus de couleur, et dépose celle-ci sur le papier qui défile mécaniquement au contact des cylindres. L'ensemble de la mécanique est mue par une machine à vapeur.

The compartments in the trough made it possible to print several stripes of colour at the same time. The advantage of this process was its ability to produce perfectly regular stripes rapidly, while with block-printing the breaking-off point at the edge of the block was always left to guesswork, and the work had to be executed very slowly. Furthermore, if the printer using the trough gave it a gentle, regular backwards-and-forwards movement in the transverse direction of the paper, undulating lines rather than stripes could be achieved.

Printing from an Engraved Metal Roller. It was also Jean Zuber who patented the process of printing from engraved metal in 1826. The principle of *taille-douce,* as it was termed, consisted of laying colour on the paper with the aid of cylinders and not of plates. These cylinders, generally of solid brass, were engraved in hollows; that is to say, small cavities were gouged into the body of the metal, one next to another. The deeper the hollow, the greater the quantity of colour that collected there, and the greater the depth of printing. By this method a print was achieved with more or less density of colour, and with shades or graduations of the same colour executed with the aid of a single cylinder. As with block-printing, there were as many cylinders as there were colours. Each cylinder was partially dipped into a vat of colour, rubbed against a doctor blade that removed the surplus colour, and deposited its colour on the paper, which unrolled mechanically on contact with the cylinders. The whole mechanism was driven by a steam-engine.

unregelmäßigen Ansatzstellen des Rapportes sah, werden mit dem Gaudet die Streifen sehr regelmäßig und sind auch viel schneller gedruckt. Bewegt man den Streifenzieher sanft und gleichmäßig über dem Papier hin und her, erhält man Wellenlinien.

Der Druck mittels Kupferstichwalze Wiederum war es Jean Zuber, der ein Druckverfahren mittels Kupferstich 1826 brevetieren ließ. Das Prinzip dieses Verfahrens besteht darin, das Papier statt mit Modeln mit Hilfe von Walzen zu bedrucken. Diese meist massiv messingenen Zylinder sind tief graviert, kleine Vertiefungen liegen dicht an dicht im Metall. Je tiefer die Höhlung, um so mehr Farbe nimmt sie auf und um so größer wird die Farbintensität beim Druck. Dadurch wird die Farbe mehr oder weniger intensiv, Schattierungen und Abtönungen einer selben Farbnuance lassen sich mit einem einzigen Zylinder drucken. Wie beim Handdruck benötigt man ebensoviele Walzen wie Farben. Jeder Zylinder hängt teilweise im Farbkasten und läuft an einer Abstreifvorrichtung zum Regulieren der Farbe vorbei. Dann überträgt er die Farbe auf das Papier, das mechanisch beim Berühren der Walze abläuft. Die ganze Mechanik wird mit einer Dampfmaschine betrieben.

Notes

[1] La comparaison entre les devants de cheminée ou dessus de porte en grisaille des années 1830–1840, avec la lithographie ou la photographie contemporaines montre une étroite proximité dans le rendu des reliefs et les dégradés de noirs gris et blancs; c'est d'ailleurs à cette période que Jean Zuber fait travailler le lithographe Engelmann et songe à un nouveau procédé d'impression dit «au cylindre lithographique».

[2] Ce n'est sans doute pas un hasard que toutes les expositions françaises et internationales insistent sur la «nouveauté» des papiers peints successivement présentés.

[3] cf. JACQUÉ, 1980.

[4] cf. S. LENORMAND, 1856.

[5] Parmi les dessinateurs cités dans cet ouvrage, les seuls qui aient composé des décors panoramiques sont: Poterlet (décor Néo-Grec, Manufacture Dauptain 1832), Wagner (Galerie de Flore, Manufacture Desfossé et Karth, 1856), Muller (Jardin d'Hiver, 1853, et Jardin d'Armide, 1854, Manufacture Desfossé et Karth), Jean Broc (Paul et Virginie, Manufacture Dufour 1823).

[6] Victor POTERLET (1811–1889) par exemple, dessinateur fort productif, et dont le Musée des Arts Décoratifs conserve une importante collection de dessins, est totalement méconnu et ne laisse presqu'aucune trace de ses activités.

[7] Une étude approfondie de brevets d'invention permet de saisir dans le détail tous les raffinements technologiques mis au point par les fabricants entre 1830 et 1860 environ dans le domaine de l'impression traditionnelle à la planche autant que dans l'emploi nouveau des cylindres.

[8] De 1800 à 1830, les bordures utilisent de 3 à 24 couleurs, tandis que dans les dessins contemporains on en trouve de 1 à 8; mais de 1840 à 1850, ceux-ci ont de 10 à 27 couleurs, sans jamais aucun veloutage. Les verdures nécessitent en moyenne moins de couleurs.

[9] Les brevets d'invention déposés par les fabricants à cette période, révèlent un attrait puissant pour les matières rugueuses, les collages de toutes sortes (grès, micas, poils de lapins, etc.) sur le papier.

Notes

[1] The comparison between chimney-screens or over-doors in grisaille from the years 1830–40 with contemporary lithography or photography shows a close proximity between them in the execution of reliefs and the shades of black, grey and white; besides, this was the period when Jean Zuber set the lithographer Engelmann to work and contemplated a new printing process called a lithographic cylinder.

[2] It was doubtless no accident that all the French and international exhibitions stressed the 'novelty' of the wall-papers successively shown.

[3] cf. Bernard Jacqué, 1980.

[4] cf. S. Lenormand, pp. 30–1.

[5] Among the designers listed in this work, the only ones who conceived panoramic decorations were Poterlet (neo-Grecian decor, Dauptain Factory, 1832), Wagner (Galerie de Flore, Desfossé and Karth Factory, 1856), Muller (Jardin d'Hiver, 1853, and Jardin d'Armide, 1854, Desfossé and Karth Factory) and Jean Broc (Paul and Virginie, Dufour Factory, 1823).

[6] Victor Poterlet (1811–89) for example, a most prolific designer, of whose designs the Musée des Arts Décoratifs holds an important collection, was totally unrecognized and left hardly any evidence of his activities.

[7] A careful study of patents for inventions enables one to grasp in detail all the technological refinements put into practice by manufacturers between about 1830 and 1860, in the field of traditional block-printing rather than in the new use of cylinders.

[8] From 1800 to 1830, borders used from 3 to 24 colours, while the numbers found in contemporary designs ranged from 1 to 8; but from 1840 to 1850, the latter constisted of 10 to 27 colours with no flocking whatsoever. Foliage required on average fewer colours.

[9] A careful study of the patented inventions registered by manufacturers at this time shows a strong liking for rough-surfaced materials and all kinds of collage (sandstone, mica, rabbit-fur, etc.) applied to the paper.

Anmerkungen

[1] Vergleicht man die aus den Jahren 1830–1840 stammenden Kaminschirme und Supraporten in Grisailletechnik mit den zeitgenössischen Lithographien oder Photographien, bemerkt man eine enge Verwandtschaft in der Wiedergabe der Reliefs und der Schwarz-Grau-Weiß-Abstufung. Zu dieser Zeit beschäftigt übrigens Jean Zuber den Lithographen Engelmann und ersinnt ein neues Druckverfahren, den »lithographischen Druckzylinder«.

[2] Es ist offensichtlich kein Zufall, wenn die französischen und die internationalen Ausstellungen großen Wert darauf legen, die Papiertapeten als »Neuheit« vorzustellen.

[3] Gemäß Bernard Jacqué, 1980

[4] Gemäß S. Lenormand, 1856, S. 30–31

[5] Von den in diesem Werk vorgestellten Entwerfern haben nur wenige Bildtapeten geschaffen: Poterlet (Neo-griechischer Dekor, Manufaktur Dauptain, 1832), Wagner (»Galerie de Flore«, Manufaktur Desfossé et Karth, 1856), Muller (»Jardin d'Hiver«, 1853, und »Jardin d'Armide«, 1854, Manufaktur Desfossé et Karth), Jean Broc (Paul et Virginie, Manufaktur Dufour, 1823).

[6] Victor Poterlet (1811–1889) zum Beispiel war ein sehr eifriger Entwerfer; das Musée des Arts Décoratifs bewahrt eine große Sammlung seiner Werke auf, doch ist er absolut verkannt worden, und man weiß fast nichts von seinem Wirken.

[7] Das Studium der Erfinderpatente erlaubt das Erfassen aller Einzelheiten der technologischen Spitzfindigkeiten, die von den Fabrikanten zwischen 1830 und 1860 sowohl für den traditionellen Handdruck wie für den neuen Maschinendruck ausgeklügelt worden sind.

[8] Zwischen 1800 und 1830 verwendet man für die Bordüren 3 bis 24 Farben, während man in den zeitgenössischen Mustern deren 1 bis 8 findet. Doch von 1840 bis 1850 haben die Dessins 10 bis 27 Farben und sind nie veloutiert. Grünpflanzenmotive haben im allgemeinen weniger Farben.

[9] Untersuchungen der Erfinderpatente der Fabrikanten dieser Zeit zeigen ihre große Vorliebe für rauhe Materialien und somit für allerlei Collagen mit Sandsteinpulver, Glimmer, Kaninchenhaaren usw.

Appendices

Appendices

Anhang

Le procédé d'impression des irisés, ou teintes fondues, a été mis au point par Michel SPOERLIN, cousin de Jean ZUBER, à Vienne, en 1819. Aussitôt la Manufacture ZUBER l'a appliqué pour ses dessins à motifs répétitifs et les ciels de ses décors panoramiques. Pendant fort longtemps elle en a gardé jalousement le secret d'exécution technique. Avec son aimable autorisation, nous publions ici de larges extraits du texte original de Michel

The technique of producing *irisé* wall-papers was developed by Michel Spoerlin, a cousin of Jean Zuber, in Vienna in 1819. The Zuber Factory immediately began to use this process for its repeat designs and for the skies of its panoramic designs, but the secret of the process was jealously guarded for a long time. We publish long extracts from Michel Spoerlin's original text here with the kind permission of the Zuber Factory. The patent registered on 10 November 1826 by the Zuber Factory, for the method of printing sometimes called metal engraving, constitutes the first attempt at adapting cylindrical machines for wall-paper. This technique was made possible thanks to Jean Zuber's perfection of his continuous papermaking process. Finally, the patent of 22 December 1842 registered by the Zuber Factory, for 'trough' printing, made it possible to print vertical, perfectly rectilinear, stripes.

Das Verfahren des Irisdruckes wurde 1819 in Wien von Michel SPOERLIN, einem Vetter von Jean ZUBER, entwickelt. Die Manufaktur ZUBER wendete diese Technik sogleich bei ihren Mustern mit repetierten Motiven an und ebenso für den Druck des Himmels bei Panorama-Dekors. Während langer Zeit hütete die Manufaktur das Geheimnis dieses Verfahrens eifersüchtig. Mit ihrer liebenswürdigen Erlaubnis können wir hier größere Auszüge aus dem Originaltext von Michel SPOERLIN veröffentlichen.

Michel Spoerlin,
Fabrication du papier peint dit *Iris* ou *Irisé*
Mulhouse, s.d.

Michel Spoerlin
Fabrication du papier peint dit *Iris* ou *Irisé*
('Manufacture of so-called *iris* or *irisé* wallpaper')
Mulhouse, undated.

Michel Spoerlin
Fabrication du papier peint dit *Iris* ou *Irisé*
(Herstellung der sogenannten Iris- oder irisierten Tapeten)
Mulhouse o. J.

Le nouveau genre de papiers peints que j'ai inventé et dont j'ai établi la fabrication dans la manufacture de MM. Jean Zuber et Comp. à Rixheim avec un succès complet, a été appelé *Iris* ou *irisé*. [. . .]

Qu'on se représente un réservoir de couleurs divisé en compartiments plus ou moins étroits, avec une brosse assez longue pour entrer à la fois dans tous les compartiments, et tout le mystère sera révélé. [. . .]

La figure 1 donnera une idée précise de mon invention, appliquée au chassis de l'imprimeur.

A représente un baquet de couleurs divisé en cinq compartiments. [. . .] Sur le fond et sur les parois intérieurs du cadre, on pratique autant de rainures qu'on veut avoir de compartiments, avec une petite scie en forme de rabot. [. . .] Ce baquet se place à côté d'un chassis ordinaire d'imprimeur, derrière lequel on fixera perpendiculairement une planche de 6 à 7 pouces de haut, qui sert de couloir à la brosse b garnie d'une poulie. La longueur du bois de cette brosse [. . .] doit correspondre à la longueur du baquet à couleurs. [. . .] Ce genre de brosses se divise facilement par les diaphragmes des compartiments, et elle est très propre pour faire le fondu sur le chassis. [. . .]

Je commencerai par décrire la manipulation pour faire les fonds unis *irisés* sur papier. [. . .]

Une table de la longueur de deux rouleaux de papiers contribuera beaucoup à l'accélération du travail. [. . .] Au milieu de cette grande

The new kind of wall-papers that have been invented and put into production at MM. Jean Zuber and Comp. at Rixheim with complete success, were called *iris* or *irisé*. . . .

If you imagine a container of colours divided into more or less narrow compartments and a brush long enough to enter all the compartments at the same time, the whole mystery will be revealed. . . .

Figure 1 gives a precise idea of my invention applied to the printer's chase.

'A' represents a tub of colours divided into five compartments. . . . On the base and on the interior surfaces of the tub you cut with a little plane-saw as many grooves as you wish to have divisions . . . . This tub is placed next to an ordinary printer's chase, behind which you fix perpendicularly a block 6 to 7 inches high, which serves as a channel for brush 'b' rigged with a pulley. The length of the wooden part of this brush . . . corresponds with the length of the tub of colours . . . This kind of brush separates very easily through the divisions of the compartments and is extremely suitable for blending the colours together on the chase . . .

I shall begin by describing the operation for making smooth *irisé* grounds on paper . . . .

A table which is two rolls of paper in length will greatly help to accelerate the work. . . . In

Die neue Sorte Papiertapeten, die ich erfunden und deren Fabrikation ich in der Manufaktur der Herren J. Zuber & Co. in Rixheim mit vollem Erfolg geleitet habe, heißt Iris oder irisiert . . .

Man stelle sich einen in mehr oder weniger schmale Fächer aufgeteilten Farbkasten vor und dazu eine Bürste, die lang genug ist, um gleichzeitig in alle Fächer zu tauchen, und schon hat man des Rätsels Lösung . . .

Figura 1, Tafel 1, gibt meine Erfindung genau wieder, die auf das Chassis des Druckers aufgebracht worden ist.

A stellt einen in fünf Fächer aufgeteilten Farbkasten dar . . . Auf dem Boden und den Innenwänden des Rahmens werden mit einer kleinen, hobelförmigen Säge so viele Rillen, wie man Fächer haben will, angebracht . . . Dieser Trog wird neben ein gewöhnliches Drucker-Chassis gesetzt, hinter welchem man ein 6 bis 7 Zoll hohes Brett senkrecht fixiert hat und das der mit einer Rolle versehenen Bürste als Lauf dient. Die Länge des Holzes dieser Bürste . . . muß der Länge des Farbkastens entsprechen . . . Die Borsten dieser Bürstensorte werden von den Fächerwänden mühelos getrennt, die Bürste eignet sich sehr gut zum Irisieren auf dem Chassis . . .

Zu Beginn möchte ich den Arbeitsgang für einen Irisgrund mit geraden Streifen erklären . . .

Ein Tisch in der Länge zweier Papierrollen wird die Arbeit sehr erleichtern . . . Auf diesem

table, garnie dans toute sa longueur d'un rebord perpendiculaire, [...] voy.fig.18, on place le baquet à compartiments, sur lequel on fixe deux racles e. Près du baquet et aux deux extrémités de la table on pratique des rainures [...] et on y ajuste une planchette taillée en bizeau, qui entre un peu serrée, en pliant le bout du rouleau dans la rainure, et serrant avec la petite planche, le rouleau restera immobile sur la table et à la distance juste du rebord. Ce travail exige un ouvrier fonceur et trois petits garçons qui se servent des trois brosses suivantes:

La première a est celle du fonceur; elle est munie d'un petit manche, d'une courroie et d'une poulie; sa longueur correspond à la largeur du papier [...] sur laquelle le poil est distribué en sept paquets. [...] La seconde brosse b est celle qui opère le *fondu*; [...] elle est munie de deux bras par devant, et d'une espèce de coussin de peau dure sur l'autre bout. La brosse c sert pour égaliser; [...] elle est munie d'une poulie et d'une courroie au milieu.

Le rouleau étant étendu et fixé par la clavette de l'extrémité de la table, un petit garçon se place près du baquet et tient le rouleau tendu pendant le travail, afin d'éviter les plis et froncis qui se forment par l'humidité. Alors le fonceur passe sa main dans la courroie de la brosse a, et la portant sur le baquet, il l'enfonce dans les compartiments, en appuyant la poulie contre le rebord, par un léger mouvement qu'il lui donne à droite et gauche, afin de bien séparer le poil par les plaques qui forment les compartiments. Quand la brosse est bien remplie de couleur, il la presse contre l'une des racles pour en enlever le superflu de couleur, ensuite il marche assez vite vers l'extrémité de la table, en distribuant la couleur sur le rouleau par un trait léger, et en suivant toujours le rebord, avec la poulie. Arrivé à ce point, il saisit le manche de la brosse par la main gauche, et en reculant du côté du baquet, il finit par garnir le rouleau entièrement de couleur, en appuyant davantage sur sa brosse, et faisant un mouvement continuel d'en avant et d'en arrière. Cet ouvrier est suivi immédiatement par un garçon, qui saisit la brosse b par les deux bras, la pose en travers sur le rouleau, et la retirant et poussant contre le rebord de la table en suivant les pas du fonceur, il opère par ce mouvement de va et vient le fondu des couleurs en ziczacs allongés. Alors le second garçon passe sa main dans la courroie de la brosse c, et l'appuyant avec la poulie contre le rebord de la table, il finit par égaliser la couleur en traits légers et allongés. Un ouvrier un peu intelligent peut faire de cette manière de 200 à 250 rouleaux de 7 aunes par jour, suivant les largeurs des compartiments. [...]

Une autre application bien intéressante de l'Iris, est celle en *forme circulaire;* elle fournit au fabricant de papiers peints le moyen de faire des rosaces de plafonds, des draperies et des bordures d'un effet merveilleux, et à peu de frais. [...]

Les brosses qui servent à ce travail sont de forme conique, les fig. 12 et 14 les démontrent clairement. Avec la brosse a, fig. 14 on fournit les couleurs en rayons concentriques, en engageant l'anneau qui y est fixé dans un des pivots de la perche; avec la brosse b, on fait le fondu par un mouvement de va et vient dirigé contre le pivot, et on termine par égaliser, en promenant légèrement la brosse autour du pivot. Il sera inutile d'observer que la longueur

the middle of this large table, fitted with a perpendicular raised edge all along its length, ... (see Fig. 18), you place the partitioned tub, on which you fix two scrapers 'e'. Near the tub and at the two ends of the table you make grooves ... and in them you fix a small bevelled plank, which fits in quite tightly. By bending the end of the roll into the groove and tightening it with the little plank, the roll will remain immobile on the table and at the correct distance from the edge. This work requires a driving operative and three small boys who use the following three brushes:

The first 'a' is the driving operative's; it is provided with a small handle, a strap and a pulley; its length corresponds with the width of the paper ..., on which the bristles divide in seven sections.... The second brush 'b' is the one that carries out the blending process; ... it is provided with two handles in front and with a sort of cushion of hard skin at the other end. Brush 'c' is used for smoothing; ... it is provided with a pulley and a strap in the middle.

The roll of paper having been stretched and fixed by the wedge at the end of the table, a small boy stands near the tub and holds the roll taut during the operation, in order to avoid the creases and wrinkles that come with dampness. Then the driving operative puts his hand into the strap of brush 'a', and carrying it over the tub, he thrusts it into the compartments, supporting the pulley against the edge, and, by a light movement to left and right, separates the bristles properly through the dividing walls. When the brush is well charged with colour, he presses it against one of the scrapers to remove the excess of colour, then he walks fairly quickly towards the end of the table, distributing the colour on to the roll with a light stroke and always holding the pulley-block against the edge. Having reached this point, he takes hold of the handle of the brush with his left hand, and, moving back towards the tub, he ends by covering the roll completely with colour, leaning more heavily upon his brush and making a continuous backwards-and-forwards movement. This workman is followed immediately by a boy who takes brush 'b' in both hands, places it across the roll, and, pulling and pushing it against the edge of the table, following the steps of the driving operative, carries out the blending of the colours in elongated zigzags by this backwards-and-forwards movement. Then the second boy puts his hand in the strap of brush 'c', and, pressing with the pulley against the edge of the table, he ends by smoothing the colour with long light strokes. A fairly competent workman can in this way make 200 to 250 rolls of 7 ells per day, according to the size of the compartments....

Another very interesting application of *irisé* papers is the one in circular form; it provides the manufacturer with the means of making ceiling roses, draperies and borders with marvellous effect and at very little cost....

The brushes used for this work are conical in shape – Figs. 12 and 14 illustrate them clearly. With brush 'a' (Fig. 14), colours are applied in concentric rays, by inserting the ring that is fixed to it in one of the pivots of the pole; with brush 'b', the blending is done with a backwards-and-forwards movement directed against the pivot, and finally the smoothing is done by lightly passing the brush around the

an einer Längsseite mit einer senkrechten Randleiste versehenen Tisch, ... siehe Fig. 18, Tf. 3, steht in der Mitte der aufgeteilte Farbtrog, auf dem man zwei Abstreifvorrichtungen für den Farbüberschuß e befestigt. Neben dem Farbkasten und an den beiden Schmalseiten des Tisches bringt man Rillen an ... und paßt darin ein keilförmiges Brettchen etwas knapp ein. Bringt man das Papierrollenende in die Rille und fixiert es mit dem Brettchen, so bleibt die Rolle schön an ihrem Platz und in der richtigen Distanz zur Randleiste. Das Irisieren erfordert einen Grundierer und drei Gehilfen, die drei verschiedene, anschließend aufgeführte Bürsten handhaben:

Die erste a gehört dem Grundierer und ist mit einem kleinen Stiel, einer Riemenschlaufe und einer Laufrolle versehen. Ihre Länge entspricht der Papierbreite ... und ihre Borsten sind in sieben Portionen aufgeteilt ... Die zweite Bürste b bewirkt das Ineinanderfließen der Farben; ... sie hat vorn zwei Stiele und am andern Ende eine Art Kissen aus hartem Leder. Mit der Bürste c wird egalisiert; ... sie hat eine Laufrolle und in der Mitte eine Riemenschlaufe.

Ist die Papierrolle am Tischende mit dem Keil fixiert, stellt sich ein Gehilfe neben den Farbkasten und hält die Rolle während des Arbeitens straff, damit sich das Papier nicht wegen der Feuchtigkeit wirft. Dann ergreift der Grundierer die Bürste a durch die Riemenschlaufe und taucht sie in den Farbtrog, indem er ihre Laufrolle auf die Randleiste drückt. Er bewegt die Bürste leicht von links nach rechts, damit sich die Borsten durch die Fächerwände leicht trennen. Ist die Bürste mit Farbe vollgesogen, drückt er sie zum Entfernen des Farbüberschusses gegen eine der Rakeln. Dann geht er raschen Schrittes gegen das andere Tischende und führt die Bürste leicht übers Papier, die Laufrolle stets auf der Randleiste haltend. Hier angelangt, faßt er den Bürstenstiel mit der linken Hand und geht bis zum Chassis zurück. Dabei drückt er etwas kräftiger auf die Bürste und fährt mit ihr stetig vor und zurück. Diesem Arbeiter auf dem Fuß folgt ein Gehilfe mit der Bürste b, die er an beiden Stielen haltend quer auf das Papier legt und sie, dem Grundierer folgend, von der Randleiste wegstößt und zu dieser zurückzieht. Diese langen, zickzackförmigen Bewegungen bewirken ein Ineinanderlaufen der Farben auf dem Papier. Der zweite Gehilfe ergreift die Bürste c durch die Riemenschlaufe und legt ihre Laufrolle auf die Randleiste, dann egalisiert er die Farben mit leichten, langen Zügen. Ein geschickter Grundierer kann auf diese Weise täglich 200 bis 250 Rollen zu 7 Ellen herstellen, je nach Breite der Fächer im Farbkasten ...

Eine andere, sehr interessante Art des Irisdruckes besteht in der runden Form, mit der sich Deckenrosetten, Draperien und herrliche Bordüren zu geringen Kosten herstellen lassen ...

Die zu diesem Zwecke benutzten Bürsten sind konisch, wie Fig. 12 und 14 deutlich zeigen. Mit der Bürste a, Fig. 14, gibt man die Farben konzentrisch strahlenförmig auf das Papier, indem man ihren Ring über einen Zapfen der Welle zieht; mit der Bürste b verwischt man die Farben in einer gegen den Zapfen laufenden Hin- und Zurückbewegung, und die Bürste leicht um den Zapfen führend, egalisiert man zum Schluß. Es ist unnötig zu sagen, daß die Länge dieser konischen Bürsten et-

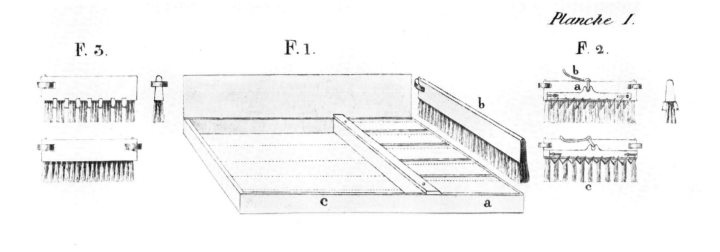

Planche I.

F. 3. F. 1. F. 2.

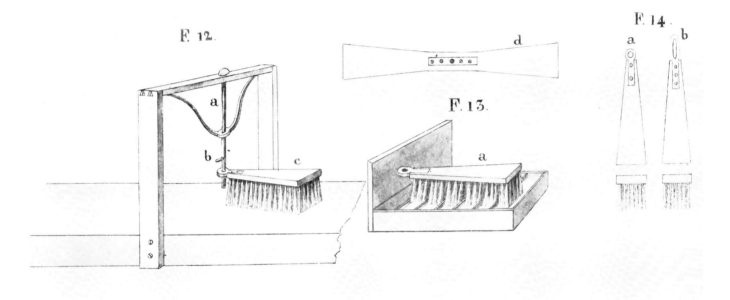

F. 12. F. 14.

F. 13.

Planche III.

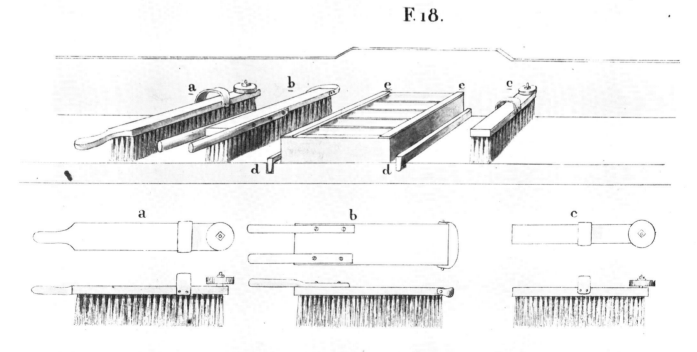

F. 18.

de ces brosses coniques doit être un peu plus grande que le rayon du demi-cercle qu'on veut faire. [. . .]

Les fig. 12 et 13 représentent l'appareil pour faire les cercles d'après ce que j'ai dit ci-dessus pour les demi-ronds; [. . .] Le pivot a est mobile et se soulève par le petit crochet b, pour le faire entrer dans l'anneau de la brosse c. [. . .]

Vienne, en Janvier 1823

SPOERLIN
Associé de Spoerlin et Rahn.

Brevets

ZUBER. Brevet du 10 Novembre 1826. Moyen de substituer au mode actuel d'impression des papiers à la main, celui d'impression au rouleau gravé en creux.

ZUBER. Brevet du 22 Décembre 1843. Description d'une machine à faire des rayures d'une et plusieurs couleurs à la fois, sur étoffes et sur papier.

pivot. It goes without saying that the length of these conical brushes should be a little greater than the radius of the desired semi-circle. . . .

Figures 12 and 13 show the apparatus for making circles in the way I have shown above for semi-circles; . . . The pivot 'a' is mobile and is raised by the little hook 'b' so that it can go into the ring on brush 'c' . . . .

Vienna, in January, 1823

SPOERLIN
Associate of Spoerlin and Rahn

Patents

ZUBER. Patent of 10 November 1826. Means of substituting for the current method of printing papers by hand, that of printing from an engraved roller.

ZUBER. Patent of 22 December 1843. Description of a machine for making stripes in one or more colours at one and the same time, on materials and on paper.

was größer als der gewünschte Halbkreisradius sein muß . . .

Die Fig. 12 und 13 stellen den Apparat dar, der die Anfertigung von Kreisen wie in der obigen Beschreibung für die Halbkreise ermöglicht; . . . Der Zapfen a ist beweglich und kann mit dem Häkchen b gehoben und in den Ring der Bürste c geschoben werden . . .

Wien, im Januar 1823

SPOERLIN
Partner von Spoerlin und Rahn

Patente

ZUBER, Patent vom 10. November 1826. Möglichkeit, das heutige Verfahren des Handdrucks auf Papier durch den Druck mittels gravierter Walze zu ersetzen.

ZUBER. Patent vom 22. Dezember 1843. Beschreibung einer Maschine für den Druck von Streifen in einer oder mehreren Farben gleichzeitig auf Stoff oder Papier.

Expositions

Paris, 1967:
Trois Siècles de Papiers Peints, Musée des Arts Décoratifs, Paris, juin-octobre 1967.

Paris, 1973:
Pompéi, Petit Palais, Paris, janvier-mars 1973.

Exhibitions

Paris, 1967
Trois siècles de Papier Peints: Musée des Arts Décoratifs, Paris, June – October, 1967

Paris, 1973
Pompéi: Petit Palais, Paris, January – March, 1973

Ausstellungen

Paris, 1967: *Trois siècles de Papiers Peints.* Musée des Arts Décoratifs, Paris, Juni–Oktober 1967
Paris, 1973: *Pompéi.* Petit Palais, Paris, Januar–März 1973

Expositions des produits de l'industrie française

1806 – QUATRIEME EXPOSITION PUBLIQUE
Notice sur les objets envoyés à l'Exposition des Produits de l'Industrie Française, rédigée par ordre de S.E.M. de Champagny, ministre de l'Intérieur. Rapport du Jury de l'Exposition présenté par M. de Champagny, 2 vol. in–8 réunis en un.

1819 – CINQUIEME EXPOSITION PUBLIQUE
Costaz (L.), Rapport du Jury de l'Exposition des Produits de l'Industrie Française, in–8, Paris, 1819.

1823 – SIXIEME EXPOSITION PUBLIQUE
Héricart de Thury et Migneron, Rapport du Jury de l'Exposition des Produits de l'Industrie Française, 1 vol. in–8, Paris, 1823.

1827 – SEPTIEME EXPOSITION PUBLIQUE
Héricart de Thury et Migneron, Rapport du Jury de l'Exposition des Produits de l'Industrie Française, in–8, Paris 1827.

1834 – HUITIEME EXPOSITION PUBLIQUE
Dupin, Rapport du Jury de l'Exposition des Produits de l'Industrie Française, 3 vol. in–8, Paris, 1834.

1839 – NEUVIEME EXPOSITION PUBLIQUE
Rapport du Jury Central de l'Exposition.

1844 – DIXIEME EXPOSITION PUBLIQUE
Rapport du Jury Central de l'Exposition.

Exhibitions of French Industrial Products

1806 – FOURTH PUBLIC EXHIBITION
Account of the objects sent to the exhibition of French Industrial Products, drawn up by order of S. E. M. de Champagny, Minister of the Interior. Report of the Exhibition Jury submitted by M. de Champagny, 2 vols. 8vo, bound in one.

1819 – FIFTH PUBLIC EXHIBITION
Costaz (L.), Report of the Jury of the Exhibition of French Industrial Products, 8vo, Paris, 1819.

1823 – SIXTH PUBLIC EXHIBITION
Héricart de Thury and Migneron, Report of the Jury of the Exhibition of French Industrial Products, 1 vol. 8vo, Paris 1823

1827 – SEVENTH PUBLIC EXHIBITION
Héricart de Thury and Migneron, Report of the Jury of the Exhibition of French Industrial Products, 8vo, Paris, 1827

1834 – EIGHTH PUBLIC EXHIBITION
Dupin, Report of the Jury of the Exhibition of French Industrial Products, 3 vols, 8vo, Paris, 1834

1839 – NINTH PUBLIC EXHIBITION
Report of the Central Jury of the Exhibition

1844 – TENTH PUBLIC EXHIBITION
Report of the Central Jury of the Exhibition

Ausstellungen französischer Industrie-Erzeugnisse

1806 – QUATRIEME EXPOSITION PUBLIQUE
(Vierte öffentliche Ausstellung)
Notice sur les objets envoyés à l'Exposition des Produits de l'Industrie Française, rédigée par ordre de S. E. M. de Champagny, ministre de l'Intérieur. Rapport du Jury de l'Exposition présenté par M. de Champagny, 2 vol. in-8 réunis en un

1819 – CINQUIEME EXPOSITION PUBLIQUE
(Fünfte öffentliche Ausstellung)
Costaz (L.), Rapport du Jury de l'Exposition des Produits de l'Industrie Française, in-8, Paris 1819

1823 – SIXIEME EXPOSITION PUBLIQUE
(Sechste öffentliche Ausstellung)
Héricart de Thury et Migneron, Rapport du Jury de l'Exposition des Produits de l'Industrie Française, 1 vol. in-8, Paris 1823

1827 – SEPTIEME EXPOSITION PUBLIQUE
(Siebente öffentliche Ausstellung)
Héricart de Thury et Migneron, Rapport du Jury de l'Exposition des Produits de l'Industrie Française, in-8, Paris 1827

1834 – HUITIEME EXPOSITION PUBLIQUE
(Achte öffentliche Ausstellung)
Dupin, Rapport du Jury de l'Exposition des Produits de l'Industrie Française, 3 vol. in-8, Paris 1834

1839 – NEUVIEME EXPOSITION PUBLIQUE
(Neunte öffentliche Ausstellung)
Rapport du Jury Central de l'Exposition

1844 – DIXIEME EXPOSITION PUBLIQUE
(Zehnte öffentliche Ausstellung)
Rapport du Jury Central de l'Exposition

Bibliographie

BRUNHAMMER et AMIC, 1967
BRUNHAMMER Yvonne et AMIC Yolande,
l'Histoire des papiers peints. Dans l'*Œil*, mai
1967, n° 149, p.42–51.

BRUNHAMMER Yvonne et RICOUR Monique.
Le Papier peint en France de 1750 à 1850.
Dans *Jardin des Arts*, n° 41, mars 1958,
p.316–322.

CALAVAS A. Bordures et ornements Empire,
photographiés d'après les originaux, Paris,
s.d.

CLOUZOT et FOLLOT, 1935
CLOUZOT Henri et FOLLOT Charles, Histoire
du Papier peint en France, Paris 1935.

FIGUIER, Louis. Les Merveilles de l'industrie.
Paris, s. d., tome 2, p.313 à 340.

FOURNY, 1967
FOURNY Anne, Trois Siècles de Papiers
Peints. Dans *Plaisir de France*, n° 346, août
1967.

GUSMAN Pierre, Panneaux décoratifs et tentures murales du XVIIIᵉ siècle et du commen-
cement du XIXᵉ siècle. Paris s.d.

HAVARD Henry, Dictionnaire de l'Ameuble-
ment et de la Décoration, TomeIV, Paris. s.d.

JACQUÉ Bernard, Les débuts de l'industrie du
papier peint à Mulhouse 1790–1794, dans *Revue d'Alsace*, 1979.

JACQUÉ, 1980
JACQUÉ Bernard, Papiers peints panorami-
ques et Jardins: l'œuvre de P.A. Mongin chez
Jean Zuber et Compagnie 1804–1827, dans
Les Nouvelles de l'Estampe, n° 49, 1980.

LENORMAND Sébastien, Nouveau manuel
complet du fabricant d'étoffes imprimées et
du fabricant de papiers peints, Paris, Roret,
1856.

MAC CLELLAND, 1924
MAC CLELLAND Nancy, Historic Wallpapers,
Philadelphie, 1924

PAPILLON Jean-Michel, Traité historique et
pratique de la gravure sur bois, Paris, 1766
3 tomes.

RIOUX DE MAILLOU, sd.
RIOUX DE MAILLOU, P., Le Papier Peint, ex-
trait de Les Arts du Bois, des Tissus et du Papier à la Septième Exposition de l'Union Centrale des Arts Décoratifs, Paris, s.d.

SEGUIN, 1968
SEGUIN J.P., Le Papier Peint en France. Dans
Flammes et Fumées, n° 53, janvier 1968.

SPOERLIN Michel, Fabrication du papier peint
dit *Iris* ou *Irisé*, Mulhouse s. d.,

La Bibliothèque Forney édite le catalogue de
sa propre collection; le premier volume est
paru: Mireille GUIBERT, Papiers peints
1800–1875, Bibliothèque Forney, Paris, 1980.
Cet ouvrage est disponible: 1, rue du Figuier,
75004 Paris.

Bibliography

BRUNHAMMER, Yvonne and AMIC, Yolande.
'L'Histoire des papiers peints' (The History of
wall-papers). In l'*Œil*. N° 149 (May, 1967):
42–51.
BRUNHAMMER, Yvonne and RICOUR, Monique. 'Le Papier peint en France de 1750 à
1850' (Wall-paper in France from 1750 to
1850). In *Jardin des Arts*. N° 41 (March, 1958):
316–22.
CALAVAS, A. *Bordures et ornements Empire,
photographiés d'après les originaux* (Empire
borders and ornaments, photographed from
originals). Paris, n. d.
CLOUZOT, Henri and FOLLOT, Charles. *Histoire du Papier peint en France* (The History of
Wall-paper in France). Paris, 1935.
FIGUIER, Louis. *Les Merveilles de l'industrie*
(The Wonders of Industry). Vol. 2. Paris, n. d.,
pp. 313–40.
FOURNY, Anne. 'Trois siècles de papiers
peints' (Three Centuries of Wall-paper). In
Plaisir de France. No. 346 (August, 1967).
GUSMAN, Pierre. *Panneaux décoratifs et tentures murales du XVIIIᵉ siècle et du com-
mencement du XIXᵉ siècle* (Decorative panels
and wall-hangings of the 18th and beginning of
the 19th centuries). Paris, n. d.
HAVARD, Henry. *Dictionnaire de l'Ameuble-
ment et de la Décoration* (Dictionary of Fur-
nishing and Decoration). Vol. IV. Paris, n. d.
JACQUÉ, Bernard. 'Les débuts de l'industrie
du papier peint à Mulhouse 1790–1794' (The
beginnings of the wall-paper industry at Mulhouse 1790–1794). In *Revue d'Alsace*. n. p.,
1979.
– 'Papiers peints panoramiques et Jardins:
l'œuvre de P. A. Mongin chez Jean Zuber et
Compagnie 1804–1827' (Panoramic Wall-
papers and Gardens: The work of P. A. Mongin at Jean Zuber and Company 1804–1827). In
Les Nouvelles de l'Estampe. N° 49 (n. p.,
1980).
LENORMAND, Sébastian. *Nouveau manuel
complet du fabricant d'étoffes imprimées et
du fabricant de papiers peints* (New complete
manual for the manufacturer of printed materials and the manufacturer of wall-papers).
Paris, 1856. [Roret].
MAC CLELLAND, Nancy. *Historic Wall-papers*. Philadelphia, 1924.
PAPILLON, Jean-Michel. *Traité historique et
pratique de la gravure sur bois* (Historic and
practical treatise on wood-engraving). 3 Vols.
Paris, 1766.
RIOUX DE MAILLOU, P. 'Le Papier Peint'
(Wall-paper). Extract from *Les Arts du Bois,
des Tissus et du Papier à la Septième Exposi-
tion de l'Union Centrale des Arts Décoratifs*
(The Arts of Wood, Woven Materials and Pa-
per at the Seventh Exhibition of the Central
Union of the Decorative Arts). Paris, n. d.
SEGUIN, Jean-Pierre. 'Le Papier Peint en
France' (Wall-paper in France). In *Flammes et
Fumées*. N° 53 (January, 1968).
SPOERLIN, Michel. *Fabrication du papier
peint dit* iris *ou* irisé (Manufacture of *Iris* or
Irisé Wall-paper). Mulhausen, n. d.

The Bibliothèque Forney is publishing a catalogue of its collections. The first volume, which
has been published, is
GUIBERT, Mireille. *Papiers peints 1800–1875*.
Paris, 1980.

Bibliographie

BRUNHAMMER und AMIC, 1967
BRUNHAMMER, Yvonne und Yolande AMIC,
L'Histoire des papiers peints, in: l'*Œil*. Nr. 149,
Mai 1967, S. 42–51

BRUNHAMMER, YVONNE und Monique RI-
COUR, Le Papier peint en France de 1750 à
1850, in: *Jardin des Arts*, Nr. 41, März 1958,
S. 316–322

CALAVAS, A., Bordures et ornements Empire,
photographiés d'après les originaux, Paris
o. J.

CLOUZOT und FOLLOT, 1935
CLOUZOT, Henri und Charles FOLLOT, Histoire du Papier peint en France, Paris 1935

FIGUIER, Louis, Les Merveilles de l'industrie.
Paris o. J., Bd. 2, S. 313–340

FOURNY, 1967
FOURNY, Anne, Trois Siècles de Papiers
Peints, in: *Plaisir de France*, Nr. 346, Au-
gust 1967

GUSMAN, Pierre, Panneaux décoratifs et tentures murales du XVIIIᵉ siècle et du commen-
cement du XIXᵉ siècle, Paris o. J.

HAVARD, Henry, Dictionnaire de l'Ameuble-
ment et de la Décoration, Bd. IV, Paris o. J.

JACQUÉ, Bernard, Les débuts de l'industrie
du papier peint à Mulhouse 1790–1794, in: *Revue d'Alsace*, 1979

JACQUÉ, 1980
JACQUÉ, Bernard, Papiers peints panorami-
ques et Jardins: l'œuvre de P. A. Mongin chez
Jean Zuber et Compagnie 1804–1827, in: *Les
Nouvelles de l'Estampe*, Nr. 49, 1980

LENORMAND, 1856
LENORMAND, Sébastien, Nouveau manuel
complet du fabricant d'étoffes imprimées et
du fabricant de papiers peints, Paris (Roret)
1856

MAC CLELLAND, 1924
MAC CLELLAND, Nancy, Historic Wallpapers,
Philadelphia 1924

PAPILLON, Jean-Michel, Traité historique et
pratique de la gravure sur bois, Paris 1766,
3 Bde.

RIOUX DE MAILLOU, o. J.
RIOUX DE MAILLOU, P., Le Papier Peint, ex-
trait de Les Arts du Bois, des Tissus et du Papier à la Septième Exposition de l'Union Centrale des Arts Décoratifs, Paris o. J.

SEGUIN, 1968
SEGUIN, J.-P., Le Papier Peint en France, in:
Flammes et Fumées, Nr. 53, Januar 1968

SPOERLIN Michel, Fabrication du papier peint
dit *Iris* ou *Irisé*, Mulhouse o. J.

Die Bibliothèque Forney gibt einen Katalog ihrer Sammlungen heraus, dessen erster Band
erschienen ist:
GUIBERT, Mireille, Papiers peints 1800–1875,
Bibliothèque Forney, Paris 1980 (erhältlich:
1, rue du Figuier, F-75004 Paris)

CATALOGUE

CATALOGUE

KATALOG

Le catalogue des 600 documents retenus est ordonné en trois grands chapitres: dessins (Nos 1 à 243) désignant les motifs répétitifs destinés à recouvrir la plus grande partie de la surface murale, les bordures (Nos 244 à 494) et les panneaux intermédiaires (Nos 495 à 600) correspondant aux décorations non répétitives, généralement prestigieuses. Chacun de ces documents est accompagné d'une notice technique indiquant successivement:
– le nom du dessinateur
– le nom de la manufacture
– la date de première édition
– les procédés de fabrications utilisés
– les dimensions du document (en cm)
– les dimensions du rapport du dessin (en cm)
– les inscriptions figurant sur le document
– la collection d'origine et le N° d'inventaire correspondant
– les indications bibliographiques
– les participations à des expositions.

The catalogue of the 600 chosen examples is set out in three chapters: repeat-pattern designs (Nos 1 to 243), intended to cover the greater part of a wall surface, borders (Nos 244 to 494), and intermediary panels (Nos 495 to 600), which are non-repetitive, usually important, decorations. Each of these examples is accompanied by a technical note, indicating in turn:
– the name of the designer (when available)
– the name of the factory
– the date of the first edition
– the manufacturing process employed
– the size of the example
– the size of the repeat of the design (in centimetres); to correspond to the original technical data, the sizes are given in the Continental form
– the inscriptions on the document
– the provenance and the corresponding inventory number
– the bibliographical references
– the inclusion in exhibitions.

Der Katalog der 600 Muster ist in drei große Kapitel gegliedert: Muster (Nr. 1 bis 243), das heißt repetierte Motive, die man zum Bedekken großer Flächen brauchte; Bordüren (Nr. 244 bis 494) und schließlich Panneaus (Nr. 495 bis 600), Einsatzstücke mit nicht repetiertem Motiv, die meist sehr prächtig waren. Jedem dieser Dokumente ist eine Notiz beigegeben, die folgendes festhält:
– Name des Entwerfers
– Name der Manufaktur
– Datum der ersten Ausgabe
– die angewendeten Fabrikationsverfahren
– die Größe des Dokumentes in cm
– die Größe in cm der Rapportzeichnung
– die Aufschriften auf dem Dokument
– die Sammlung, der das Dokument entstammt, mit entsprechender Inventarnummer
– bibliographische Anmerkungen
– Beteiligung an Ausstellungen.

Abréviations

Coul.	= couleurs
Imp. pl.	= Impression à la planche
BF	= Bibliothèque Forney, Paris
MISE	= Musée de l'Impression sur Etoffes – Mulhouse
UCAD	= Union Centrale des Arts Décoratifs, Paris

Abbreviations

col.	= colours
engr.	= engraving
BF	= Bibliothèque Forney, Paris
MISE	= Musée de l'Impression sur Etoffes, Mulhouse
UCAD	= Union Centrale des Arts Décoratifs, Paris

The French term *manufacture,* used throughout the catalogue, is equivalent to 'factory' in English. Env. (*environ*) means *circa.*

Abkürzungen

BF	= Bibliothèque Forney, Paris
MISE	= Musée de l'Impression sur Etoffes, Mulhouse
UCAD	= Union Centrale des Arts Décoratifs, Paris

Dessins à motifs répétitifs

Repeat-pattern Designs

Muster mit repetierten Motiven

Fleurs au naturel

1 Manufacture ZUBER / 1801 / Fond mat. Imp. pl. 14 coul. / 46 × 50 / MISE 980 PP 23 / Archives Zuber n° 587

2 EBERT et BUFFARD / Manufacture JAC-QUEMART et BENARD / 1826 / Fond mat. Imp. pl. 2 coul. / 27,5 × 18 / 11,5 × 11 / Recto, manuscrit: «N° 77 N Mrs Ebert et Buffard» / UCAD HH 2275

3 Manufacture ZUBER / 1826 / Fond mat. irisé. Imp. Taille douce 1 coul. / 56 × 51 / 36 × 47 / MISE 826 n° 2 PP / Archives Zuber TD 2

4 Manufacture JACQUEMART et BENARD / 1826 / Fond mat. Imp. pl. 3 coul. / 28 × 17 / 12 × 11,5 / Recto, manuscrit: «N° 72 (Brûlé) A» / UCAD HH 2271

5 Fritz ZUBER / Manufacture ZUBER / 1827 / Fond satin irisé. Imp. pl. 2 coul. Irisé / 49,5 × 50 / 30 × 23,5 / MISE 827 2380 PP / Archives Zuber n° 2380

6 Joseph-Laurent MALAINE / Manufacture ZUBER / 1829 / Fond satin. Imp. pl. 8 coul. / 73 × 48 / 55 × 47 / MISE 829 2580 PP / Archives Zuber n° 2580

7 MERY / Manufacture ZUBER / 1829 / Fond satin. Imp. pl. 3 coul. / 50 × 49,5 / MISE 829 2748 PP / Archives Zuber n° 2748

8 Manufacture ZUBER / 1832 / Fond mat. Imp. pl. 2 coul. Irisé / 43,5 × 50,5 / 31,5 × 23,5 / MISE 832 2772 PP / Archives Zuber n° 2772

9 EBERT et BUFFARD / Manufacture JAC-QUEMART et BENARD / 1828–1830 / Fond mat. Imp. pl. 2 coul. / 28 × 17,5 / 11,7 × 11,7 / Recto, manuscrit: «N° 117 Mrs Ebert et Buffard f^d ord^re et vert 1.60» / UCAD HH 2315

10 D'après LAGRENEE / Manufacture ZU-BER / 1833 / Fond satin. Imp. pl. 2 coul. Irisés / 60 × 50 / 23,5 × 11,7 / MISE 980 PP 88 / Archives Zuber n° 2880

11 Manufacture ZUBER / 1833 / Fond satin. Imp. pl. 4 coul. Taille douce, irisés / 55 × 50 / 47 × 23,5 / MISE 980 PP 103 / Archives Zuber n° 2932

12 D'après A. R. / Manufacture ZUBER / 1833 / Fond satin. Imp. pl. 8 coul. Taille douce / 52 × 50 / 39,5 × 45 / MISE 980 PP 104 / Archives Zuber n° 2934

Naturalistic Flowers

1 Manufacture ZUBER / 1801 / Matt ground. Block-print 14 col. / 46 × 50 / MISE 980 PP 23 / Archives Zuber n° 587

2 EBERT et BUFFARD / Manufacture JACQUEMART et BENARD / 1826 / Matt ground. Block-print 2 col. / 27,5 × 18 / 11,5 × 11 / Recto, inscribed: 'N° 77 N Mrs Ebert et Buffard' / UCAD HH 2275

3 Manufacture ZUBER / 1826 / Matt ground *irisé*. Copper-plate engr. 1 col. / 56 × 51 / 36 × 47 / MISE 826 n° 2 PP / Archives Zuber n°TD 2

4 Manufacture JACQUEMART et BENARD / 1826 / Matt ground. Block-print 3 col. / 28 × 17 / 12 × 11,5 / Recto, inscribed: 'N° 72 (Brûlé) A' / UCAD HH 2271

5 Fritz ZUBER / Manufacture ZUBER / 1827 / Satin ground *irisé*. Block-print 2 col. *Irisé* / 49,5 × 50 / 30 × 23,5 / MISE 827 2380 PP / Archives Zuber n° 2380

6 Joseph-Laurent MALAINE / Manufacture ZUBER / 1829 / Satin ground. Block-print 8 col. / 73 × 48 / 55 × 47 / MISE 829 2580 PP / Archives Zuber n° 2580

7 MERY / Manufacture ZUBER / 1829 / Satin ground. Block-print 3 col. / 50 × 49,5 / MISE 829 2748 PP / Archives Zuber n° 2748

8 Manufacture ZUBER / 1832 / Matt ground. Block-print 2 col. *Irisé* / 43,5 × 50,5 / 31,5 × 23,5 / MISE 832 2772 PP / Archives Zuber n° 2772

9 EBERT et BUFFARD / Manufacture JACQUEMART et BENARD / 1828–1830 / Matt ground. Block-print 2 col. / 28 × 17,5 / 11,7 × 11,7 / Recto, inscribed: 'N° 117 Mrs Ebert et Buffard f^d ord^re et vert 1.60'. / UCAD HH 2315

10 After LAGRENEE / Manufacture ZUBER / 1833 / Satin ground. Block-print 2 col. *Irisé* / 60 × 50 / 23,5 × 11,7 / MISE 980 PP 88 / Archives Zuber n° 2880

11 Manufacture ZUBER / 1833 / Satin ground. Block-print 4 col. Metal engr., *irisé* / 55 × 50 / 47 × 23,5 / MISE 980 PP 103 / Archives Zuber n° 2932

12 After A. R. / Manufacture ZUBER / 1833 / Satin ground. Block-print 8 col. Metal engr. / 52 × 50 / 39,5 × 45 / MISE 980 PP 104 / Archives Zuber n° 2934

Naturalistische Blumen

1 Manufaktur ZUBER / 1801 / Matter Grund. Handdruck, 14 Farben / 46 × 50 / MISE 980 PP 23 / Archives Zuber Nr. 587

2 EBERT und BUFFARD / Manufaktur JAC-QUEMART et BENARD / 1826 / Matter Grund. Handdruck, 2 Farben / 27,5 × 18 / 11,5 × 11 / Vorderseite beschriftet: »N° 77 N Mrs Ebert et Buffard« / UCAD HH 2275

3 Manufaktur ZUBER / 1826 / Matter, irisierter Grund. Druck mittels Kupferstichwalze, 1 Farbe / 56 × 51 / 36 × 47 / MISE 826 2 PP / Archives Zuber Nr. TD 2

4 Manufaktur JACQUEMART et BENARD / 1826 / Matter Grund. Handdruck, 3 Farben / 28 × 17 / 12 × 11,5 / Vorderseite beschriftet: »N° 72 (Brûlé) A« / UCAD HH 2271

5 Fritz ZUBER / Manufaktur ZUBER / 1827 / Satinierter, irisierter Grund. Handdruck, 2 Farben. Irisiert / 49,5 × 50 / 30 × 23,5 / MISE 827 2380 PP / Archives Zuber Nr. 2380

6 Joseph-Laurent MALAINE / Manufaktur ZUBER / 1829 / Satinierter Grund. Handdruck, 8 Farben / 73 × 48 / 55 × 47 / MISE 829 2580 PP / Archives Zuber Nr. 2580

7 MERY / Manufaktur ZUBER / 1829 / Satinierter Grund. Handdruck, 3 Farben / 50 × 49,5 / MISE 829 2748 PP / Archives Zuber Nr. 2748

8 Manufaktur ZUBER / 1832 / Matter Grund. Handdruck, 2 Farben. Irisiert / 43,5 × 50,5 / 31,5 × 23,5 / MISE 832 2772 PP / Archives Zuber Nr. 2772

9 EBERT und BUFFARD / Manufaktur JAC-QUEMART et BENARD / 1828–1830 / Matter Grund. Handdruck, 2 Farben / 28 × 17,5 / 11,7 × 11,7 / Vorderseite beschriftet: »N° 117 Mrs Ebert et Buffard f^d ord^re et vert 1.60« / UCAD HH 2315

10 Nach LAGRENEE / Manufaktur ZUBER / 1833 / Satinierter Grund. Handdruck, 2 Farben. Irisiert / 60 × 50 / 23,5 × 11,7 / MISE 980 PP 88 / Archives Zuber Nr. 2880

11 Manufaktur ZUBER / 1833 / Satinierter Grund. Handdruck, 4 Farben. Kupferstich, irisiert / 55 × 50 / 47 × 23,5 / MISE 980 PP 103 / Archives Zuber Nr. 2932

12 Nach A. R. / Manufaktur ZUBER / 1833 / Satinierter Grund. Handdruck, 8 Farben. Kupferstich / 52 × 50 / 39,5 × 45 / MISE 980 PP 104 / Archives Zuber Nr. 2934

1

2

3

4

5

6

7

8

9

10

11

12

13 MERII / 1833 / Fond satin. Dessin original 1 coul. / 56 × 48 / 47 × 47 / Verso, manuscrit: «A. Mérii le 24 août 1833.» / UCAD HH 924 / Paris, 1967, N° 359

14 Manufacture ZUBER ? / 1835–1840 / Fond satin. Imp. pl. 13 coul. / 67 × 50 / 46,5 × 47 / UCAD HH 852 / Paris, 1967, n° 251

15 France / 1835–1840 / Fond satin. Imp. pl. 6 coul. / 67 × 52,5 / Verso, tampon «1124» / UCAD HH 851

16 France / 1835–1840 / Fond mat. Dessin original 4 coul. / 61 × 49 / 53 × 47,5 / Recto, manuscrit: «2442» / UCAD HH 2356

17 France / 1835–1840 / Fond satin. Imp. pl. 8 coul. Irisés / 57,5 × 47,5 / 47 × 47,5 / Verso, tampon «2443» / UCAD HH 889

18 France / 1835–1840 / Fond lissé, Dessin original 4 coul. / 55 × 50 / 47 × 47 / Verso, manuscrit: «2490» et énumération des couleurs / UCAD HH 2353

19 D'après S. K. / Manufacture ZUBER / 1841 / Fond mat. Imp. pl. 5 coul. Lissage / 63 × 48 / 47 × 47 / MISE 980 PP 45 / Archives Zuber n° 3486

20 D'après S. K. et Cie / Manufacture ZUBER / 1843 / Fond lissé. Imp. pl. 7 coul. / 69 × 50 / 26 × 23,5 / MISE 980 PP 610 / Archives Zuber n° 3602

21 D'après n° 343 de S. K. G. (Dreux) / Manufacture ZUBER / 1843 / Fond mat. Imp. pl. 15 coul. Lissage / 96 × 50 / 53 × 47 / MISE 980 PP 637 / Archives Zuber n° 3668

22 Manufacture RIOTTOT et PACON / 1845–1850 / Fond satin. Imp. pl. 14 coul. / 72 × 47 / 53 × 44 / BF 14

23 Manufacture RIOTTOT / 1845–1850 / Fond satin. Imp. pl. 16 coul. / 77 × 48,5 / 47 × 47 / Recto, tampon: «J. R.» / BF 203

24 France / 1845–1850 / Fond satin. Imp. pl. 12 coul. Taille douce / 62 × 50 / 47 × 47 / BF 121

13 MERII / 1833 / Satin ground. Original design 1 col. / 56 × 48 / 47 × 47 / Verso, inscribed: 'A. Mérii le 24 août 1833.' / UCAD HH 924 / Paris, 1967, n° 359

14 Manufacture ZUBER? / 1835–1840 / Satin ground. Block-print 13 col. / 67 × 50 / 46,5 × 47 / UCAD HH 852 / Paris, 1967, n° 251

15 France / 1835–1840 / Satin ground. Block-print 6 col. / 67 × 52,5 / Verso, stamped: '1124' / UCAD HH 851

16 France / 1835–1840 / Matt ground. Original design 4 col. / 61 × 49 / 53 × 47,5 / Recto, inscribed: '2442' / UCAD HH 2356

17 France / 1835–1840 / Satin ground. Block-print 8 col. *Irisé* / 57,5 × 47,5 / 47 × 47,5 / Verso, stamped '2443' / UCAD HH 889

18 France / 1835–1840 / Smooth ground. Original design 4 col. / 55 × 50 / 47 × 47 / Verso, inscribed: '2490' with enumeration of colours / UCAD HH 2353

19 After S. K. / Manufacture ZUBER / 1841 / Matt ground. Block-print 5 col. Smoothing / 63 × 48 / 47 × 47 / MISE 980 PP 45 / Archives Zuber n° 3486

20 After S. K. et Cie / Manufacture ZUBER / 1843 / Smooth ground. Block-print 7 col. / 69 × 50 / 26 × 23,5 / MISE 980 PP 610 / Archives Zuber n° 3602

21 After n° 343 of S. K. G. (Dreux) / Manufacture ZUBER / 1843 / Matt ground. Block-print 15 col Smoothing / 96 × 50 / 53 × 47 / MISE 980 PP 637 / Archives Zuber n° 3668

22 Manufacture RIOTTOT et PACON / 1845–1850 / Satin ground. Block-print 14 col. / 72 × 47 / 53 × 44 / BF 14

23 Manufacture RIOTTOT / 1845–1850 / Satin ground. Block-print 16 col. / 77 × 48,5 / 47 × 47 / Recto, stamped: 'J. R.' / BF 203

24 France / 1845–1850 / Satin ground. Block-print 12 col. / Metal engr. / 62 × 50 / 47 × 47 / BF 121

13 MERII / 1833 / Satinierter Grund. Originalentwurf, 1 Farbe / 56 × 48 / 47 × 47 / Rückseitig beschriftet: »A. Mérii le 24 août 1833.« / UCAD HH 924 / Paris, 1967, Nr. 359

14 Manufaktur ZUBER? / 1835–1840 / Satinierter Grund. Handdruck, 13 Farben / 67 × 50 / 46,5 × 47 / UCAD HH 852 / Paris, 1967, Nr. 251

15 Frankreich / 1835–1840 / Satinierter Grund. Handdruck, 6 Farben / 67 × 52,5 / Rückseitig Stempel: »1124« / UCAD HH 851

16 Frankreich / 1835–1840 / Matter Grund. Originalentwurf, 4 Farben / 61 × 49 / 53 × 47,5 / Vorderseite beschriftet: »2442« / UCAD HH 2356

17 Frankreich / 1835–1840 / Satinierter Grund. Handdruck, 8 Farben. Irisiert / 57,5 × 47,5 / 47 × 47,5 / Rückseitig Stempel: »2443« / UCAD HH 889

18 Frankreich / 1835–1840 / Geglätteter Grund. Originalentwurf, 4 Farben / 55 × 50 / 47 × 47 / Rückseitig beschriftet: »2490« und Aufzählung der Farben / UCAD HH 2353

19 Nach S. K. / Manufaktur ZUBER / Matter Grund. Handdruck, 5 Farben. Geglättet / 63 × 48 / 47 × 47 / MISE 980 PP 45 / Archives Zuber Nr. 3486

20 Nach S. K. et Cie / Manufaktur ZUBER / 1843 / Geglätteter Grund. Handdruck, 7 Farben / 69 × 50 / 26 × 23,5 / MISE 980 PP 610 / Archives Zuber Nr. 3602

21 Nach Nr. 343 von S. K. G. (Dreux) / Manufaktur Zuber / 1843 / Matter Grund. Handdruck, 15 Farben. Geglättet / 96 × 50 / 53 × 47 / MISE 980 PP 637 / Archives Zuber Nr. 3668

22 Manufaktur RIOTTOT et PACON / 1845–1850 / Satinierter Grund. Handdruck, 14 Farben / 72 × 47 / 53 × 44 / BF 14

23 Manufaktur RIOTTOT / 1845–1850 / Satinierter Grund. Handdruck, 16 Farben / 77 × 48,5 / 47 × 47 / Vorderseite Stempel: »J. R.« / BF 203

24 Frankreich / 1845–1850 / Satinierter Grund. Handdruck, 12 Farben. Kupferstich / 62 × 50 / 47 × 47 / BF 121

13

14

15

16

17

18

19

20

21

22

23

24

25 France / 1845–1850 / Fond satin. Imp. pl. 27 coul. / 77 × 50 / BF 201

26 France / 1845–1850 / Dessin original 10 coul. / 62 × 49 / 47,5 × 47 / Recto, manuscrit: «2421» / UCAD HH 2375

27 Manufacture RIOTTOT et PACON / 1850 env. / Fond mat. Imp. pl. 12 coul. / 68,5 × 50 / 50 × 47 / Recto, tampon: «Riottot et Pacon» / UCAD HH 888

28 HENRY / Manufacture RIOTTOT / 1850–1855 / Fond lissé. Imp. pl. 19 coul. / 55 × 49 / Recto, tampon: «J. R.». Verso, manuscrit: «Henry» / BF 296

29 MULLER / 1850–1855 / Fond mat. Imp. pl. 55 coul. / 39,5 × 40 / Verso, manuscrit: «Muller» / BF 341

30 France / 1850–1855 / Fond satin. Imp. pl. 16 coul. / 60 × 49 / 54,5 × 47 / UCAD HH 768 / Paris, 1967, n° 295

31 France / 1850–1855 / Fond satin. Imp. pl. 10 coul. / 60 × 50 / 46 × 47 / UCAD HH 774

32 France / 1850–1855 / Fond lissé. Imp. pl. 15 coul. / 70 × 50 / 53 × 47 / BF 120

33 France / 1850–1855 / Fond satin. Imp. pl. 16 coul. / 67 × 50 / 58 × 47 / BF 199

34 France / 1850–1855 / Fond lissé. Imp. pl. 15 coul. / 63 × 49 / 57 × 47 / BF 200

35 France / 1850–1855 / Fond lissé. Imp. pl. 21 coul. / 63 × 49 / BF 205

25 France / 1845–1850 / Satin ground. Block-print 27 col. / 77 × 50 / BF 201

26 France / 1845–1850 / Original design 10 col. / 62 × 49 / 47,5 × 47 / Recto, inscribed: '2421' / UCAD HH 2375

27 Manufacture RIOTTOT et PACON / 1850 env. / Matt ground. Block-print 12 col. / 68,5 × 50 / 50 × 47 / Recto, stamped: 'Riottot et Pacon' / UCAD HH 888

28 HENRY / Manufacture RIOTTOT / 1850–1855 / Smooth ground. Block-print 19 col. / 55 × 49 / Recto, stamped: 'J. R.' / Verso, inscribed: 'Henry' / BF 296

29 MULLER / 1850–1855 / Matt ground. Block-print 55 col. / 39,5 × 40 / Verso, inscribed: 'Muller' / BF 341

30 France / 1850–1855 / Satin ground. Block-print 16 col. / 60 × 49 / 54,5 × 47 / UCAD HH 768 / Paris, 1967, n° 295

31 France / 1850–1855 / Satin ground. Block-print 10 col. / 60 × 50 / 46 × 47 / UCAD HH 774

32 France / 1850–1855 / Smooth ground. Block-print 15 col. / 70 × 50 / 53 × 47 / BF 120

33 France / 1850–1855 / Satin ground. Block-print 16 col. / 67 × 50 / 58 × 47 / BF 199

34 France / 1850–1855 / Smooth ground. Block-print 15 col. / 63 × 49 / 57 × 47 / BF 200

35 France / 1850–1855 / Smooth ground. Block-print 21 col. / 63 × 49 / BF 205

25 Frankreich / 1845–1850 / Satinierter Grund. Handdruck, 27 Farben / 77 × 50 / BF 201

26 Frankreich / 1845–1850 / Originalentwurf, 10 Farben / 62 × 49 / 47,5 × 47 / Vorderseite beschriftet: »2421« / UCAD HH 2375

27 Manufaktur RIOTTOT et PACON / Um 1850 / Matter Grund. Handdruck, 12 Farben / 68,5 × 50 / 50 × 47 / Vorderseite Stempel: »Riottot et Pacon« / UCAD HH 888

28 HENRY / Manufaktur RIOTTOT / 1850–1855 / Geglätteter Grund. Handdruck, 19 Farben / 55 × 49 / Vorderseite Stempel: »J. R.«. Rückseitig beschriftet: »Henry« / BF 296

29 MULLER / 1850–1855 / Matter Grund. Handdruck, 55 Farben / 39,5 × 40 / Rückseitig beschriftet: »Muller« / BF 341

30 Frankreich / 1850–1855 / Satinierter Grund. Handdruck, 16 Farben / 60 × 49 / 54,5 × 47 / UCAD HH 768 / Paris, 1967, Nr. 295

31 Frankreich / 1850–1855 / Satinierter Grund. Handdruck, 10 Farben / 60 × 50 / 46 × 47 / UCAD HH 774

32 Frankreich / 1850–1855 / Geglätteter Grund. Handdruck, 15 Farben / 70 × 50 / 53 × 47 / BF 120

33 Frankreich / 1850–1855 / Satinierter Grund. Handdruck, 16 Farben / 67 × 50 / 58 × 47 / BF 199

34 Frankreich / 1850–1855 / Geglätteter Grund. Handdruck, 15 Farben / 63 × 49 / 57 × 47 / BF 200

35 Frankreich / 1850–1855 / Geglätteter Grund. Handdruck, 21 Farben / 63 × 49 / BF 205

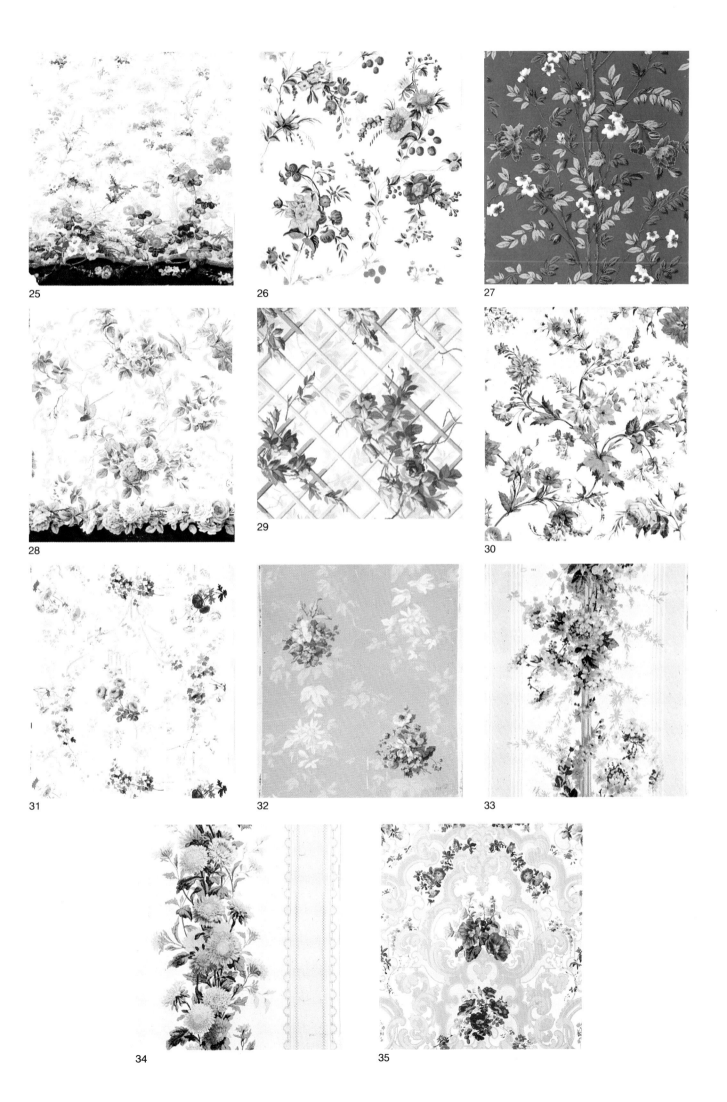

25

26

27

28

29

30

31

32

33

34

35

Verdures

36 Manufacture JACQUEMART et BENARD / 1805–1810 / Fond mat. Imp. pl. 2 coul. / 27 × 17,5 / 5,8 × 5,8 / Recto, manuscrit: «N° 18 (Brûlé) » / UCAD HH 2217

37 Manufacture DUFOUR / 1805–1810 / Fond mat. Imp. pl. 8 coul. / 56 × 75 / 53 × 41 / BF 1417

38 Manufacture DUFOUR / 1805–1810 / Fond mat. Imp. pl. 13 coul. / 56 × 95 / 54 × 78 / BF 1416

39 France / 1815–1820 / Fond mat. Imp. pl. 6 coul. / 55,5 × 54 / UCAD HH 938 B / Paris, 1967, N° 274

40 France / 1815–1820 / Fond mat. Imp. pl. 11 coul. / 51 × 48,5 / 47,5 × 47,5 / UCAD HH 2376

41 France / 1820–1825 / Fond satin. Dessin original 4 coul. / 50 × 54 / 42,5 × 47,5 / Recto, manuscrit: «n° 2013» / UCAD HH 2365

42 France / 1820–1825 / Fond satin. Dessin original 3 coul. / 57 × 53 / 43 × 47 / Recto, manuscrit: «2711» / UCAD HH 2363

43 D'après SPOERLIN et RAHN / Manufacture ZUBER / 1826 / Fond mat. Imp. pl. 14 coul. / 54 × 50 / MISE 826 2293 a PP / Archives Zuber n° 2293

44 Fritz ZUBER / Manufacture ZUBER / 1826 / Fond satin irisé. Imp. pl. 1 coul. Irisé / 28 × 49 / 24 × 23,5 / MISE 826 2348 a PP / Archives Zuber n° 2348

45 Fritz ZUBER / Manufacture ZUBER / 1826 / Fond satin irisé. Imp. pl. 1 coul. Irisé / 41 × 50 / 16 × 47 / MISE 826 2358 a PP / Archives Zuber n° 2358

46 LAPEYRE / Manufacture ZUBER / 1826 / Fond mat. Imp. pl. 3 coul. / 41 × 48 / 8 × 23,5 / MISE 826 2362 PP / Archives Zuber n° 2362

47 D'après SPOERLIN et RAHN / Manufacture ZUBER / 1827 / Fond satin irisé. Imp. pl. 3 coul. Irisé / 46 × 49 / 17 × 23,5 / MISE 827 2386 PP / Archives Zuber n° 2386

48 Fritz ZUBER / Manufacture ZUBER / 1829 / Fond mat. Imp. pl. 4 coul. Irisé / 43 × 47 / 36 × 47 / Recto, manuscrit: «2552 perse s. bleu fin en irisé rose-jaune» / Archives Zuber n° 2552

49 France / 1845–1850 / Fond lissé. Imp. pl. 2 coul. Poudre dorée, veloutage / 70 × 50 / 51 × 47 / UCAD HH 2054

50 France / 1850 env. / Fond mat. Imp. pl. 7 coul. / 68 × 50 / 60 × 47 / UCAD HH 795

Foliage

36 Manufacture JACQUEMART et BENARD / 1805–1810 / Matt ground. Block-print 2 col. / 27 × 17,5 / 5,8 × 5,8 / Recto, inscribed: 'N° 18 (Brûlé)'. / UCAD HH 2217

37 Manufacture DUFOUR / 1805–1810 / Matt ground. Block-print 8 col. / 56 × 75 / 53 × 41 / BF 1417

38 Manufacture Dufour / 1805–1810 / Matt ground. Block-print 13 col. / 56 × 95 / 54 × 78 / BF 1416

39 France / 1815–1820 / Matt ground. Block-print 6 col. / 55,5 × 54 / UCAD HH 938 B / Paris, 1967, n° 274

40 France / 1815–1820 / Matt ground. Block-print 11 col. / 51 × 48,5 / 47,5 × 47,5 / UCAD HH 2376

41 France / 1820–1825 / Satin ground. Original design 4 col. / 50 × 54 / 42,5 × 47,5 / Recto, inscribed: 'n° 2013' / UCAD HH 2365

42 France / 1820–1825 / Satin ground. Original design 3 col. / 57 × 53 / 43 × 47 / Recto, inscribed: '2711' / UCAD HH 2363

43 After SPOERLIN et RAHN / Manufacture ZUBER / 1826 / Matt ground. Block-print 14 col. / 54 × 50 / MISE 826 2293 a PP / Archives Zuber n° 2293

44 Fritz ZUBER / Manufacture ZUBER / 1826 / Satin *irisé* ground. Block-print 1 col. *Irisé* / 28 × 49 / 24 × 23,5 / MISE 826 2348 a PP / Archives Zuber n° 2348

45 Fritz ZUBER / Manufacture ZUBER / 1826 / Satin *irisé* ground. Block-print 1 col. *Irisé* / 41 × 50 / 16 × 47 / MISE 826 2358 a PP / Archives Zuber n° 2358

46 LAPEYRE / Manufacture ZUBER / 1826 / Matt ground. Block-print 3 col. / 41 × 48 / 8 × 23,5 / MISE 826 2362 PP / Archives Zuber n° 2362

47 After SPOERLIN et RAHN / Manufacture ZUBER / 1827 / Satin *irisé* ground. Block-print 3 col. *Irisé* / 46 × 49 / 17 × 23,5 / MISE 827 2386 PP / Archives Zuber n° 2386

48 Fritz ZUBER / Manufacture ZUBER / 1829 / Matt ground. Block-print 4 col. *Irisé* / 43 × 47 / 36 × 47 / Recto, inscribed: '2552 perse S. bleu fin en irisé rose-jaune' / UCAD HH 2367 / Archives Zuber n° 2552

49 France / 1845–1850 / Smooth ground. Block-print 2 col. Gold dust, flocking / 70 × 50 / 51 × 47 / UCAD HH 2054

50 France / 1850 env. / Matt ground. Block-print 7 col. / 68 × 50 / 60 × 47 / UCAD HH 795

Blattwerk

36 Manufaktur JACQUEMART et BENARD / 1805–1810 / Matter Grund. Handdruck, 2 Farben / 27 × 17,5 / 5,8 × 5,8 / Vorderseite beschriftet: »N° 18 (Brûlé)« / UCAD HH 2217

37 Manufaktur DUFOUR / 1805–1810 / Matter Grund. Handdruck, 8 Farben / 56 × 75 / 53 × 41 / BF 1417

38 Manufaktur DUFOUR / 1805–1810 / Matter Grund. Handdruck, 13 Farben / 56 × 95 / 54 × 78 / BF 1416

39 Frankreich / 1815–1820 / Matter Grund. Handdruck, 6 Farben / 55,5 × 54 / UCAD HH 938 / Paris, 1967, Nr. 274

40 Frankreich / 1815–1820 / Matter Grund. Handdruck, 11 Farben / 51 × 48,5 / 47,5 × 47,5 / UCAD HH 2376

41 Frankreich / 1820–1825 / Satinierter Grund. Originalentwurf, 4 Farben / 50 × 54 / 42,5 × 47,5 / Vorderseite beschriftet: »n° 2013« / UCAD HH 2365

42 Frankreich / 1820–1825 / Satinierter Grund. Originalentwurf, 3 Farben / 57 × 53 / 43 × 47 / Vorderseite beschriftet: »2711« / UCAD HH 2363

43 Nach SPOERLIN und RAHN / Manufaktur ZUBER / 1826 / Matter Grund. Handdruck, 14 Farben / 54 × 50 / MISE 826 2293 a PP / Archives Zuber Nr. 2293

44 Fritz ZUBER / Manufaktur ZUBER / 1826 / Satinierter, irisierter Grund. Handdruck, 1 Farbe. Irisiert. / 28 × 49 / 24 × 23,5 / MISE 826 2348 a PP / Archives Zuber Nr. 2348

45 Fritz ZUBER / Manufaktur ZUBER / 1826 / Satinierter, irisierter Grund. Handdruck, 1 Farbe. Irisiert / 41 × 50 / 16 × 47 / MISE 826 2358 a PP / Archives Zuber Nr. 2358

46 LAPEYRE / Manufaktur ZUBER / 1826 / Matter Grund. Handdruck, 3 Farben / 41 × 48 / 8 × 23,5 / MISE 826 2362 PP / Archives Zuber Nr. 2362

47 Nach SPOERLIN und RAHN / Manufaktur ZUBER / 1827 / Satinierter, irisierter Grund. Handdruck, 3 Farben. Irisiert / 46 × 49 / 17 × 23,5 / MISE 827 2386 PP / Archives Zuber Nr. 2386

48 Fritz ZUBER / Manufaktur ZUBER / 1829 / Matter Grund. Handdruck, 4 Farben. Irisiert / 43 × 47 / 36 × 47 / Vorderseite beschriftet: »2552 perse S.bleu fin en irisé rose-jaune« / UCAD HH 2367 / Archives Zuber Nr. 2552

49 Frankreich / 1845–1850 / Geglätteter Grund. Handdruck, 2 Farben. Goldstaub. Veloutiert / 70 × 50 / 51 × 47 / UCAD HH 2054

50 Frankreich / Um 1850 / Matter Grund. Handdruck, 7 Farben / 68 × 50 / 60 × 47 / UCAD HH 795

36

37

39

38

40

43

41

42

48

45

44

47

46

49

50

Fleurs en rosace

51 EBERT et BUFFARD / Manufacture JAC-QUEMART et BENARD / 1810–1815 / Fond mat. Imp. pl. 3 coul. / 23 × 17,5 / 6 × 6 / Recto, manuscrit: «Mrs Ebert et Buffard N° 35, f^d ord^re toute couleur 1.70» / UCAD HH 2234

52 Manufacture JACQUEMART et BENARD / 1815–1820 / Fond mat. Imp. pl. 3 coul. / 15,5 × 18,5 / 11,5 × 12 / Recto, manuscrit: «Mr XXX rue de Provence n° 10 ou 12 N° 47» / UCAD HH 2245

53 Manufacture JACQUEMART et BENARD / 1815–1820 / Fond mat. Imp. pl. 3 coul. / 18,5 × 20 / 12 × 12 / Recto, manuscrit: «N° 56 (Brûlé) » / UCAD HH 2254

54 France / 1820–1825 / Fond satin. Imp. pl. 2 coul. Veloutage et repiquage / 66 × 51 / 20 × 24 / UCAD HH 957

55 France / 1820–1825 / Fond satin. Imp. pl. 2 coul. / 69 × 52 / 24 × 24 / UCAD HH 958

56 France / 1820–1825 / Fond satin irisé. Dessin original 4 coul. / 51 × 51/ 47 × 47 / Recto, manuscrit: «1716 – Vous avez le choix de met-tre ou non un repiqué sur la laine. Si vous le mettez les parties des coins serviront de mo-dèle.» / UCAD HH 925 / Paris, 1967 n° 365

57 France / 1820–1825 / Fond mat. Imp. pl. 8 coul. / 128 × 59 / 56 × 56 / UCAD HH 2790

58 France / 1820–1825 / Fond satin. Imp. pl. 7 coul. / 68 × 56 / 54 × 47 / UCAD HH 960

59 France / 1820–1825 / Fond satin irisé. Imp. pl. 2 coul. Irisés / 54 × 49 / 47,5 × 47,5 / UCAD HH 936 / Paris, 1967, n° 272

60 France / 1820–1825 / Fond mat irisé. Dessin original 3 coul. / 54,5 × 51 / 11,5 × 11,5 / Recto, manuscrit: «Bordure 1823. n° 1788». Verso, énumération des couleurs / UCAD HH 926

61 France / 1820–1825 / Fond satin. Dessin original 4 coul. / 52,5 × 50 / 47,5 × 47,5 / Rec-to, manuscrit: «Projet n° 1791.» / UCAD HH 927 / Paris, 1967, n° 365

62 Manufacture ZUBER / 1824 / Fond satin. Imp. pl. 6 coul. Irisés / 47 × 51 / 47 × 47 / MISE 824 2181 PP / Archives Zuber n° 2181

Rosettes

51 EBERT et BUFFARD / Manufacture JACQUEMART et BENARD / 1810–1815 / Matt ground. Block-print 3 col./ 23 × 17,5 / 6 × 6 / Recto, inscribed: 'Mrs Ebert et Buffard N° 35, f^d ord^re toute couleur 1.70' / UCAD HH 2234

52 Manufacture JACQUEMART et BENARD / 1815–1820 / Matt ground. Block-print 3 col. / 15,5 × 18,5 / 11,5 × 12 / Recto inscribed: 'Mr XXX rue de Provence n° 10 ou 12 N° 47' / UCAD HH 2245

53 Manufacture JACQUEMART et BENARD / 1815–1820 / Matt ground. Block-print 3 col. / 18,5 × 20 / 12 × 12 / Recto, inscribed: 'N° 56 (Brûlé)' / UCAD HH 2254

54 France / 1820–1825 / Satin ground. Block-print 2 col. Flocking and over-printing / 66 × 51 / 20 × 24 / UCAD HH 957

55 France / 1820–1825 / Satin ground. Block-print 2 col. / 69 × 52 / 24 × 24 / UCAD HH 958

56 France / 1820–1825 / Satin *irisé* ground. Original design 4 col. / 51 × 51 / 47 × 47 / Recto, inscribed: '1716 – Vous avez le choix de mettre ou non un repiqué sur la laine. Si vous le mettez les parties des coins serviront de modèle.' / UCAD HH 925 / Paris, 1967, n^0 365

57 France / 1820–1825 / Matt ground. Block-print 8 col. 128 × 59 / 56 × 56 / UCAD HH 2790

58 France / 1820–1825 / Satin ground. Block-print 7 col. / 68 × 56 / 54 × 47 / UCAD HH 960

59 France / 1820–1825 / Satin *irisé* ground. Block-print 2 col. *Irisé* 54 × 49 / 47,5 × 47,5 / UCAD HH 936 / Paris, 1967, n° 272

60 France / 1820–1825 / Matt *irisé* ground. Original design 3 col. / 54,5 × 51 / 11,5 × 11,5 / Recto, inscribed: 'Bordure 1823. n° 1788'. / Verso with enumeration of colours / UCAD HH 926

61 France / 1820–1825 / Satin ground. Original design 4 col. / 52,5 × 50 / 47,5 × 47,5 / Recto inscribed: 'Projet n° 1791.' / UCAD HH 927 / Paris, 1967, n° 365

62 Manufacture ZUBER / 1824 / Satin ground. Block-print 6 col. *Irisé* / 47 × 51 / 47 × 47 / MISE 824 2181 PP / Archives Zuber n° 2181

Blütenrosetten

51 EBERT und BUFFARD / Manufaktur JAC-QUEMART et BENARD / 1810–1815 / Matter Grund. Handdruck, 3 Farben / 23 × 17,5 / 6 × 6 / Vorderseite beschriftet: »Mrs Ebert et Buffard N° 35, f^d ord^re toute couleur 1.70« / UCAD HH 2234

52 Manufaktur JACQUEMART et BENARD / 1815–1820 / Matter Grund. Handdruck, 3 Far-ben / 15,5 × 18,5 / 11,5 × 12 / Vorderseite be-schriftet: »Mr XXX rue de Provence n° 10 ou 12 N° 47« / UCAD HH 2245

53 Manufaktur JACQUEMART et BENARD / 1815–1820 / Matter Grund. Handdruck, 3 Far-ben / 18,5 × 20 / 12 × 12 / Vorderseite be-schriftet: N° 56 (Brûlé)« / UCAD HH 2254

54 Frankreich / 1820–1825 / Satinierter Grund. Handdruck, 2 Farben. Veloutiert und repiquiert / 66 × 51 / 20 × 24 / UCAD HH 957

55 Frankreich / 1820–1825 / Satinierter Grund. Handdruck, 2 Farben / 69 × 52 / 24 × 24 / UCAD HH 958

56 Frankreich / 1820–1825 / Satinierter, iri-sierter Grund. Originalentwurf, 4 Farben / 51 × 51 / 47 × 47 / Vorderseite beschriftet: »1716 – Vous avez le choix de mettre ou non un repiqué sur la laine. Si vous le mettez les parties des coins serviront de modèle.« / UCAD HH 925 / Paris, 1967, Nr. 365

57 Frankreich / 1820–1825 / Matter Grund. Handdruck, 8 Farben / 128 × 59 / 56 × 56 / UCAD HH 2790

58 Frankreich / 1820–1825 / Satinierter Grund. Handdruck, 7 Farben / 68 × 56 / 54 × 47 / UCAD HH 960

59 Frankreich / 1820–1825 / Satinierter, iri-sierter Grund. Handdruck, 2 Farben. Irisiert / 54 × 49 / 47,5 × 47,5 / UCAD HH 936 / Paris, 1967, Nr. 272

60 Frankreich / 1820–1825 / Matter, irisierter Grund. Originalentwurf, 3 Farben / 54,5 × 51 / 11,5 × 11,5 / Vorderseite beschriftet: »Bordu-re 1823. n° 1788«. Rückseitig Aufzählung der Farben / UCAD HH 926

61 Frankreich / 1820–1825 / Satinierter Grund. Originalentwurf, 4 Farben / 52,5 × 50 / 47,5 × 47,5 / Vorderseite beschriftet: »Projet n° 1791.« / UCAD HH 927 / Paris, 1967, Nr. 365

62 Manufaktur ZUBER / 1824 / Satinierter Grund. Handdruck, 6 Farben. Irisiert / 47 × 51 / 47 × 47 / MISE 824 2181 PP / Archives Zu-ber Nr. 2181

51

52

53

54

58

55

56

57

59

60

61

62

63 France / 1825 env. / Fond satin irisé. Dessin original 3 coul. / 52 × 52 / 47,5 × 47,5 / Recto, manuscrit: «n° 1868». Verso, liste des variantes de couleurs / UCAD HH 929 / Paris, 1967, n° 365

64 MERII / 1825 / Fond satin. Dessin original 2 coul. / 55 × 52 / 47,5 × 47,5 / Verso, manuscrit: «Au. Mérii rue de la Muette n° 15. Le 3 décembre 1825. Projet n° 1881.» / UCAD HH 922 / Paris, 1967, n° 357

65 Manufacture JACQUEMART et BENARD / 1826 / Fond mat. Imp. pl. 3 coul. / 28 × 19 / 11,5 × 11,5 / Recto, manuscrit: «N° 78 Brûlé Collection 1826 A» / UCAD HH 2269

66 JULIEN / Manufacture ZUBER / 1826 / Fond satin. Imp. pl. 2 coul. Irisés / 41 × 49 / 23,5 × 23,5 / MISE 826 2290 a PP / Archives Zuber n° 2290

67 Fritz ZUBER / Manufacture ZUBER / 1826 / Fond satin. Imp. pl. 2 coul. Irisés / 39 × 47 / 24 × 24 / MISE 826 2368 b PP / Archives Zuber n° 2368

68 France / 1820–1825 / Fond satin. Dessin original 2 coul. / 54,5 × 54,5 / 47,5 × 47,5 / Recto, manuscrit: «n° 2016» / UCAD HH 2359

69 France / 1825–1830 / Fond satin irisé. Dessin original 1 coul. / 55 × 54,5 / 47,5 × 47,5 / Recto, manuscrit: «Projet n° 2017» / UCAD HH 931 / Paris, 1967, n° 365

70 France / 1825–1830 / Fond satin. Dessin original 5 coul. / 52 × 52 / 47,5 × 47,5 / Recto, manuscrit: «n° 2060» / UCAD HH 930 / Paris, 1967, n° 365

71 France / 1825–1830 / Fond mat. Dessin original 1 coul. / 56 × 54 / 56 × 52 / Recto, manuscrit: «n° 2444» / UCAD HH 933 / Paris, 1967, n° 366

72 EBERT et BUFFARD / Manufacture JACQUEMART et BENARD / 1827 / Fond mat. Imp. 2 coul. / 25,5 × 17 / 11,5 × 11,5 / Recto, manuscrit: «N° 80 A Mrs Ebert et Buffard» / UCAD HH 2278

73 EBERT et BUFFARD / Manufacture JACQUEMART et BENARD / 1827 / Fond mat. Imp. pl. 2 coul. / 22 × 16 / 8,5 × 11,5 / Recto, manuscrit: «N° 82 A Mrs Ebert et Buffard» / UCAD HH 2280

63 France/ 1825 env. / Satin irisé ground. Original design 3 col. / 52 × 52 / 47,5 × 47,5 / Recto, inscribed: 'n° 1868' / Verso, with list of colour variants / UCAD HH 929 / Paris, 1967, n° 365

64 MERII / 1825 / Satin ground. Original design 2 col. / 55 × 52 / 47,5 × 47,5 / Verso, inscribed: 'Au. Mérii rue de la Muette n° 15. Le 3 décembre 1825. Projet n° 1881' / UCAD HH 922 / Paris, 1967, n° 357

65 Manufacture JACQUEMART et BENARD / 1826 / Matt ground. Block-print 3 col. / 28 × 19 / 11,5 × 11,5 / Recto, inscribed: 'N° 78 Brûlé Collection 1826 A' / UCAD HH 2269

66 JULIEN / Manufacture ZUBER / 1826 / Satin ground. Block-print 2 col. Irisé / 41 × 49 / 23,5 × 23,5 / MISE 826 2290 a PP / Archives Zuber n° 2290

67 Fritz ZUBER / Manufacture ZUBER / 1826 / Satin ground. Block-print 2 col. Irisé / 39 × 47 / 24 × 24 / MISE 826 2368 b PP / Archives Zuber n° 2368

68 France / 1820–1825 / Satin ground. Original design 2 col. / 54,5 × 54,5 / 47,5 × 47,5 / Recto, inscribed: 'n° 2016' / UCAD HH 2359

69 France / 1825–1830 / Satin irisé ground. Original design 1 col. / 55 × 54,5 / 47,5 × 47,5 / Recto, inscribed: 'Projet n° 2017' / UCAD HH 931 / Paris, 1967, n° 365

70 France/1825–1830 / Satin ground. Original design 5 col. / 52 × 52 / 47,5 × 47,5 / Recto, inscribed: 'n° 2060' / UCAD HH 930 / Paris, 1967, n° 365

71 France / 1825–1830 / Matt ground. Original design 1 col. / 56 × 54 / 56 × 52 / Recto, inscribed: 'n° 2444' / UCAD HH 933 / Paris, 1967, n° 366

72 EBERT et BUFFARD / Manufacture JACQUEMART et BENARD / 1827 / Matt ground. Block-print 2 col. / 25,5 × 17 / 11,5 × 11,5 / Recto, inscribed: 'N° 80 A Mrs Ebert et Buffard' / UCAD HH 2278

73 EBERT et BUFFARD / Manufacture JACQUEMART et BENARD / 1827 / Matt ground. Block-print 2 col. / 22 × 16 / 8,5 × 11,5 / Recto, inscribed: 'N° 82 A Mrs Ebert et Buffard' / UCAD HH 2280

63 Frankreich / Um 1825 / Satinierter, irisierter Grund. Originalentwurf, 3 Farben / 52 × 52 / 47,5 × 47,5 / Vorderseite beschriftet: »n° 1868«. Rückseitig Liste der Farbvarianten / UCAD HH 929 / Paris, 1967, Nr. 365

64 MERII / 1825 / Satinierter Grund. Originalentwurf, 2 Farben / 55 × 52 / 47,5 × 47,5 / Rückseitig beschriftet: »Au. Mérii rue de la Muette n° 15. Le 3 décembre 1825. Projet n° 1881.« / UCAD HH 922 / Paris, 1967, Nr. 357

65 Manufaktur JACQUEMART et BENARD / 1826 / Matter Grund. Handdruck, 3 Farben / 28 × 19 / 11,5 × 11,5 / Vorderseite beschriftet: »N° 78 Brûlé Collection 1826 A« / UCAD HH 2269

66 JULIEN / Manufaktur ZUBER / 1826 / Satinierter Grund. Handdruck, 2 Farben. Irisiert / 41 × 49 / 23,5 × 23,5 / MISE 826 2290 a PP / Archives Zuber Nr. 2290

67 Fritz ZUBER / Manufaktur ZUBER / 1826 / Satinierter Grund. Handdruck, 2 Farben. Irisiert / 39 × 47 / 24 × 24 / MISE 826 2368 b PP / Archives Zuber Nr. 2368

68 Frankreich / 1820–1825 / Satinierter Grund. Originalentwurf, 2 Farben / 54,5 × 54,5 / 47,5 × 47,5 / Vorderseite beschriftet: »n° 2016« / UCAD HH 2359

69 Frankreich / 1825–1830 / Satinierter, irisierter Grund. Originalentwurf, 1 Farbe / 55 × 54,5 / 47,5 × 47,5 / Vorderseite beschriftet: »Projet n° 2017« / UCAD HH 932 / Paris, 1967, Nr. 365

70 Frankreich / 1825–1830 / Satinierter Grund. Originalentwurf, 5 Farben / 52 × 52 / 47,5 × 47,5 / Vorderseite beschriftet: »n° 2060« / UCAD HH 930 / Paris, 1967, Nr. 365

71 Frankreich / 1825–1830 / Matter Grund. Originalentwurf, 1 Farbe / 56 × 54 / 56 × 52 / Vorderseite beschriftet: »n° 2444« / UCAD HH 933 / Paris, 1967, Nr. 366

72 EBERT und BUFFARD / Manufaktur JACQUEMART et BENARD / 1827 / Matter Grund, Handdruck, 2 Farben / 25,5 × 17 / 11,5 × 11,5 / Vorderseite beschriftet: »N° 80 A Mrs Ebert et Buffard« / UCAD HH 2278

73 EBERT und BUFFARD / Manufaktur JACQUEMART et BENARD / 1827 / Matter Grund. Handdruck, 2 Farben / 22 × 16 / 8,5 × 11,5 / Vorderseite beschriftet: »N° 82 A Mrs Ebert et Buffard« / UCAD HH 2280

63

64

66

65

67

68

69

72

73

70

71

Fleurs d'ornement

74 EBERT et BUFFARD / Manufacture JAC-QUEMART et BENARD / 1825 / Fond mat. Imp. pl. 3 coul. / 18,5 × 18,5 / 5 × 6,5 / Recto, manuscrit: «N° 64 Mrs. Ebert et Buffard» / UCAD HH 2262

75 D'après LAGRENEE / Manufacture ZU-BER / 1827 / Fond satin irisé. Imp. pl. 2 coul. Irisés / 53,5 × 49,5 / 42 × 27,5 / MISE 827 2400 PP / Archives Zuber n° 2400

76 FLAMENT et BIZET / Manufacture JAC-QUEMART et BENARD / 1828–1830 / Fond mat. Imp. pl. 2 coul. / 27 × 17,5 / 23,5 × 11,5 / Recto, manuscrit: «n° 101 A Mrs Flament et Bizet F^d ord^{re} 1.50» / UCAD HH 2299

77 EBERT et BUFFARD / Manufacture JAC-QUEMART et BENARD / 1828–1830 / Fond mat. Imp. pl. 1 coul. / 28,5 × 18 / 5,2 × 5,2 / Recto, manuscrit: «N° 115 Mrs. Ebert et Buffard. F^d ord^{re} 1.30» / UCAD HH 2313

78 Manufacture ZUBER / 1828 / Fond satin irisé. Imp. pl. 1 coul. Irisé / 69 × 49,5 / 47,5 × 47,5 / UCAD HH 848 / Paris, 1967, n° 248

79 Manufacture ZUBER / 1829 / Fond mat. Imp. pl. 2 coul. Irisés / 65 × 50 / MISE 829 2776 PP / Archives Zuber n° 2776

80 France / 1830 env. / Fond satin. Dessin original 1 coul. / 64 × 52 / 58,5 × 47,5 / Recto, manuscrit: «Damas velouté à l'antique. 1712» / UCAD HH 2370

81 Manufacture ZUBER / 1832 / Fond satin irisé. Imp. pl. 2 coul. Irisés / 58 × 49,5 / 47 × 47 / MISE 832 2752 PP / Archives Zuber n° 2752

82 D'après ZIPELIUS / Manufacture ZUBER / 1832 / Fond satin irisé. Imp. pl. 4 coul. Irisés / 58,5 × 50 / MISE 832 2756 PP / Archives Zuber n° 2756

83 Victor POTERLET / 1835–1840 / Fond lissé. Imp. pl. 2 coul. / 136 × 51 / 117 × 47 / Verso, manuscrit: «Poterlet. Grand damas» / BF 565

84 GRUCHY / Manufacture GENOUX / 1835–1840 / Fond satin. Imp. pl. 2 coul. / 62,5 × 47 / 55 × 47 / Recto, manuscrit: «Gruchy-Genoux.» / UCAD HH 2794

Ornamental Flowers

74 EBERT et BUFFARD / Manufacture JACQUEMART et BENARD / 1825 / Matt ground. Block-print 3 col. 18,5 × 18,5 / 5 × 6,5 / Recto, inscribed: 'N° 64 Mrs. Ebert et Buffard' / UCAD HH 2262

75 After LAGRENEE / Manufacture ZUBER / 1827 / Satin *irisé* ground. Block-print 2 col. *Irisé* / 53,5 × 49,5 / 42 × 27,5 / MISE 827 2400 PP / Archives Zuber n° 2400

76 FLAMENT et BIZET / Manufacture JACQUEMART et BENARD / 1828–1830 / Matt ground. Block-print 2 col. / 27 × 17,5 / 23,5 × 11,5 / Recto, inscribed: 'n° 101 A Mrs Flament et Bizet F^d ord^{re} 1.50' / UCAD HH 2299

77 EBERT et BUFFARD / Manufacture JACQUEMART et BENARD / 1828–1830 / Matt ground. Block-print 1 col. / 28,5 × 18 / 5,2 × 5,2 / Recto, inscribed: 'N° 115 Mrs. Ebert et Buffard. F^d ord^{re} 1.30' / UCAD HH 2313

78 Manufacture ZUBER / 1828 / Satin *irisé* ground. Block-print 1 col. *Irisé* / 69 × 49,5 / 47,5 × 47,5 / UCAD HH 848 / Paris, 1967, n° 248

79 Manufacture ZUBER / 1829 / Matt ground. Block-print 2 col *Irisé* / 65 × 50 / MISE 829 2776 PP / Archives Zuber n° 2776

80 France / 1830 env. / Satin ground. Original design 1 col / 64 × 52 / 58,5 × 47,5 / Recto, inscribed: 'Damas velouté à l'antique. 1712' / UCAD HH 2370

81 Manufacture ZUBER / 1832 / Satin *irisé* ground. Block-print 2 col. *Irisé* / 58 × 49,5 / 47 × 47 / MISE 832 2752 PP / Archives Zuber n° 2752

82 After ZIPELIUS / Manufacture ZUBER / 1832 / Satin *irisé* ground. Block-print 4 col. *Irisé* / 58,5 × 50 / MISE 832 2756 PP / Archives Zuber n° 2756

83 Victor POTERLET / 1835–1840 / Smooth ground. Block-print 2 col. / 136 × 51 / 117 × 47 / Verso, inscribed: 'Poterlet. Grand damas' / BF 565

84 GRUCHY / Manufacture GENOUX / 1835–1840 / Satin ground. Block-print 2 col. / 62,5 × 47 / 55 × 47 / Recto, inscribed: 'Gruchy-Genoux.' / UCAD HH 2794

Ornamentale Blumen

74 EBERT und BUFFARD / Manufaktur JAC-QUEMART et BENARD / 1825 / Matter Grund. Handdruck, 3 Farben / 18,5 × 18,5 / 5 × 6,5 / Vorderseite beschriftet: »N° 64 Mrs. Ebert et Buffard« / UCAD HH 2262

75 Nach LAGRENEE / Manufaktur ZUBER / 1827 / Satinierter, irisierter Grund. Handdruck, 2 Farben. Irisiert / 53,5 × 49,5 / 42 × 27,5 / MISE 827 2400 PP / Archives Zuber Nr. 2400

76 FLAMENT und BIZET / Manufaktur JAC-QUEMART et BENARD / 1828–1830 / Matter Grund. Handdruck, 2 Farben / 27 × 17,5 / 23,5 × 11,5 / Vorderseite beschriftet: »n° 101 A Mrs Flament et Bizet F^d ord^{re} 1.50« / UCAD HH 2299

77 EBERT und BUFFARD / Manufaktur JAC-QUEMART et BENARD / 1828–1830 / Matter Grund. Handdruck, 1 Farbe / 28,5 × 18 / 5,2 × 5,2 / Vorderseite beschriftet: »N° 115 Mrs. Ebert et Buffard. F^d ord^{re} 1.30« / UCAD HH 2313

78 Manufaktur ZUBER / 1828 / Satinierter, irisierter Grund. Handdruck, 1 Farbe. Irisiert / 69 × 49,5 / 47,5 × 47,5 / UCAD HH 848 / Paris, 1967, Nr. 248

79 Manufaktur ZUBER / 1829 / Matter Grund. Handdruck, 2 Farben. Irisiert / 65 × 50 / MISE 829 2776 PP / Archives Zuber Nr. 2776

80 Frankreich / Um 1830 / Satinierter Grund. Originalentwurf, 1 Farbe / 64 × 52 / 58,5 × 47,5 / Vorderseite beschriftet: »Damas velouté à l'antique. 1712« / UCAD HH 2370

81 Manufaktur ZUBER / 1832 / Satinierter, irisierter Grund. Handdruck, 2 Farben. Irisiert / 58 × 49,5 / 47 × 47 / MISE 832 2752 PP / Archives Zuber Nr. 2752

82 Nach ZIPELIUS / Manufaktur ZUBER / 1832 / Satinierter, irisierter Grund. Handdruck, 4 Farben. Irisiert / 58,5 × 50 / MISE 832 2756 PP / Archives Zuber Nr. 2756

83 Victor POTERLET / 1835–1840 / Geglätteter Grund. Handdruck, 2 Farben / 136 × 51 / 117 × 47 / Rückseitig beschriftet: »Poterlet. Grand damas« / BF 565

84 GRUCHY / Manufaktur GENOUX / 1835–1840 / Satinierter Grund. Handdruck, 2 Farben / 62,5 × 47 / 55 × 47 / Vorderseite beschriftet: »Gruchy-Genoux.« / UCAD HH 2794

74

75

76

77

78

84

79

80

81

83

82

85 Victor POTERLET? / 1835–1840 / Fond mat. Imp. pl. 2 coul. Poudre dorée / 73 × 50 / UCAD HH 914 / Paris, 1967, n° 193

86 France / 1835–1840 / Fond satin. Imp. pl. 2 coul. / 60 × 50 / 68 × 47 / UCAD HH 707

87 France / 1835–1840 / Fond satin. Imp. pl. 2 coul. Poudre dorée, veloutage / 126 × 55 / UCAD HH 2792

88 France / 1835–1840 / Fond satin. Imp. pl. 5 coul. / 52 × 50,5 / UCAD HH 833 / Paris, 1967, n° 323

89 Victor POTERLET / Manufacture GELOT / 1837 / Fond satin. Imp. pl. 3 coul. / 69 × 47 / 56,5 × 47 / Recto, manuscrit: «Gelot. V. P. 1837» / UCAD HH 2793

90 France / 1840 env. / Fond satin. Imp. pl. 3 coul. / 69 × 50 / 47,5 × 47,5 / UCAD HH 844

91 ZIPELIUS / Manufacture ZUBER / 1843 / Fond lissé. Imp. pl. 4 coul. Poudre d'argent. Gauffrage en moire / 122 × 57 / 105,5 × 53 / MISE 980 PP 620 / Archives Zuber n° 3630

92 France / 1840–1845 / Fond satin. Imp. pl. 2 coul. / 59 × 50 / UCAD HH 2002

93 France / 1840–1845 / Fond satin. Imp. pl. 2 coul. Poudre dorée. Gauffrage en pointe de diamant / 66,5 × 49 / 60 × 45,5 / UCAD HH 702

94 France / 1840–1845 / Fond lissé. Imp. pl. 5 coul. / 67 × 50 / 64 × 47 / UCAD HH 2047

85 Victor POTERLET? / 1835–1840 / Matt ground. Block-print 2 col. Gold dust / 73 × 50 / UCAD HH 914 / Paris, 1967, n° 193

86 France / 1835–1840 / Satin ground. Block-print 2 col. / 60 × 50 / 68 × 47 / UCAD HH 707

87 France / 1835–1840 / Satin ground. Block-print 2 col. Gold dust, flocking / 126 × 55 / UCAD HH 2792

88 France / 1835–1840 / Satin ground. Block-print 5 col. / 52 × 50,5 / UCAD HH 833 / Paris, 1967, n° 323

89 Victor POTERLET / Manufacture GELOT / 1837 / Satin ground. Block-print 3 col. / 69 × 47 / 56,5 × 47 / Recto, inscribed: 'Gelot. V. P. 1837' / UCAD HH 2793

90 France / 1840 env. / Satin ground. Block-print 3 col. / 69 × 50 / 47,5 × 47,5 / UCAD HH 844

91 ZIPELIUS / Manufacture ZUBER / 1843 / Smooth ground. Block-print 4 col. Silver dust. Embossing in moiré / 122 × 57 / 105,5 × 53 / MISE 980 PP 620 / Archives Zuber n° 3630

92 France / 1840–1845 / Satin ground. Block-print 2 col. / 59 × 50 / UCAD HH 2002

93 France / 1840–1845 / Satin ground. Block-print 2 col. Gold dust. Light embossing in diamond point / 66,5 × 49 / 60 × 45,5 / UCAD HH 702

94 France / 1840–1845 / Smooth ground. Block-print 5 col. / 67 × 50 / 64 × 47 / UCAD HH 2047

85 Victor POTERLET? / 1835–1840 / Matter Grund. Handdruck, 2 Farben. Goldstaub / 73 × 50 / UCAD HH 914 / Paris, 1967, Nr. 193

86 Frankreich / 1835–1840 / Satinierter Grund. Handdruck, 2 Farben / 60 × 50 / 68 × 47 / UCAD HH 707

87 Frankreich / 1835–1840 / Satinierter Grund. Handdruck, 2 Farben. Goldstaub. Veloutiert / 126 × 55 / UCAD HH 2792

88 Frankreich / 1835–1840 / Satinierter Grund. Handdruck, 5 Farben / 52 × 50,5 / UCAD HH 833 / Paris, 1967, Nr. 323

89 Victor POTERLET / Manufaktur GELOT / 1837 / Satinierter Grund. Handdruck, 3 Farben / 69 × 47 / 56,5 × 47 / Vorderseite beschriftet: »Gelot. V.P. 1837« / UCAD HH 2793

90 Frankreich / Um 1840 / Satinierter Grund. Handdruck, 3 Farben / 69 × 50 / 47,5 × 47,5 / UCAD HH 844

91 ZIPELIUS / Manufaktur ZUBER / 1843 / Geglätteter Grund. Handdruck, 4 Farben. Silberstaub. Moiré-Gaufrierung / 122 × 57 / 105,5 × 53 / MISE 980 PP 620 / Archives Zuber Nr. 3630

92 Frankreich / 1840–1845 / Satinierter Grund. Handdruck, 2 Farben / 59 × 50 / UCAD HH 2002

93 Frankreich / 1840–1845 / Satinierter Grund. Handdruck, 2 Farben. Goldstaub. »Pointe de diamant«-Gaufrierung / 66,5 × 49 / 60 × 45,5 / UCAD HH 702

94 Frankreich / 1840–1845 / Geglätteter Grund. Handdruck, 5 Farben / 67 × 50 / 64 × 47 / UCAD HH 2047

85

88

87

86

89

92

90

94

91

93

95 France / 1840–1845 / Fond satin. Imp. pl. 4 coul. / 73 × 51,5 / 73 × 47 / UCAD HH 905 / Paris, 1967, n° 320

96 France / 1840–1845 / Fond satin. Imp. pl. 5 coul. / 69 × 50 / 56,5 × 46,5 / UCAD HH 823

97 France / 1840–1845 / Fond satin. Imp. pl. 2 coul. / 68 × 50,5 / UCAD HH 734

98 France / 1840–1845 / Fond satin. Imp. pl. 3 coul. / 58 × 48 / UCAD HH 201

99 Victor POTERLET / Manufacture J. H. et Cie -? / 1845–1850 / Fond satin. Imp. pl. 1 coul. Veloutage / 70 × 47 / 60 × 47 / Recto, manuscrit: «V. P.» et tampons «2297», «J. H. et Cie Paris» / UCAD 29816

100 France / 1845–1850 / Fond satin. Imp. pl. 3 coul. Poudre dorée, veloutage / 65 × 47,5 / 53 × 47 / UCAD HH 800

101 France / 1845–1850 / Fond main poudre dorée. Imp. pl. 1 coul. Veloutage / 68 × 54 / UCAD HH 821

102 Victor POTERLET / 1845–1850 / Fond mat. Imp. pl. 5 coul. Veloutage / 131 × 61 / 120 × 60 / Verso, manuscrit: «Poterlet» / BF 586

103 Manufacture RIOTTOT / 1845–1850 / Fond satin. Imp. pl. 5 coul. Poudre dorée / 122 × 70 / Verso, tampon: «J. R.» / BF 489

104 Victor POTERLET / Manufacture DELICOURT / 1850 / Fond satin. Imp. pl. 2 coul. Poudre dorée. Veloutage / 69 × 53 / 55,5 × 46,5 / Verso, manuscrit: «Victor Poterlet. Impression de Delicourt 1850» / UCAD HH 171

105 Victor POTERLET / Manufacture DAUPTAIN / 1850 / Fond satin. Imp. pl. 1 coul. Velouté / 70 × 47 / 60,5 × 46,5 / Verso, manuscrit: «Poterlet 1850 impression de Dauptain» / UCAD 29815 / Paris, 1967, n° 92

95 France / 1840–1845 / Satin ground. Block-print 4 col. / 73 × 51,5 / 73 × 47 / UCAD HH 905 / Paris, 1967, n° 320

96 France / 1840–1845 / Satin ground. Block-print 5 col. / 69 × 50 / 56,5 × 46,5 / UCAD HH 823

97 France / 1840–1845 / Satin ground. Block-print 2 col. / 68 × 50,5 / UCAD HH 734

98 France / 1840–1845 / Satin ground. Block-print 3 col. / 58 × 48 / UCAD HH 201

99 Victor POTERLET / Manufacture J. H. et Cie? / 1845–1850 / Satin ground. Block-print 1 col. Flocking / 70 × 47 / 60 × 47 / Recto, inscribed: 'V. P' and stamped '2297' J. H. et Cie Paris' / UCAD 29816

100 France / 1845–1850 / Satin ground. Block-print 3 col. Gold dust. Flocking / 65 × 47,5 / 53 × 47 / UCAD HH 800

101 France / 1845–1850 / Ground gold-dusted by hand. Block-print 1 col. Flocking / 68 × 54 / UCAD HH 821

102 Victor POTERLET / 1845–1850 / Matt ground. Block-print 5 col. Flocking / 131 × 61 / 120 × 60 / Verso, inscribed: 'Poterlet' / BF 586

103 Manufacture RIOTTOT / 1845–1850 / Satin ground. Block-print 5 col. Gold dust / 122 × 70 / Verso, stamped: 'J. R.' / BF 489

104 Victor POTERLET / Manufacture DELICOURT / 1850 / Satin ground. Block-print 2 col. Gold dust. Flocking / 69 × 53 / 55,5 × 46,5 / Verso, inscribed: 'Victor Poterlet. Impression de Delicourt 1850' / UCAD HH 171

105 Victor POTERLET / Manufacture DAUPTAIN / 1850 / Satin ground. Block-print 1 col. Flocking / 70 × 47 / 60,5 × 46,5 / Verso, inscribed: 'Poterlet 1850 impression de Dauptain' / UCAD 29815 / Paris, 1967, n° 92

95 Frankreich / 1840–1845 / Satinierter Grund, Handdruck, 4 Farben / 73 × 51,5 / 73 × 47 / UCAD HH 905 / Paris, 1967, Nr. 320

96 Frankreich / 1840–1845 / Satinierter Grund. Handdruck, 5 Farben / 69 × 50 / 56,5 × 46,5 / UCAD HH 823

97 Frankreich / 1840–1845 / Satinierter Grund. Handdruck, 2 Farben / 68 × 50,5 / UCAD HH 734

98 Frankreich / 1840–1845 / Satinierter Grund. Handdruck, 3 Farben / 58 × 48 / UCAD HH 201

99 Victor POTERLET / Manufaktur J. H. et Cie? / 1845–1850 / Satinierter Grund. Handdruck, 1 Farbe. Veloutiert / 70 × 47 / 60 × 47 / Vorderseite beschriftet: »V.P.« und Stempel: »2297«, »J. H. et Cie Paris« / UCAD 29816

100 Frankreich / 1845–1850 / Satinierter Grund. Handdruck, 3 Farben. Goldstaub. Veloutiert / 65 × 47,5 / 53 × 47 / UCAD HH 800

101 Frankreich / 1845–1850 / Von Hand goldbestäubter Grund. Handdruck, 1 Farbe. Veloutiert. / 68 × 54 / UCAD HH 821

102 Victor POTERLET / 1845–1850 / Matter Grund. Handdruck, 5 Farben. Veloutiert / 131 × 61 / 120 × 60 / Rückseitig beschriftet: »Poterlet« / BF 586

103 Manufaktur RIOTTOT / 1845–1850 / Satinierter Grund. Handdruck, 5 Farben. Goldstaub / 122 × 70 / Rückseitig Stempel: »J.R.« / BF 489

104 Victor POTERLET / Manufaktur DELICOURT / 1850 / Satinierter Grund. Handdruck, 2 Farben. Goldstaub. Veloutiert / 69 × 53 / 55,5 × 46,5 / Rückseitig beschriftet: »Victor Poterlet. Impression de Delicourt 1850« / UCAD HH 171

105 Victor POTERLET / Manufaktur DAUPTAIN / 1850 / Satinierter Grund. Handdruck, 1 Farbe. Veloutiert / 70 × 47 / 60,5 × 46,5 / Rückseitig beschriftet: »Poterlet 1850 impression de Dauptain« / UCAD 29815 / Paris, 1967, Nr. 92

Ramages de tiges

106 ZIPELIUS / Manufacture ZUBER / 1843 / Fond lissé. Imp. pl. 3 coul. / 66 × 50 / 23,5 × 23,5 / MISE 980 PP 615 / Archives Zuber n° 3620

107 Manufacture ZUBER / 1842 / Fond lissé. Imp. pl. 16 coul. / 52 × 51 / MISE 980 PP 663 / Archives Zuber n° 3596

108 Fritz ZUBER / Manufacture ZUBER / 1843 / Fond lissé. Imp. taille douce 1 coul. poudre dorée. Imp. pl. 2 coul. / 82 × 50 / 35 × 47 / MISE 980 PP 621-1 / Archives Zuber n° 3632

Branches

106 ZIPELIUS / Manufacture ZUBER / 1843 / Smooth ground. Block-print 3 col. / 66 × 50 / 23,5 × 23,5 / MISE 980 PP 615 / Archives Zuber n° 3620

107 Manufacture ZUBER / 1842 / Smooth ground. Block-print 16 col. / 52 × 51 / MISE 980 PP 663 / Archives Zuber n° 3596

108 Fritz ZUBER / Manufacture ZUBER / 1843 / Smooth ground. Metal engr. 1 col. Gold dust. Block-print 2 col. / 82 × 50 / 35 × 47 / MISE 980 PP 621-1 / Archives Zuber n° 3632

Rankenwerk

106 ZIPELIUS / Manufaktur ZUBER / 1843 / Geglätteter Grund. Handdruck, 3 Farben / 66 × 50 / 23,5 × 23,5 / MISE 980 PP 615 / Archives Zuber Nr. 3620

107 Manufaktur ZUBER / 1842 / Geglätteter Grund. Handdruck, 16 Farben / 52 × 51 / MISE 980 PP 663 / Archives Zuber Nr. 3596

108 Fritz ZUBER / Manufaktur ZUBER / 1843 / Geglätteter Grund. Druck mittels Kupferstichwalze, 1 Farbe, Goldstaub. Handdruck, 2 Farben / 82 × 50 / 35 × 47 / MISE 980 PP 621-1 / Archives Zuber Nr. 3632

95

96

97

98

99

100

101

102

103

104

105

106

107

108

Chinois

109 MULLER et Victor POTERLET / Manufacture ZUBER / 1840 / Fond mat. Imp. pl. 5 coul. Vernis / 62 × 49 / 58,5 × 47 / Verso, tampon «JZ Cie»; et manuscrit: «3370 ; 3,50-» / UCAD HH 145 / Paris, 1967, n° 256 / Archives Zuber n° 3370

110 GUICHARD, Victor POTERLET et ZIPELIUS / Manufacture ZUBER / 1842 / Fond mat. Imp. pl. 5 coul. Vernis / 61,5 × 50 / 55,5 × 47 / Verso, tampon «JZ Cie», et manuscrit «3514; 2,50-» / UCAD HH 29734 B / Paris, 1967, n° 256 / Archives Zuber n° 3514

111 GUICHARD et Victor POTERLET / Manufacture ZUBER / 1842 / Fond mat. Imp. pl. 5 coul. Vernis / 71 × 48 / 54 × 47 / UCAD HH 29734 A

Gothique

112 ZIPELIUS, d'après HEIDELOFF / Manufacture ZUBER / 1833 / Fond satin. Imp. pl. 5 coul. / 48,5 × 50 / 33 × 23,5 / MISE 980 PP 92 / Archives Zuber n° 2888

113 France / 1835–1840 / Fond satin. Imp. pl. 3 coul. Feuille d'or / 60 × 50 / UCAD HH 903

114 Manufacture Jules RIOTTOT / 1840 env. / Fond mat. Imp. pl. 6 coul. / 74 × 52 / 58 × 47 / Verso, manuscrit «Riottot», tampon «J-R» / BF 450

115 Victor POTERLET / Manufacture DAUPTAIN / 1840–1845 / Fond mat. Imp. pl. 7 coul. Poudre dorée. Veloutage et repiquage / 70 × 47 / 31,5 × 24,5 / UCAD 29814 / 1967 Paris, n° 92

116 DURAND / Manufacture ZUBER / 1843 / Fond satin. Imp. pl. 4 coul. / 90 × 49 / 58,5 × 49 / MISE 980 PP 623 / Archives Zuber n° 3638

117 Manufacture Isidore LEROY / Abbaye de Jumièges / 1845 / Fond mat, irisé. Imp. pl. 8 coul. / 98 × 50 / Recto, manuscrit «Jumièges». Verso, manuscrit: «Leroy. Abbaye de Jumièges. 1845» / BF 449

Chinoiseries

109 MULLER et Victor POTERLET / Manufacture ZUBER / 1840 / Matt ground. Block-print 5 col. Varnish / 62 × 49 / 58,5 × 47 / Verso, stamped: 'JZ Cie', and inscribed: '3370; 3,50–' / UCAD HH 145 / Paris, 1967, n° 256 / Archives Zuber, n° 3370

110 GUICHARD, Victor POTERLET et ZIPELIUS / Manufacture ZUBER / 1842 / Matt ground. Block-print 5 col. Varnish / 61,5 × 50 / 55,5 × 47 / Verso stamped: 'JZ Cie', and inscribed: '3514; 2,50–'. / UCAD HH 29734 B / Paris, 1967, n° 256 / Archives Zuber n° 3514

111 GUICHARD et Victor POTERLET / Manufacture ZUBER / 1842 / Matt ground. Block-print 5 col. Varnish / 71 × 48 / 54 × 47 / UCAD HH 29734 A

Gothic Designs

112 ZIPELIUS, after HEIDELOFF / Manufacture ZUBER / 1833 / Satin ground. Block-print 5 col. / 48,5 × 50 / 33 × 23,5 / MISE 980 PP 92 / Archives Zuber n° 2888

113 France / 1835–1840 / Satin ground. Block-print 3 col. Gold leaf / 60 × 50 / UCAD HH 903

114 Manufacture Jules RIOTTOT / 1840 env. / Matt ground. Block-print 6 col. / 74 × 52 / 58 × 47 / Verso, inscribed: 'Riottot', stamped: 'J–R' / BF 450

115 Victor POTERLET / Manufacture DAUPTAIN / 1840–1845 / Matt ground. Block-print 7 col. Gold dust. Flocking and over-printing / 70 × 47 / 31,5 × 24,5 / UCAD 29814 / 1967 Paris, n° 92

116 DURAND / Manufacture ZUBER / 1843 / Satin ground. Block-print 4 col. / 90 × 49 / 58,5 × 49 / MISE 980 PP 623 / Archives Zuber n° 3638

117 Manufacture Isidore LEROY / Jumièges Abbey / 1845 / Matt *irisé* ground. Block-print 8 col. / 98 × 50 / Recto, inscribed: 'Jumièges'. / Verso, inscribed: 'Leroy. Abbaye de Jumièges. 1845' / BF 449

Chinoise Muster

109 MULLER und Victor POTERLET / Manufaktur ZUBER / 1840 / Matter Grund. Handdruck, 5 Farben. Firnis / 62 × 49 / 58,5 × 47 / Rückseitig Stempel: »JZ Cie« und handschriftlich: »3370; 3,50–« / UCAD HH 145 / Paris, 1967, Nr. 256 / Archives Zuber Nr. 3370

110 GUICHARD, Victor POTERLET und ZIPELIUS / Manufaktur ZUBER / 1842 / Matter Grund. Handdruck, 5 Farben. Firnis / 61,5 × 50 / 55,5 × 47 / Rückseitig Stempel: »JZ Cie« und handschriftlich: »3514; 2,50–« / UCAD HH 29734 B / Paris, 1967, Nr. 256 / Archives Zuber Nr. 3514

111 GUICHARD und Victor POTERLET / Manufaktur ZUBER / 1842 / Matter Grund. Handdruck, 5 Farben. Firnis / 71 × 48 /54 × 47 / UCAD HH 29734 A

Gotische Muster

112 ZIPELIUS nach HEIDELOFF / Manufaktur ZUBER / 1833 / Satinierter Grund. Handdruck, 5 Farben / 48,5 × 50 / 33 × 23,5 / MISE 980 PP 92 / Archives Zuber Nr. 2888

113 Frankreich / 1835–1840 / Satinierter Grund. Handdruck, 3 Farben. Blattgold / 60 × 50 / UCAD HH 903

114 Manufaktur Jules RIOTTOT / Um 1840 / Matter Grund. Handdruck, 6 Farben / 74 × 52 / 58 × 47 / Rückseitig beschriftet: »Riottot«; Stempel: »J-R« / BF 450

115 Victor POTERLET / Manufaktur DAUPTAIN / 1840–1845 / Matter Grund. Handdruck, 7 Farben. Goldstaub. Veloutiert und repiquiert / 70 × 47 / 31,5 × 24,5 / UCAD 29814 / 1967 Paris, Nr. 92

116 DURAND / Manufaktur ZUBER / 1843 / Satinierter Grund. Handdruck, 4 Farben / 90 × 49 / 58,5 × 49 / MISE 980 PP 623 / Archives Zuber Nr. 3638

117 Manufaktur Isidore LEROY, Abtei Jumièges / 1845 / Matter, irisierter Grund. Handdruck, 8 Farben / 98 × 50 / Vorderseite beschriftet: »Jumièges«. Rückseitig beschriftet: »Leroy. Abbaye de Jumièges. 1845« / BF 449

109

110

111

112

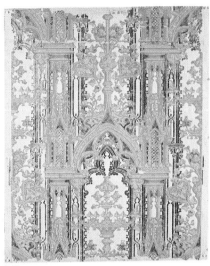

113

114

117

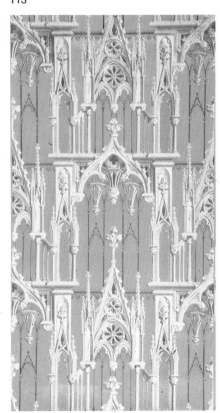

116

115

Rocaille

118 Victor POTERLET / 1840–1845 / Fond satin. Imp. pl. 3 coul. Poudre dorée / 67 × 50 / 63 × 47 / Recto, manuscrit: «V. P.» / UCAD HH 716 / Paris, 1967, n° 334

119 France / 1840–1845 / Fond satin. Imp. pl. 3 coul. Poudre dorée / 62 × 49 / 53 × 47 / UCAD HH 752 A / Paris, 1967, n° 331

120 Victor POTERLET / 1845–1850 / Fond satin. Imp. pl. 14 coul. / 116,5 × 50 / 59 × 47 / UCAD HH 489

121 France / 1845–1850 / Fond satin. Imp. pl. 4 coul. / 61,5 × 51 / 61,5 × 47 / UCAD HH 708

122 Victor PORTERLET / 1845–1850 / Fond satin. Imp. pl. 16 coul. / 81 × 50 / 59 × 47 / UCAD HH 477 B / Paris, 1967, n° 197

123 France / 1845–1850 / Fond satin. Imp. pl. 8 coul. Veloutage et repiquage / 231 × 70 / 117 × 66 / BD 576

124 France / 1850–1855 / Fond mat. Imp. pl. 11 coul. Veloutage et repiquage / 70 × 50 / 59 × 47 / BF 51

125 France / 1850–1855 Fond lissé. Imp. pl. 18 coul. / 56 × 49 / 53 × 47 / BF 204

Volutes

126 France / 1840–1845 / Fond satin. Imp. pl. 4 coul. / 61 × 49 / 53 × 47 / UCAD HH 725 / Paris, 1967, n° 171

127 France / 1840–1845 / Fond satin. Imp. pl. 2 coul. Poudre dorée, veloutage / 59,5 × 53 / UCAD HH 729

128 France / 1840–1845 / Fond lissé. Imp. pl. 2 coul. Poudre dorée, veloutage / 69 × 49 / 58 × 47 / UCAD HH 2000

129 France / 1840–1845 / Fond satin. Imp. pl. 2 coul. / 53,5 × 50,5 / UCAD HH 728

Rocaille

118 Victor POTERLET / 1840–1845 / Satin ground. Block-print 3 col. Gold dust / 67 × 50 / 63 × 47 / Recto, inscribed: 'V. P.'. / UCAD HH 716 / Paris, 1967, n° 334

119 France / 1840–1845 / Satin ground. Block-print 3 col. Gold dust / 62 × 49 / 53 × 47 / UCAD HH 752 A / Paris, 1967, n° 331

120 Victor POTERLET / 1845–1850 / Satin ground. Block-print 14 col. / 116,5 × 50 / 59 × 47 / UCAD HH 489

121 France / 1845–1850 / Satin ground. Block-print 4 col. / 61,5 × 51 / 61,5 × 47 / UCAD HH 708

122 Victor POTERLET / 1845–1850 / Satin ground. Block-print 16 col. / 81 × 50 / 59 × 47 / UCAD HH 477 B / Paris, 1967, n° 197

123 France / 1845–1850 / Satin ground. Block-print 8 col. Flocking and over-printing / 231 × 70 / 117 × 66 / BF 576

124 France / 1850–1855 / Matt ground. Block-print 11 col. Flocking and over-printing / 70 × 50 / 59 × 47 / BF 51

125 France / 1850–1855 / Smooth ground. Block-print 18 col. / 56 × 49 / 53 × 47 / BF 204

Volutes

126 France / 1840–1845 / Satin ground. Block-print 4 col. / 61 × 49 / 53 × 47 / UCAD HH 725 / Paris, 1967, n° 171

127 France / 1840–1845 / Satin ground. Block-print 2 col. Gold dust, flocking / 59,5 × 53 / UCAD HH 729

128 France / 1840–1845 / Smooth ground. Block-print 2 col. Gold dust, flocking / 69 × 49 / 58 × 47 / UCAD HH 2000

129 France / 1840–1845 / Satin ground. Block-print 2 col. / 53,5 × 50,5 / UCAD HH 728

Rocaille-Muster

118 Victor POTERLET / 1840–1845 / Satinierter Grund. Handdruck, 3 Farben. Goldstaub / 67 × 50 / 63 × 47 / Rückseitig beschriftet: »V.P.« / UCAD HH 716 / Paris, 1967, Nr. 334

119 Frankreich / 1840–1845 / Satinierter Grund. Handdruck, 3 Farben. Goldstaub / 62 × 49 / 53 × 47 / UCAD HH 752 A / Paris, 1967, Nr. 331

120 Victor POTERLET / 1845–1850 / Satinierter Grund. Handdruck, 14 Farben / 116,5 × 50 / 59 × 47 / UCAD HH 489

121 Frankreich / 1845–1850 / Satinierter Grund. Handdruck, 4 Farben / 61,5 × 51 / 61,5 × 47 / UCAD HH 708

122 Victor POTERLET / 1845–1850 / Satinierter Grund. Handdruck, 16 Farben / 81 × 50 / 59 × 47 / UCAD HH 477 B / Paris, 1967, Nr. 197

123 Frankreich / 1845–1850 / Satinierter Grund. Handdruck, 8 Farben. Veloutiert und repiquiert / 231 × 70 / 117 × 66 / BF 576

124 Frankreich / 1850–1855 / Matter Grund. Handdruck, 11 Farben. Veloutiert und repiquiert / 70 × 50 / 59 × 47 / BF 51

125 Frankreich / 1850–1855 / Geglätteter Grund. Handdruck, 18 Farben / 56 × 49 / 53 × 47 / BF 204

Voluten

126 Frankreich / 1840–1845 / Satinierter Grund. Handdruck, 4 Farben / 61 × 49 / 53 × 47 / UCAD HH 725 / Paris, 1967, Nr. 171

127 Frankreich / 1840–1845 / Satinierter Grund. Handdruck, 2 Farben. Goldstaub. Veloutiert / 59,5 × 53 / UCAD HH 729

128 Frankreich / 1840–1845 / Geglätteter Grund. Handdruck, 2 Farben. Goldstaub. Veloutiert / 69 × 49 / 58 × 47 / UCAD HH 2000

129 Frankreich / 1840–1845 / Satinierter Grund. Handdruck, 2 Farben / 53,5 × 50,5 / UCAD HH 728

118

119

120

121

122

123

124

125

126

127

128

129

130 France / 1840–1845 / Fond satin. Imp. pl. 3 coul. / 72,5 × 49,5 / 50 × 46,5 / UCAD HH 906/ Paris, 1967, n° 313

131 Victor POTERLET / Manufacture LA-PEYRE / 1841/ Fond satin. Imp. pl. 2 coul. / 68 × 52 / 31,5 × 23 / Recto, manuscrit: «S. Lapeyre V. P. 1841» / UCAD HH 703

132 Victor POTERLET / Manufacture SEVES-TRE / 1844 / Fond satin. Imp. pl. 3 coul. Feuille d'or, veloutage / 73 × 52 / 47 × 47 / UCAD HH 904 B / Paris, 1967, n° 212

133 Victor POTERLET / Manufacture DUMAS / 1845 / Fond satin. Imp. pl. 2 coul. Poudre dorée, veloutage. Gauffrage en pointe de diamant / Verso, manuscrit: «Poterlet, Dumas 1845» / UCAD HH 172 / Paris, 1967, n° 138

134 Victor POTERLET / Manufacture DUMAS / 1845 / Fond satin. Imp. pl. 2 coul. Poudre dorée, veloutage. Verso, manuscrit: «Poterlet, Dumas 1845» / UCAD HH 190 / Paris, 1967, n° 139

135 Victor POTERLET / 1845–1850 / Fond satin. Imp. pl. 3 coul. / 70 × 47 / 62 × 46,5 / Recto, manuscrit: «V. P.» / UCAD HH 2004

136 Victor POTERLET / 1845–1850 / Fond mat. Imp. pl. 3 coul. Veloutage / 61 × 49 / UCAD HH 720 / Paris, 1967, n° 192

137 Victor POTERLET / 1845–1850 / Fond lissé. Imp. pl. 2 coul. / 75 × 51 / 62 × 47 / Verso, manuscrit: «grand damas Poterlet» / BF 405

138 France / 1845–1850 / Fond satin. Imp. pl. 2 coul. Poudre dorée, veloutage / 110 × 55,5 / UCAD HH 482 / Paris, 1967, n° 191

139 Victor POTERLET / Manufacture DAUP-TAIN / 1850 / Fond lissé. Imp. pl. 2 coul. Poudre dorée, veloutage / 66 × 57 / Verso, manuscrit: «Poterlet Dauptain 1850» / UCAD HH 169 / Paris, 1967, n° 92

140 Victor POTERLET / Manufacture DAUP-TAIN / 1850 / Fond mat. Imp. pl. 2 coul. Poudre dorée, veloutage / 68 × 48 / 48 × 47 / Verso, manuscrit: «Poterlet 1850 Dauptain» / UCAD HH 167 / Paris, 1967, n° 92

141 Victor POTERLET / Manufacture DELI-COURT / 1850 / Fond satin. Imp. pl. 2 coul. Veloutage / 68 × 52 / 58 × 46,5 / UCAD HH 183 / Paris, 1967, n° 95

142 France / 1850 / Fond satin. Imp. pl. 2 coul. Poudre dorée, veloutage / 107 × 64 / 98 × 64 / UCAD HH 483

130 France / 1840–1845 / Satin ground. Block-print 3 col. / 72,5 × 49,5 / 50 × 46,5 / UCAD HH 906 / Paris, 1967, n° 313

131 Victor POTERLET / Manufacture LA-PEYRE / 1841 / Satin ground. Block-print 2 col. / 68 × 52 / 31,5 × 23 / Recto, inscribed: 'S. Lapeyre V. P. 1841' / UCAD HH 703

132 Victor POTERLET / Manufacture SEVES-TRE / 1844 / Satin ground. Block-print 3 col. Gold-leaf, flocking / 73 × 52 / 47 × 47 / UCAD HH 904 B / Paris, 1967, n° 212

133 Victor POTERLET / Manufacture DUMAS / 1845 / Satin ground. Block-print 2 col. Gold dust, flocking, light embossing in diamond point / Verso, inscribed: 'Poterlet, Dumas 1845' / UCAD HH 172 / Paris, 1967 n° 138

134 Victor POTERLET / Manufacture DUMAS / 1845 / Satin ground. Block-print 2 col. Gold dust, flocking / Verso, inscribed: 'Poterlet Dumas 1845'. / UCAD HH 190 / Paris, 1967, n° 139

135 Victor POTERLET / 1845–1850 / Satin ground. Block-print 3 col. / 70 × 47 / 62 × 46,5 / Recto, inscribed: 'V. P.' / UCAD HH 2004

136 Victor POTERLET / 1845–1850 / Matt ground. Block-print 3 col. Flocking / 61 × 49 / UCAD HH 720 / Paris, 1967, n° 192

137 Victor POTERLET / 1845–1850 / Smooth ground. Block-print 2 col. / 75 × 51 / 62 × 47 / Verso, inscribed: 'grand damas Poterlet' / BF 405

138 France / 1845–1850 / Satin ground. Block-print 2 col. Gold dust, flocking / 110 × 55,5 / UCAD HH 482 / Paris, 1967, n° 191

139 Victor POTERLET / Manufacture DAUP-TAIN / 1850 / Glossy ground. Block-print 2 col. Gold dust, flocking / 66 × 57 / Verso, inscribed: 'Poterlet Dauptain 1850'. / UCAD HH 169 / Paris, 1967, n° 92

140 Victor POTERLET / Manufacture DAUP-TAIN / 1850 / Matt ground. Block-print 2 col. Gold dust, flocking / 68 × 48 / 48 × 47 / Verso inscribed: 'Poterlet 1850 Dauptain' / UCAD HH 167 / Paris, 1967, n° 92

141 Victor POTERLET / Manufacture DELI-COURT / 1850 / Satin ground. Block-print 2 col. Flocking / 68 × 52 / 58 × 46,5 / UCAD HH 183 / Paris, 1967, n° 95

142 France / 1850 / Satin ground. Block-print 2 col. Gold dust, flocking / 107 × 64 / 98 × 64 / UCAD HH 483

130 Frankreich / 1840–1845 / Satinierter Grund. Handdruck, 3 Farben / 72,5 × 49,5 / 50 × 46,5 / UCAD HH 906 / Paris, 1967, Nr. 313

131 Victor POTERLET / Manufaktur LAPEY-RE / 1841 / Satinierter Grund, Handdruck, 2 Farben / 68 × 52 / 31,5 × 23 / Vorderseite beschriftet: »S. Lapeyre V.P. 1841« / UCAD HH 703

132 Victor POTERLET / Manufaktur SEVES-TRE / 1844 / Satinierter Grund. Handdruck, 3 Farben. Blattgold. Veloutiert / 73 × 52 / 47 × 47 / UCAD HH 904 B / Paris, 1967, Nr. 212

133 Victor POTERLET / Manufaktur DUMAS / 1845 / Satinierter Grund. Handdruck, 2 Farben. Goldstaub. Veloutiert. »Pointe de diamant«-Gaufrierung / Rückseitig beschriftet: »Poterlet, Dumas 1845« / UCAD HH 172 / Paris, 1967, Nr. 138

134 Victor POTERLET / Manufaktur DUMAS / 1845 / Satinierter Grund. Handdruck, 2 Farben. Goldstaub. Veloutiert / Rückseitig beschriftet: »Poterlet Dumas 1845« / UCAD HH 190 / Paris, 1967, Nr. 139

135 Victor POTERLET / 1845–1850 / Satinierter Grund. Handdruck, 3 Farben / 70 × 47 / 62 × 46,5 / Vorderseite beschriftet: »V.P.« / UCAD HH 2004

136 Victor POTERLET / 1845–1850 / Matter Grund. Handdruck, 3 Farben. Veloutiert / 61 × 49 / UCAD HH 720 / Paris, 1967, Nr. 192

137 Victor POTERLET / 1845–1850 / Geglätteter Grund. Handdruck, 2 Farben / 75 × 51 / 62 × 47 / Rückseitig beschriftet: »grand damas Poterlet« / BF 405

138 Frankreich / 1845–1850 / Satinierter Grund. Handdruck, 2 Farben. Goldstaub. Veloutiert / 110 × 55,5 / UCAD HH 482 / Paris, 1967, Nr. 191

139 Victor POTERLET / Manufaktur DAUP-TAIN / 1850 / Geglätteter Grund. Handdruck, 2 Farben. Goldstaub. Veloutiert / 66 × 57 / Rückseitig beschriftet: »Poterlet Dauptain 1850« / UCAD HH 169 / Paris, 1967, Nr. 92

140 Victor POTERLET / Manufaktur DAUP-TAIN / 1850 / Matter Grund. Handdruck, 2 Farben. Goldstaub. Veloutiert / 68 × 48 / 48 × 47 / Rückseitig beschriftet: »Poterlet 1850 Dauptain« / UCAD HH 167 / Paris, 1967, Nr. 92

141 Victor POTERLET / Manufaktur DELI-COURT / 1850 / Satinierter Grund. Handdruck, 2 Farben. Veloutiert / 68 × 52 / 58 × 46,5 / UCAD HH 183 / Paris, 1967, Nr. 95

142 Frankreich / 1850 / Satinierter Grund. Handdruck, 2 Farben. Goldstaub. Veloutiert / 107 × 64 / 98 × 64 / UCAD HH 483

130

134

136

132

131

133

137

135

139

138

140

141

142

Imbrications

143 Victor POTERLET / Manufacture DAUP-TAIN / 1832 / Fond satin. Imp. pl. 2 coul. / 72,5 × 50,5 / 29,5 × 23,5 / Recto, manuscrit: «1832, V. P. Dauptain» / UCAD HH 911 / Paris, 1967, n° 314

144 Victor POTERLET / Manufacture SEVES-TRE / 1834 / Fond satin. Imp. pl. 2 coul. Gauffrage en pointe de diamants / 70 × 48 / Recto, manuscrit: «Fabrication de Sevestre, 1834 V. P.» / UCAD HH 1949

145 Manufacture DAUPTAIN / 1835–1840 / Fond satin. Imp. pl. 3 coul. / 52 × 49,5 / 47 × 47 / UCAD HH 907 B / Paris, 1967, n° 94

146 France / 1835–1840 / Fond satin. Imp. pl. 3 coul. / 61,5 × 51 / UCAD HH 713 / Paris, 1967, n° 325

147 France / 1835–1840 / Fond mat. Imp. pl. 2 coul. Poudre dorée / 56 × 50 / 47 × 47 / UCAD HH 742 / Paris, 1967, n° 343

148 France / 1835–1840 / Fond satin. Imp. pl. 2 coul. / 60 × 48 / 47 × 47 / UCAD HH 1987

149 France/ 1835–1840 / Fond lissé. Imp. pl. 2 coul. Feuille d'or et veloutage / 59 × 54 / 53,5 × 52,5 / UCAD HH 801

150 France / 1835–1840 / Fond satin. Imp. pl. 2 coul. / 31 × 49 / 23,5 × 23,5 / UCAD HH 2361

151 France / 1840–1845 / Fond satin. Imp. pl. 16 coul. / 61 × 50 / 55 × 47 /UCAD HH 777

152 France / 1840–1845 / Fond satin. Imp. pl. 2 coul. Poudre dorée / 34 × 50 / UCAD HH 1986

Overlapping Work

143 Victor POTERLET / Manufacture DAUP-TAIN / 1832 / Satin ground. Block-print 2 col. / 72,5 × 50,5 / 29,5 × 23,5 / Recto, inscribed: '1832. V. P. Dauptain' / UCAD HH 911 / Paris, 1967, n° 314

144 Victor POTERLET / Manufacture SEVES-TRE / 1834 / Satin ground. Block-print 2 col. Light embossing in diamond point / 70 × 48 / Recto, inscribed: 'Fabrication de Sevestre, 1834, V. P.' / UCAD HH 1949

145 Manufacture DAUPTAIN / 1835–1840 / Satin ground. Block-print 3 col. / 52 × 49,5 / 47 × 47 / UCAD HH 907 B / Paris, 1967, n° 94

146 France / 1835–1840 / Satin ground. Block-print 3 col. / 61,5 × 51 / UCAD HH 713 / Paris, 1967, n° 325

147 France / 1835–1840 / Matt ground. Block-print 2 col. Gold dust / 56 × 50 / 47 × 47 / UCAD HH 742 / Paris, 1967, n° 343

148 France / 1835–1840 / Satin ground. Block-print 2 col. / 60 × 48 / 47 × 47 / UCAD HH 1987

149 France / 1835–1840 / Smooth ground. Block-print 2 col. Gold leaf and flocking / 59 × 54 / 53,5 × 52,5 / UCAD HH 801

150 France / 1835–1840 / Satin ground. Block-print 2 col. / 31 × 49 / 23,5 × 23,5 / UCAD HH 2361

151 France / 1840–1845 / Satin ground. Block-print 16 col. / 61 × 50 / 55 × 47 / UCAD HH 777

152 France / 1840–1845 / Satin ground. Block-print 2 col. Gold dust / 34 × 50 / UCAD HH 1986

Ineinandergreifende und verzahnte Muster

143 Victor POTERLET / Manufaktur DAUP-TAIN / 1832 / Satinierter Grund. Handdruck, 2 Farben / 72,5 × 50,5 / 29,5 × 23,5 / Vorderseite beschriftet: »1832. V.P. Dauptain« / UCAD HH 911 / Paris, 1967, Nr. 314

144 Victor POTERLET / Manufaktur SEVES-TRE / 1834 / Satinierter Grund. Handdruck, 2 Farben. »Pointe de diamant«-Gaufrierung / 70 × 48 / Vorderseite beschriftet: »Fabrication de Sevestre, 1834 V.P.« / UCAD HH 1949

145 Manufaktur DAUPTAIN / 1835–1840 / Satinierter Grund. Handdruck, 3 Farben / 52 × 49,5 / 47 × 47 / UCAD HH 907 B / Paris, 1967, Nr. 94

146 Frankreich / 1835–1840 / Satinierter Grund. Handdruck, 3 Farben / 61,5 × 51 / UCAD HH 713 / Paris, 1967, Nr. 325

147 Frankreich / 1835–1840 / Matter Grund. Handdruck, 2 Farben. Goldstaub / 56 × 50 / 47 × 47 / UCAD HH 742 / Paris, 1967, Nr. 343

148 Frankreich / 1835–1840 / Satinierter Grund. Handdruck, 2 Farben / 60 × 48 / 47 × 47 / UCAD HH 1987

149 Frankreich / 1835–1840 / Geglätteter Grund. Handdruck, 2 Farben. Blattgold. Veloutiert / 59 × 54 / 53,5 × 52,5 / UCAD HH 801

150 Frankreich / 1835–1840 / Satinierter Grund. Handdruck, 2 Farben / 31 × 49 / 23,5 × 23,5 / UCAD HH 2361

151 Frankreich / 1840–1845 / Satinierter Grund. Handdruck, 16 Farben / 61 × 50 / 55 × 47 / UCAD HH 777

152 Frankreich / 1840–1845 / Satinierter Grund. Handdruck, 2 Farben. Goldstaub / 34 × 50 / UCAD HH 1986

143

144

145

146

151

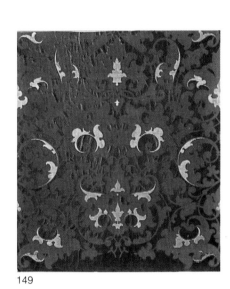

149

147

150

152

148

153 ZIPELIUS / Manufacture ZUBER / 1841 / Fond lissé. Imp. pl. 4 coul. / 112 × 53 / 102 × 52 / MISE 980 PP 650 / Archives Zuber n° 3498

154 ZIPELIUS / Manufacture ZUBER / 1843 / Fond lissé. Imp. pl. 3 coul. / 99 × 49 / 59 × 47 / MISE 980 PP 338 /Archives Zuber n° 3610

155 Manufacture ZUBER / 1843 / Fond peigné? Imp. pl. 2 coul. / 76 × 50 / 47 × 15,5 / MISE 980 PP 626 / Archives Zuber n° 3646

156 Manufacture ZUBER / 1843 / Fond satin. Imp. pl. 5 coul. / 88 × 50 / 50,5 × 23,5 / MISE 980 PP 633 / Archives Zuber n° 3660

157 Victor POTERLET / Manufacture SEVES-TRE / 1843 / Fond satin. Imp. pl. 1 coul. / 72,5 × 48 / 57,5 × 47 / Recto, manuscrit: «V. P. Victor Poterlet 1843. Sevestre» / UCAD HH 910 / Paris, 1967, n° 141

158 France / 1845 env. / Fond satin. Imp. pl. 2 coul. Feuille d'or, veloutage / 72 × 53,5 / 58 × 47 / UCAD HH 912

159 France/ 1845–1850 / Fond satin. Imp. pl. 2 coul. / 60,5 × 52,5 / 59,5 × 47 / UCAD HH 714

160 France / 1845–1850 / Fond mat. Imp. 3 coul. Feuille d'or, veloutage / 47 × 50 / 41,5 × 47 / UCAD HH 743 / Paris, 1967, n° 345

161 France / 1845–1850 / Fond satin. Imp. pl. 3 coul. Feuille d'or, veloutage / 61 × 50 / 47,5 × 47 / UCAD HH 749 A / Paris, 1967, n° 340

162 France / 1845–1850 / Fond satin. Imp. pl. 13 coul. / 60,5 × 52 / 53,5 × 47 / UCAD HH 772

163 France / 1845–1850 / Fond lissé. Imp. pl. 4 coul. / 68,5 × 50 / 54 × 47 / UCAD HH 874

164 Victor POTERLET / 1850–1855 / Fond lissé. Imp. pl. 26 coul. / 131 × 50 / Verso, manuscrit: «Poterlet» / BF 437

153 ZIPELIUS / Manufacture ZUBER / 1841 / Smooth ground. Block-print 4 col. / 112 × 53 / 102 × 52 / MISE 980 PP 650 / Archives Zuber n° 3498

154 ZIPELIUS / Manufacture ZUBER / 1843 / Smooth ground. Block-print 3 col. / 99 × 49 / 59 × 47 / MISE 980 PP 338 / Archives Zuber n° 3610

155 Manufacture ZUBER / 1843 / Combed ground? Block-print 2 col. / 76 × 50 / 47 × 15,5 / MISE 980 PP 626 / Archives Zuber n° 3646

156 Manufacture ZUBER / 1843 / Satin ground. Block-print 5 col. / 88 × 50 / 50,5 × 23,5 / MISE 980 PP 633 / Archives Zuber n° 3660

157 Victor POTERLET / Manufacture SEVES-TRE / 1843 / Satin ground. Block-print 1 col. / 72,5 × 48 / 57,5 × 47 /Recto, inscribed: 'V. P. Victor Poterlet 1843, Sevestre' / UCAD HH 910 / Paris, 1967, n° 141

158 France / 1845 env. / Satin ground. Block-print 2 col. Gold leaf, flocking / 72 × 53,5 / 58 × 47 / UCAD HH 912

159 France / 1845–1850 / Satin ground. Block-print 2 col. / 60,5 × 52,5 / 59,5 × 47 / UCAD HH 714

160 France / 1845–1850 / Matt ground. Block-print 3 col. Gold leaf, flocking / 47 × 50 / 41,5 × 47 / UCAD HH 743 / Paris, 1967, n° 345

161 France / 1845–1850 / Satin ground. Block-print 3 col. Gold leaf, flocking / 61 × 50 / 47,5 × 47 / UCAD HH 749 A / Paris, 1967, n° 340

162 France / 1845–1850 / Satin ground. Block-print 13 col. / 60,5 × 52 / 53,5 × 47 / UCAD HH 772

163 France / 1845–1850 / Smooth ground. Block-print 4 col. / 68,5 × 50 / 54 × 47 / UCAD HH 874

164 Victor POTERLET / 1850–1855 / Smooth ground. Block-print 26 col. / 131 × 50 / Verso, inscribed: 'Poterlet' / BF 437

153 ZIPELIUS / Manufaktur ZUBER / 1841 / Geglätteter Grund. Handdruck, 4 Farben / 112 × 53 / 102 × 52 / MISE 980 PP 650 / Archives Zuber Nr. 3498

154 ZIPELIUS / Manufaktur ZUBER / 1843 / Geglätteter Grund. Handdruck, 3 Farben / 99 × 49 / 59 × 47 / MISE 980 PP 338 / Archives Zuber Nr. 3610

155 Manufaktur ZUBER / 1843 / Gekämmter Grund. Handdruck, 2 Farben / 76 × 50 / 47 × 15,5 / MISE 980 PP 626 / Archives Zuber Nr. 3646

156 Manufaktur ZUBER / 1843 / Satinierter Grund. Handdruck, 5 Farben / 88 × 50 / 50,5 × 23,5 / MISE 980 PP 633 / Archives Zuber Nr. 3660

157 Victor POTERLET / Manufaktur SEVES-TRE / 1843 / Satinierter Grund. Handdruck, 1 Farbe / 72,5 × 48 / 57,5 × 47 / Vorderseite beschriftet: »V.P. Victor Poterlet 1843. Sevestre« / UCAD HH 910 / Paris, 1967, Nr. 141

158 Frankreich / Um 1845 / Satinierter Grund. Handdruck, 2 Farben. Blattgold. Veloutiert / 72 × 53,5 / 58 × 47 / UCAD HH 912

159 Frankreich / 1845–1850 / Satinierter Grund. Handdruck, 2 Farben / 60,5 × 52,5 / 59,5 × 47 / UCAD HH 714

160 Frankreich / 1845–1850 / Matter Grund. Handdruck, 3 Farben. Blattgold. Veloutiert / 47 × 50 / 41,5 × 47 / UCAD HH 743 / Paris, 1967, Nr. 345

161 Frankreich / 1845–1850 / Satinierter Grund. Handdruck, 3 Farben. Blattgold. Veloutiert / 61 × 50 / 47,5 × 47 / UCAD HH 749 A / Paris, 1967, Nr. 340

162 Frankreich / 1845–1850 / Satinierter Grund. Handdruck, 13 Farben / 60,5 × 52 / 53,5 × 47 / UCAD HH 772

163 Frankreich / 1845–1850 / Geglätteter Grund. Handdruck, 4 Farben / 68,5 × 50 / 54 × 47 / UCAD HH 874

164 Victor POTERLET / 1850–1855 / Geglätteter Grund. Handdruck, 26 Farben / 131 × 50 / Rückseitig beschriftet: »Poterlet« / BF 437

155

156

157

158

153

154

160

164

159

161

162

163

Géométriques

165 EBERT et BUFFARD / Manufacture JAC-QUEMART et BENARD / 1800–1805 / Fond mat Imp. pl. 1 coul. / 28,5 × 18 / 5 × 5 / Recto, manuscrit: «N° 9. 1.ᶠ64. Mrs Ebert et Buffard» / UCAD HH 2208

166 EBERT et BUFFARD / Manufacture JAC-QUEMART et BENARD / 1800–1805 / Fond mat. Imp. pl. 2 coul. / 27 × 18 / 8,5 × 6 / Recto, manuscrit: «Mrs Ebert et Buffard N° 19» / UCAD HH 2218

167 Manufacture ZUBER / 1812 / Fond mat. Imp. pl. 4 coul. / 22,5 × 16 / 2,2 × 2,2 / MISE 980 PP 25 / Archives Zuber n° 1224

168 Manufacture ZUBER / 1824 / Fond mat irisé. Imp. pl. 2 coul. Irisés / 33,5 × 49 / MISE 824 PP 2182 / Archives ZUBER n° 2182

169 MERII / 1825 / Fond satin. Dessin original 5 coul. / 53,5 × 52 / 12 × 23,5 / Verso, manuscrit: «Le 22 8ᵇʳ 1825 . . . tu Mérii rue de la Muette n° 15» / UCAD HH 921 / Paris, 1967, n° 356

170 MERII / 1827 / Fond mat. Dessin original 4 coul. / 56 × 55,5 / 23,5 × 47 / Verso, manuscrit: «Le 29 août 1827. AV. Mérii rue de la Muette n° 15» / UCAD HH 923 / Paris, 1967, n° 358

171 HAITY/ Manufacture ZUBER / 1827 / Fond satin irisé. Imp. pl. 1 coul. Irisés / 23 × 49 / MISE 827 2410 PP / Archives Zuber n° 2410

172 EBERT et BUFFARD / Manufacture JAC-QUEMART et BENARD / 1827 / Fond mat. Imp. pl. 2 coul. / 25 × 16 / 5,5 × 6 / Recto, manuscrit: «Mrs Ebert et Buffard. Collection 1827–1828 N° 78 A» / UCAD HH 2276

173 EBERT et BUFFARD / Manufacture JAC-QUEMART et BENARD / 1828 / Fond mat. Imp. pl. 3 coul. / 21 × 16,5 / 2 × 3 / Recto, manuscrit: «N° 83 Mrs Ebert et Buffard» / UCAD HH 2281

174 EBERT et BUFFARD / Manufacture JAC-QUEMART et BENARD / 1828 / Fond mat. Imp. pl. 3 coul. / 24 × 18 / 6,5 × 12 / Recto, manuscrit: «N° 93 A Mrs Ebert et Buffard» / UCAD HH 2291

175 Manufacture JACQUEMART et BENARD / 1828 / Fond mat. Imp. pl. 4 coul. / 16 × 25,5 / 8 × 7,5 / Recto, manuscrit: «N° 98 (Brûlé) » / UCAD HH 2296

176 Manufacture ZUBER / 1828 / Fond satin irisé. Imp. pl. 2 coul. Irisés / 26 × 49 / MISE 828 2250 PP / Archives Zuber n° 2250

Geometric Designs

165 EBERT et BUFFARD / Manufacture JACQUEMART et BENARD / 1800–1805 / Matt ground. Block-print 1 col. / 28,5 × 18 / 5 × 5 / Recto, inscribed: 'N° 9. 1, ᶠ64. Mrs Ebert et Buffard' / UCAD HH 2208

166 EBERT et BUFFARD / Manufacture JACQUEMART et BENARD / 1800–1805 / Matt ground. Block-print 2 col. / 27 × 18 / 8,5 × 6 / Recto, inscribed: 'Mrs Ebert et Buffard N° 19' / UCAD HH 2218

167 Manufacture ZUBER / 1812 / Matt ground. Block-print 4 col. / 22,5 × 16 / 2,2 × 2,2 / MISE 980 PP 25 / Archives Zuber n° 1224

168 Manufacture ZUBER / 1824 / Matt *irisé* ground. Block-print 2 col. *Irisé* / 33,5 × 49 / MISE 824 PP 2182 / Archives ZUBER n° 2182

169 MERII / 1825 / Satin ground. Original design 5 col. / 53,5 × 52 / 12 × 23,5 / Verso, inscribed: 'Le 22 8ᵇʳᵉ 1825 . . . tu Mérii rue de la Muette n° 15' / UCAD HH 921 / Paris, 1967, n° 356

170 MERII / 1827 / Matt ground. Original design 4 col. / 56 × 55,5 / 23,5 × 47 / Verso, inscribed: 'Le 29 août 1827. AV. Mérii rue de la Muette n° 15' / UCAD HH 923 / Paris, 1967, n° 358

171 HAITY / Manufacture ZUBER / 1827 / Satin *irisé* ground. Block-print 1 col. *Irisé* / 23 × 49 / MISE 827 2410 PP / Archives Zuber n° 2410

172 EBERT et BUFFARD / Manufacture JACQUEMART et BENARD / 1827 / Matt ground. Block-print 2 col. / 25 × 16 / 5,5 × 6 / Recto, inscribed: 'Mrs Ebert et Buffard. Collection 1827–1828 N° 78 A' / UCAD HH 2276

173 EBERT et BUFFARD / Manufacture JACQUEMART et BENARD / 1828 / Matt ground. Block-print 3 col. / 21 × 16,5 / 2 × 3 / Recto, inscribed: 'N° 83 Mrs Ebert et Buffard' / UCAD HH 2281

174 EBERT et BUFFARD / Manufacture JACQUEMART et BENARD / 1828 / Matt ground. Block-print 3 col. / 24 × 18 / 6,5 × 12 / Recto, inscribed: 'N° 93 A Mrs Ebert et Buffard' / UCAD HH 2291

175 Manufacture JACQUEMART et BENARD / 1828 / Matt ground. Block-print 4 col. / 16 × 25,5 / 8 × 7,5 / Recto, inscribed: 'N° 98 (Brûlé)' / UCAD HH 2296

176 Manufacture ZUBER / 1828 / Satin *irisé* ground. Block-print 2 col. *Irisé* / 26 × 49 / MISE 828 2250 PP / Archives Zuber n° 2250

Geometrische Muster

165 EBERT und BUFFARD / Manufaktur JAC-QUEMART et BENARD / 1800–1805 / Matter Grund. Handdruck, 1 Farbe / 28,5 × 18 / 5 × 5 / Vorderseite beschriftet: »N° 9. 1. ᶠ 64. Mrs Ebert et Buffard« / UCAD HH 2208

166 EBERT und BUFFARD / Manufaktur JAC-QUEMART et BENARD / 1800–1805 / Matter Grund. Handdruck, 2 Farben / 27 × 18 / 8,5 × 6 / Vorderseite beschriftet: »Mrs Ebert et Buffard N° 19« / UCAD HH 2218

167 Manufaktur ZUBER / 1812 / Matter Grund. Handdruck, 4 Farben / 22,5 × 16 / 2,2 × 2,2 / MISE 980 PP 25 / Archives Zuber Nr. 1224

168 Manufaktur ZUBER / 1824 / Matter, irisierter Grund. Handdruck, 2 Farben. Irisiert / 33,5 × 49 / MISE 824 PP 2182 / Archives Zuber Nr. 2182

169 MERII / 1825 / Satinierter Grund. Originalentwurf, 5 Farben / 53,5 × 52 / 12 × 23,5 / Rückseitig beschriftet: »Le 22 8ᵇʳᵉ 1825 . . . tu Mérii rue de la Muette n° 15« / UCAD HH 921 / Paris, 1967, Nr. 356

170 MERII / 1827 / Matter Grund. Originalentwurf, 4 Farben / 56 × 55,5 / 23,5 × 47 / Rückseitig beschriftet: »Le 29 août 1827. AV. Mérii rue de la Muette n° 15« / UCAD HH 923 / Paris, 1967, Nr. 358

171 HAITY / Manufaktur ZUBER / 1827 / Satinierter, irisierter Grund. Handdruck, 1 Farbe. Irisiert / 23 × 49 / MISE 827 2410 PP / Archives Zuber Nr. 2410

172 EBERT und BUFFARD / Manufaktur JAC-QUEMART et BENARD / 1827 / Matter Grund. Handdruck, 2 Farben / 25 × 16 / 5,5 × 6 / Vorderseite beschriftet: »Mrs Ebert et Buffard. Collection 1827–1828 N° 78 A« / UCAD HH 2276

173 EBERT und BUFFARD / Manufaktur JAC-QUEMART et BENARD / 1828 / Matter Grund. Handdruck, 3 Farben / 21 × 16,5 / 2 × 3 / Vorderseite beschriftet: »N° 83 Mrs Ebert et Buffard« / UCAD HH 2281

174 EBERT und BUFFARD / Manufaktur JAC-QUEMART et BENARD / 1828 / Matter Grund. Handdruck, 3 Farben / 24 × 18 / 6,5 × 12 / Vorderseite beschriftet: »N° 93 Mrs Ebert et Buffard« / UCAD HH 2291

175 Manufaktur JACQUEMART et BENARD / 1828 / Matter Grund. Handdruck, 4 Farben / 16 × 25,5 / 8 × 7,5 / Vorderseite beschriftet: »N° 98 (Brûlé)« / UCAD HH 2296

176 Manufaktur ZUBER / 1828 / Satinierter, irisierter Grund. Handdruck, 2 Farben. Irisiert / 26 × 49 / MISE 828 2250 PP / Archives Zuber Nr. 2250

165

166

167

169

173

170

168

172

171

175

174

176

177 Manufacture ZUBER / 1828 / Fond satin irisé. Imp. pl. 2 coul. Irisés / 37 × 49 / 23,5 × 23,5 / Mise 828 2253 PP / Archives Zuber n° 2253

178 Manufacture ZUBER / 1828 / Fond satin irisé. Imp. pl. 2 coul. Irisés / 39 × 49 / MISE 828 2261 PP / Archives Zuber n° 2261

179 Manufacture ZUBER / 1828 / Fond satin irisé. Imp. pl. 2 coul. Irisés / 31 × 46 / 23,5 × 1,5 / MISE 828 PP 2572 / Archives Zuber n° 2572

180 Fritz ZUBER / Manufacture Zuber / 1829 / Fond satin. Imp. pl. 3 coul. / 55 × 49 / 23,5 × 23,5 / MISE 829 PP 2534 A / Archives Zuber n° 2534

181 CHEVALIER / Manufacture JACQUEMART et BENARD / 1828–1830 / Fond mat. Imp. pl. 3 coul. / 27,5 × 16,5 / 12 × 12 / Recto, manuscrit: «N° 113. Mr. Chevalier. f^d et couleur ord^{re} 1.40» / UCAD HH 2311

182 France / 1840–1850 / Fond poudre d'or. Imp. pl. 1 coul. Veloutage / 53 × 51 / 27 × 23,5 / UCAD HH 2088

Cannages

183 Manufacture ZUBER / 1824 / Fond satin. Imp. pl. 2 coul. / 23,5 × 50 / 2 × 4 / MISE 824 2170 PP Archives Zuber n° 2170

184 Manufacture ZUBER / 1824 / Fond mat. Imp. pl. 2 coul. / 22,5 × 49 / 2 × 2 / MISE 824 2189 PP / Archives Zuber n° 2189

Caissons

185 France / 1815–1820 / Fond mat. Imp. pl. 3 coul. / 65 × 49 / 12 × 12 / UCAD HH 2712

186 Manufacture ZUBER / 1827 / Fond mat. Imp. pl. 2 coul. / 45 × 50 / 14 × 12 / MISE 827 2383 PP / Archives Zuber n° 2383

Marbre

187 Manufacture ZUBER / 1824 / Fond satin irisé. Imp. pl. 2 coul. / 36 × 50 / MISE 824 2200 PP / Archives Zuber N° 2200

---

177 Manufacture ZUBER / 1828 / Satin *irisé* ground. Block-print 2 col. *Irisé* / 37 × 49 / 23,5 × 23,5 / MISE 828 2253 PP / Archives Zuber n° 2253

178 Manufacture ZUBER / 1828 / Satin *irisé* ground. Block-print 2 col. *Irisé* / 39 × 49 / MISE 828 2261 PP / Archives Zuber n° 2261

179 Manufacture ZUBER / 1828 / Satin *irisé* ground. Block-print 2 col. *Irisé* / 31 × 46 / 23,5 × 1,5 / MISE 828 PP 2572 / Archives Zuber n° 2572

180 Fritz ZUBER / Manufacture Zuber / 1829 / Satin ground. Block-print 3 col. / 55 × 49 / 23,5 × 23,5 / MISE 829 PP 2534 A / Archives Zuber n° 2534

181 CHEVALIER / Manufacture JACQUEMART et BENARD / 1828–1830 / Matt ground. Block-print 3 col. / 27,5 × 16,5 / 12 × 12 / Recto, inscribed: 'N° 113. Mr. Chevalier. f^d et couleur ord^{re} 1.40' / UCAD HH 2311

182 France / 1840–1850 / Gold dust base. Block-print 1 col. Flocking / 53 × 51 / 27 × 23,5 / UCAD HH 2088

Cane-work

183 Manufacture ZUBER / 1824 / Satin ground. Block-print 2 col. / 23,5 × 50 / 2 × 4 / MISE 824 2170 PP / Archives Zuber n° 2170

184 Manufacture ZUBER / 1824 / Matt ground. Block-print 2 col. / 22,5 × 49 / 2 × 2 / MISE 824 2189 PP / Archives Zuber n° 2189

Coffering

185 France / 1815–1820 / Matt ground. Block-print 3 col. / 65 × 49 / 12 × 12 / UCAD HH 2712

186 Manufacture ZUBER / 1827 / Matt ground. Block-print 2 col. / 45 × 50 / 14 × 12 / MISE 827 2383 PP / Archives Zuber n° 2383

Marble

187 Manufacture ZUBER / 1824 / Satin *irisé* ground. Block-print 2 col. / 36 × 50 / MISE 824 2200 PP / Archives Zuber N° 2200

---

177 Manufaktur ZUBER / 1828 / Satinierter, irisierter Grund. Handdruck, 2 Farben. Irisiert / 37 × 49 / 23,5 × 23,5 / MISE 828 2253 PP / Archives Zuber Nr. 2253

178 Manufaktur ZUBER / 1828 / Satinierter, irisierter Grund. Handdruck, 2 Farben. Irisiert / 39 × 49 / MISE 828 2261 PP / Archives Zuber Nr. 2261

179 Manufaktur ZUBER / 1828 / Satinierter, irisierter Grund. Handdruck, 2 Farben. Irisiert / 31 × 46 / 23,5 × 1,5 / MISE 828 PP 2572 / Archives Zuber Nr. 2572

180 Fritz ZUBER / Manufaktur ZUBER / 1829 / Satinierter Grund. Handdruck, 3 Farben / 55 × 49 / 23,5 × 23,5 / MISE 829 PP 2534 A / Archives Zuber Nr. 2534

181 CHEVALIER / Manufaktur JACQUEMART et BENARD / 1828–1830 / Matter Grund. Handdruck, 3 Farben / 27,5 × 16,5 / 12 × 12 / Vorderseite beschriftet: »N° 113. Mr. Chevalier. f^d et couleur ord^{re} 1.40« / UCAD HH 2311

182 Frankreich / 1840–1850 / Grund Goldstaub. Handdruck, 1 Farbe. Veloutiert / 53 × 51 / 27 × 23,5 / UCAD HH 2088

Geflechte

183 Manufaktur ZUBER / 1824 / Satinierter Grund. Handdruck, 2 Farben / 23,5 × 50 / 2 × 4 / MISE 824 2170 PP / Archives Zuber Nr. 2170

184 Manufaktur ZUBER / 1824 / Matter Grund. Handdruck, 2 Farben / 22,5 × 49 / 2 × 2 / MISE 824 2189 PP / Archives Zuber Nr. 2189

Kassetten

185 Frankreich / 1815–1820 / Matter Grund. Handdruck, 3 Farben / 65 × 49 / 12 × 12 / UCAD HH 2712

186 Manufaktur ZUBER / 1827 / Matter Grund. Handdruck, 2 Farben / 45 × 50 / 14 × 12 / MISE 827 2383 PP Archives Zuber Nr. 2383

Marmor

187 Manufaktur ZUBER / 1824 / Satinierter, irisierter Grund. Handdruck, 2 Farben / 36 × 50 / MISE 824 2200 PP / Archives Zuber Nr. 2200

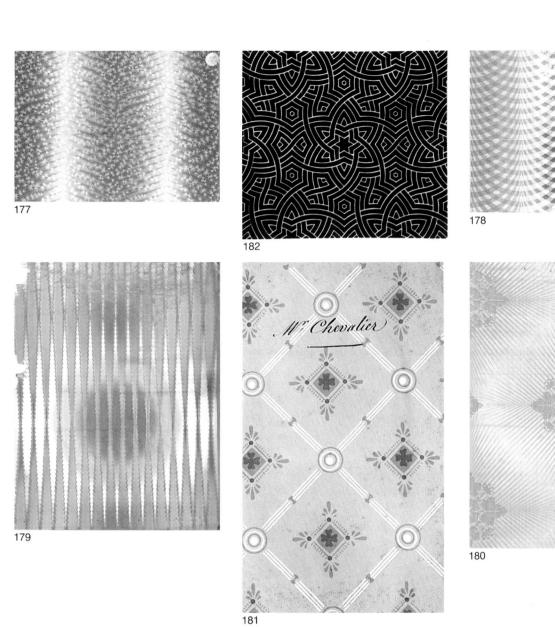

177

182

178

179

Mr Chevalier

181

180

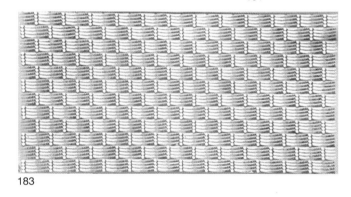

183

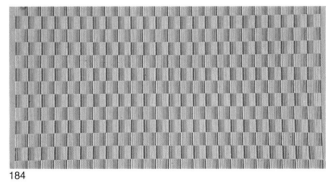

184

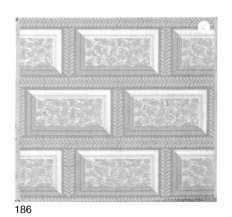

186

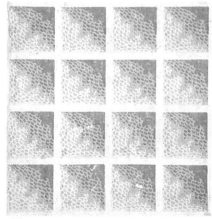

185

187

Rayures & écossais

188 EBERT et BUFFARD / Manufacture JAC-QUEMART et BENARD / 1805–1810 / Fond mat. Imp. pl. 3 coul. / 29,5 × 17,5 / 12 × 12 / Recto, manuscrit: «Mrs Ebert et Buffard. N° 6» / UCAD HH 2205

189 Fritz ZUBER / Manufacture ZUBER / 1826 / Fond satin irisé. Imp. pl. 3 coul. Irisés/ 38 × 50 / 13,5 × 23,5 / MISE 826 PP 2300 b / Archives Zuber n° 2300

190 Manufacture ZUBER / 1826 / Fond satin irisé. Imp. pl. 2 coul. Irisés / 52 × 49,5 / 23,5 × 23,5 / MISE 826 PP 2354 d. / Archives Zuber n° 2354

191 EBERT et BUFFARD / Manufacture JAC-QUEMART et BENARD / 1825–1830 / Fond mat. Imp. pl. 3 coul. / 24 × 17,5 / 12 × 12 / Recto, manuscrit: «N° 92, Mrs Ebert et Buffard» / UCAD HH 2290

192 France / 1825–1830 / Fond satin. Dessin original 4 coul. / 52 × 50 / 46 × 47,5 / Recto, manuscrit: «1714» / UCAD HH 2373

193 Manufacture ZUBER / 1826 / Fond satin. Imp. taille douce 1 coul. / 40 × 49 / MISE 826 TD 1

194 MERY / Manufacture ZUBER / 1826 / Fond satin irisé. Imp. pl. 2 coul. Irisé / 41,5 × 50 / 23,5 × 50 / MISE 826 2350 PP / Archives Zuber n° 2350

195 Manufacture ZUBER / 1826 / Fond satin irisé. Imp. pl. 2 coul. Feuille d'argent / 48 × 48 / 11,5 × 11,5 / MISE 826 2371 PP / Archives Zuber n° 2371

196 TERNE / Manufacture ZUBER / 1827 / Fond satin Imp. pl. 2 coul. Irisés / 49 × 50 / 30,5 × 23,5 / MISE 827 2388 PP / Archives Zuber n° 2388

197 D'après SPOERLIN et RAHN / Manufacture ZUBER / 1827 / Fond mat. irisé. Imp. pl. 3 coul. Irisé / 54 × 50 / 47 × 47 / MISE 827 2404 PP / Archives Zuber n° 2404

198 Fritz ZUBER / Manufacture ZUBER / 1828 / Fond satin irisé. Imp. taille douce 2 coul. / 42 × 49,5 / 33 × 48 / MISE 828 TD 13 a / Archives Zuber TD 13

199 Victor POTERLET / Manufacture SEVES-TRE / 1840 / Fond satin. Imp. pl. 2 coul. / 69 × 47 / 23,5 × 11,5 / Recto, manuscrit: «V. P. Sevestre 1840» / UCAD HH 2788

200 Manufacture ZUBER / 1845 / Imp. auge 7 coul. Imp. taille douce 1 coul. / 5,5 × 47 / 21 × 23,5 / MISE 980 PP 7 / Archives Zuber n° 335 Carré 57

Stripes and Plaids

188 EBERT et BUFFARD / Manufacture JACQUEMART et BENARD / 1805–1810 / Matt ground. Block-print 3 col. / 29,5 × 17,5 / 12 × 12 / Recto, inscribed: 'Mrs Ebert et Buffard. N° 6' / UCAD HH 2205

189 Fritz ZUBER / Manufacture ZUBER / 1826 / Satin *irisé* ground. Block-print 3 col. *Irisé* / 38 × 50 / 13,5 × 23,5 / MISE 826 PP 2300 b / Archives Zuber n° 2300

190 Manufacture ZUBER / 1826 / Satin *irisé* ground. Block-print 2 col. *Irisé* / 52 × 49,5 / 23,5 × 23,5 / MISE 826 PP 2354 d. / Archives Zuber n° 2354

191 EBERT et BUFFARD / Manufacture JACQUEMART et BENARD / 1825–1830 / Matt ground. Block-print 3 col. / 24 × 17,5 / 12 × 12 / Recto, inscribed: 'N° 92, Mrs Ebert et Buffard' / UCAD HH 2290

192 France / 1825–1830 / Satin ground. Original design 4 col. / 52 × 50 / 46 × 47,5 / Recto, inscribed: '1714' / UCAD HH 2373

193 Manufacture ZUBER / 1826 / Satin ground. Metal engr. 1 col. / 40 × 49 / MISE 826 TD 1

194 MERY / Manufacture ZUBER / 1826 / Satin *irisé* ground. Block-print 2 col. *Irisé* / 41,5 × 50 / 23,5 × 50 / MISE 826 2350 PP / Archives Zuber n° 2350

195 Manufacture ZUBER / 1826 / Satin *irisé* ground. Block-print 2 col. Silver leaf / 48 × 48 / 11,5 × 11,5 / MISE 826 2371 PP / Archives Zuber n° 2371

196 TERNE / Manufacture ZUBER / 1827 / Satin ground. Block-print 2 col. *Irisé* / 49 × 50 / 30,5 × 23,5 / MISE 827 2388 PP / Archives Zuber n° 2388

197 After SPOERLIN et RAHN / Manufacture ZUBER / 1827 / Matt *irisé* ground. Block-print 3 col. *Irisé* / 54 × 50 / 47 × 47 / MISE 827 2404 PP / Archives Zuber n° 2404

198 Fritz ZUBER / Manufacture ZUBER / 1828 / Satin *irisé* ground. Metal engr. 2 col. / 42 × 49,5 / 33 × 48 / MISE 828 TD 13 a / Archives Zuber TD 13

199 Victor POTERLET / Manufacture SEVES-TRE / 1840 / Satin ground. Block-print 2 col. / 69 × 47 / 23,5 × 11,5 / Recto, inscribed: 'V. P. Sevestre 1840' / UCAD HH 2788

200 Manufacture ZUBER / 1845 / Trough-print 7 col. Metal engr. 1 col. / 55,5 × 47 / 21 × 23,5 / MISE 980 PP 7 / Archives Zuber n° 335 Carré 57

Streifen und Schottenmuster

188 EBERT und BUFFARD / Manufaktur JAC-QUEMART et BENARD / 1805–1810 / Matter Grund. Handdruck, 3 Farben / 29,5 × 17,5 / 12 × 12 / Vorderseite beschriftet: »Mrs Ebert et Buffard. N° 6« / UCAD HH 2205

189 Fritz ZUBER / Manufaktur ZUBER / 1826 / Satinierter, irisierter Grund. Handdruck, 3 Farben. Irisiert / 38 × 50 / 13,5 × 23,5 / MISE 826 PP 2300 b / Archives Zuber Nr. 2300

190 Manufaktur ZUBER / 1826 / Satinierter, irisierter Grund. Handdruck, 2 Farben. Irisiert / 52 × 49,5 / 23,5 × 23,5 / MISE 826 PP 2354 d / Archives Zuber Nr. 2354

191 EBERT und BUFFARD / Manufaktur JAC-QUEMART et BENARD / 1825–1830 / Matter Grund. Handdruck, 3 Farben / 24 × 17,5 / 12 × 12 / Vorderseite beschriftet: »N° 92 Mrs Ebert et Buffard« / UCAD HH 2290

192 Frankreich / 1825–1830 / Satinierter Grund. Originalentwurf, 4 Farben / 52 × 50 / 46 × 47,5 / Vorderseite beschriftet: »1714« / UCAD HH 2373

193 Manufaktur ZUBER / 1826 / Satinierter Grund. Druck mittels Kupferstichwalze, 1 Farbe / 40 × 49 / MISE 826 TD 1

194 MERY / Manufaktur ZUBER / 1826 / Satinierter, irisierter Grund. Handdruck, 2 Farben. Irisiert / 41,5 × 50 / 23,5 × 50 / MISE 826 2350 PP / Archives Zuber Nr. 2350

195 Manufaktur ZUBER / 1826 / Satinierter, irisierter Grund. Handdruck, 2 Farben. Blattsilber / 48 × 48 / 11,5 × 11,5 / MISE 826 2371 PP / Archives Zuber Nr. 2371

196 TERNE / Manufaktur ZUBER / 1827 / Satinierter Grund. Handdruck, 2 Farben. Irisiert / 49 × 50 / 30,5 × 23,5 / MISE 827 2388 PP / Archives Zuber Nr. 2388

197 Nach SPOERLIN und RAHN / Manufaktur ZUBER / 1827 / Matter, irisierter Grund. Handdruck, 3 Farben. Irisiert / 54 × 50 / 47 × 47 / MISE 827 2404 PP / Archives Zuber Nr. 2404

198 Fritz ZUBER / Manufaktur ZUBER / 1828 / Satinierter, irisierter Grund. Druck mittels Kupferstichwalze, 2 Farben / 42 × 49,5 / 33 × 48 / MISE 828 TD 13 a / Archives Zuber Nr. TD 13

199 Victor POTERLET / Manufaktur SEVES-TRE / 1840 / Satinierter Grund. Handdruck, 2 Farben / 69 × 47 / 23,5 × 11,5 / Vorderseite beschriftet: »V.P. Sevestre 1840« / UCAD HH 2788

200 Manufaktur ZUBER / 1845 / Druck mittels Streifenzieher, 7 Farben. Druck mittels Kupferstichwalze, 1 Farbe / 55,5 × 47 / 21 × 23,5 / MISE 980 PP 7 / Archives Zuber Nr. 335 Carré 57

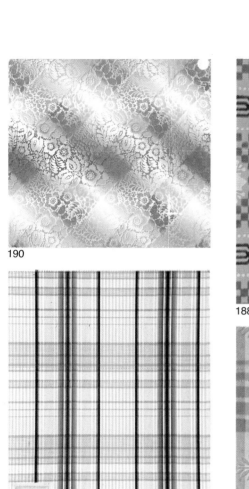

190

188

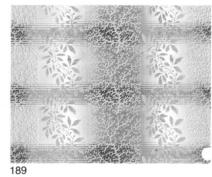

189

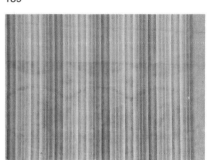

193

192

191

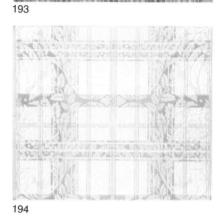

194

195

196

197

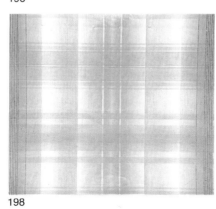

198

199

200

Etoffes et dentelles

201 France / 1825–1830 / Fond satin. Imp. pl. 2 coul. / 67,5 × 51 / 52,5 × 48/ UCAD HH 944 / Paris, 1967 N° 275

202 KUPFER / Manufacture ZUBER / 1827 / Fond satin, irisé. Imp. pl. 2 coul. Irisé / 48 × 50 / 23,5 × 47 / MISE 827 2416 PP / Archives Zuber N° 2416

203 Manufacture ZUBER / 1831 / Fond mat, irisé. Imp. taille douce 2 coul. / 66 × 49,5 / 37,5 × 47 / Recto, étiquette manuscrite: «n° 1928 de l'Exposition de 1834. Papiers Peints Mr Jn Zuber et Cie à Rixheim. n° 1915 à l'exposition de 1834. Ce dessin et la gravure ont été faits par Mrs Koechlin-Ziegler à Mulhouse» / MISE 177 PP Y / Archives Zuber TD 30

204 Manufacture DAUPTAIN / 1828 / Fond mat. Imp. pl. 2 coul. / 69 × 47 / Recto, manuscrit: «1828 Dauptain» / UCAD HH 981 / Paris, 1967, n° 86

205 Manufacture ZUBER / 1833 / Fond satin. Imp. pl. 1 coul. imp. taille douce 1 coul. / 41 × 50 / MISE 980 PP 100 / Archives Zuber N° 2910

206 France / 1835–1840 / Fond satin. Imp. pl. 2 coul. Poudre dorée / 62 × 52 / 32 × 47 / UCAD HH 701 / Paris, 1967, n° 338

207 France / 1835–1840 / Fond mat. Imp. pl. 2 coul. Feuille d'argent / 60 × 51 / 47 × 23,5 / UCAD HH 740 / Paris, 1967, N° 339

208 France / 1840–1845 / Fond satin. Imp. pl. 8 coul. / 61 × 50 / 48,5 × 47 / UCAD HH 762

209 France / 1840–1845 / Fond satin. Imp. pl. 3 coul. / 50,5 × 50 / 30 × 23 / UCAD HH 763 B

210 France / 1840–1845 / Fond satin. Imp. pl. 3 coul. / 53 × 51 / 47 × 47 / UCAD HH 764 / Paris, 1967, N° 307

211 France / 1840–1845 / Fond satin. Imp. pl. 3 coul. / 59 × 52 / UCAD HH 765 / Paris, 1967, N° 306

Materials and Lace

201 France / 1825–1830 / Satin ground. Block-print 2 col. / 67,5 × 51 / 52,5 × 48 / UCAD HH 944 / Paris, 1967 N° 275

202 KUPFER / Manufacture ZUBER / 1827 / Satin *irisé* ground. Block-print 2 col. *Irisé* / 48 × 50 / 23,5 × 47 / MISE 827 2416 PP / Archives Zuber N° 2416

203 Manufacture ZUBER / 1831 / Matt *irisé* ground. Metal engr. 2 col. / 66 × 49,5 / 37,5 × 47 / Recto, inscribed on a label: 'n° 1928 de l'Exposition de 1834. Papiers Peints Mr Jn Zuber et Cie à Rixheim. n° 1915 à l'exposition de 1834. Ce dessin et la gravure ont été faits par Mrs Koechlin-Ziegler à Mulhouse'. / MISE 177 PP Y / Archives Zuber n° TD 30

204 Manufacture DAUPTAIN / 1828 / Matt ground. Block-print. 2 col. / 69 × 47 / Recto, inscribed: '1828 Dauptain' / UCAD HH 981 / Paris, 1967, n° 86

205 Manufacture ZUBER / 1833 / Satin ground. Block-print 1 col. Metal engr. 1 col. / 41 × 50 / MISE 980 PP 100 / Archives Zuber N° 2910

206 France / 1835–1840 / Satin ground. Block-print 2 col. Gold dust / 62 × 52 / 32 × 47 / UCAD HH 701 / Paris, 1967, n° 338

207 France / 1835–1840 / Matt ground. Block-print 2 col. Silver leaf / 60 × 51 / 47 × 23,5 / UCAD HH 740 / Paris, 1967, n° 339

208 France / 1840–1845 / Satin ground. Block-print 8 col. / 61 × 50 / 48,5 × 47 / UCAD HH 762

209 France / 1840–1845 / Satin ground. Block-print 3 col. / 50,5 × 50 / 30 × 23 / UCAD HH 763 B

210 France / 1840–1845 / Satin ground. Block-print 3 col. / 53 × 51 / 47 × 47 / UCAD HH 764 / Paris, 1967, N° 307

211 France / 1840–1845 / Satin ground. Block-print 3 col. / 59 × 52 / UCAD HH 765 / Paris, 1967, N° 306

Stoff- und Spitzenimitationen

201 Frankreich / 1825–1830 / Satinierter Grund. Handdruck, 2 Farben / 67,5 × 51 / 52,5 × 48 / UCAD HH 944 / Paris, 1967, Nr. 275

202 KUPFER / Manufaktur ZUBER / 1827 / Satinierter, irisierter Grund. Handdruck, 2 Farben. Irisiert / 48 × 50 / 23,5 × 47 / MISE 827 2416 PP / Archives Zuber Nr. 2416

203 Manufaktur ZUBER / 1831 / Matter, irisierter Grund. Druck mittels Kupferstichwalze, 2 Farben / 66 × 49,5 / 37,5 × 47 / Auf der Vorderseite beschriftete Etikette: »n° 1928 de l'Exposition de 1834. Papiers Peints Mr Jn Zuber et Cie à Rixheim. n° 1915 à l'exposition de 1834. Ce dessin et la gravure ont été faits par Mrs Koechlin-Ziegler à Mulhouse« / MISE 177 PP Y / Archives Zuber Nr. TD 30

204 Manufaktur DAUPTAIN / 1828 / Matter Grund. Handdruck, 2 Farben / 69 × 47 / Vorderseite beschriftet: »1828 Dauptain« / UCAD HH 981 / Paris, 1967, Nr. 86

205 Manufaktur ZUBER / 1833 / Satinierter Grund. Handdruck, 1 Farbe. Druck mittels Kupferstichwalze, 1 Farbe / 41 × 50 / MISE 980 PP 100 / Archives Zuber Nr. 2910

206 Frankreich / 1835–1840 / Satinierter Grund. Handdruck, 2 Farben. Goldstaub / 62 × 52 / 32 × 47 / UCAD HH 701 / Paris, 1967, Nr. 338

207 Frankreich / 1835–1840 / Matter Grund. Handdruck, 2 Farben. Blattsilber / 60 × 51 / 47 × 23,5 / UCAD HH 740 / Paris, 1967, Nr. 339

208 Frankreich / 1840–1845 / Satinierter Grund. Handdruck, 8 Farben / 61 × 50 / 48,5 × 47 / UCAD HH 762

209 Frankreich / 1840–1845 / Satinierter Grund. Handdruck, 3 Farben / 50,5 × 50 / 30 × 23 / UCAD HH 763 B

210 Frankreich / 1840–1845 / Satinierter Grund. Handdruck, 3 Farben / 53 × 51 / 47 × 47 / UCAD HH 764 / Paris, 1967, Nr. 307

211 Frankreich / 1840–1845 / Satinierter Grund. Handdruck, 3 Farben / 59 × 52 / UCAD HH 765 / Paris, 1967, Nr. 306

205

203

202

201

206

207

204

208

209

211

210

212 France / 1840–1845 / Fond satin.Imp. pl. 2 coul. / 52 × 50 / Verso tampon: «1392» / uCAD HH 902

213 France / 1840 / Fond mat. Imp. pl. 15 coul. / 57 × 88 / 17 × 45 / BF 528

214 France / 1845 env. / Fond satin. Imp. pl. 5 coul. / 68 × 48 / 50 × 47 / UCAD HH 2785

215 Victor POTERLET / 1845 / Fond satin. Imp. pl. 1 coul. Veloutage / 97 × 49 / UCAD HH 487

216 Manufacture ZUBER / 1845–1850 / Fond satin. Imp. taille douce 1 coul. Imp. pl. 6 coul. / 44,5 × 49 / UCAD HH 2784

217 France / 1845–1850 / Fond satin. Imp. pl. 10 coul. / 61 × 50 / 54 × 47,5 / UCAD HH 757 / Paris, 1967 N° 303

218 France / 1845–1850 / Fond mat. Imp. pl. 19 coul. / 70 × 49 / 64 × 47 / BF 31

219 France / 1845–1850 / Fond lissé. Imp. pl. 21 coul. / 48 × 49 / BF 156

220 Victor POTERLET / Manufacture MAR-CHAND / 1848 / Fond mat. Imp. pl. 6 coul. / 69,5 × 47 / 54 × 47 / Recto, manuscrit: «Poterlet-Marchand 1848» / UCAD HH 761 / Paris, 1967 N° 181

221 France / 1850 / Fond satin. Imp. pl. 8 coul. / 61 × 52 / BF 20

222 Manufacture RIOTTOT et PACON / 1850 env. / Fond satin. Imp. pl. 18 coul. / 69 × 50,5 / Recto, tampon: «Riottot et Pacon» / UCAD HH 917 / Paris, 1967, N° 206

212 France / 1840–1845 / Satin ground. Block-print 2 col. / 52 × 50 / Verso, stamped: '1392' / UCAD HH 902

213 France / 1840 / Matt ground. Block-print 15 col. / 57 × 88 / 17 × 45 / BF 528

214 France / 1845 env. / Satin ground. Block-print 5 col. / 68 × 48 / 50 × 47 / UCAD HH 2785

215 Victor POTERLET / 1845 / Satin ground. Block-print 1 col. Flocking / 97 × 49 / UCAD HH 487

216 Manufacture ZUBER / 1845–1850 / Satin ground. Metal engr. 1 col. Block-print 6 col. / 44,5 × 49 / UCAD HH 2784

217 France / 1845–1850 / Satin ground. Block-print 10 col. / 61 × 50 / 54 × 47,5 / UCAD HH 757 / Paris, 1967, N° 303

218 France / 1845–1850 / Matt ground. Block-print 19 col. / 70 × 49 / 64 × 47 / BF 31

219 France / 1845–1850 / Smooth ground. Block-print 21 col. / 48 × 49 / BF 156

220 Victor POTERLET / Manufacture MAR-CHAND / 1848 / Matt ground. Block-print 6 col. / 69,5 × 47 / 54 × 47 / Recto, inscribed: 'Poterlet-Marchand 1848' / UCAD HH 761 / Paris, 1967, N° 181

221 France / 1850 / Satin ground. Block-print 8 col. / 61 × 52 / BF 20

222 Manufacture RIOTTOT et PACON / 1850 env. / Satin ground. Block-print 18 col. / 69 × 50,5 / Recto, stamped: 'Riottot et Pacon' / UCAD HH 917 / Paris, 1967, N° 206

212 Frankreich / 1840–1845 / Satinierter Grund. Handdruck, 2 Farben / 52 × 50 / Rückseitig Stempel: »1392« / UCAD HH 902

213 Frankreich / 1840 / Matter Grund. Handdruck, 15 Farben / 57 × 88 / 17 × 45 / BF 528

214 Frankreich / Um 1845 / Satinierter Grund. Handdruck, 5 Farben / 68 × 48 / 50 × 47 / UCAD HH 2785

215 Victor POTERLET / 1845 / Satinierter Grund. Handdruck, 1 Farbe. Veloutiert / 97 × 49 / UCAD HH 487

216 Manufaktur ZUBER / 1845–1850 / Satinierter Grund. Druck mittels Kupferstichwalze, 1 Farbe. Handdruck, 6 Farben / 44,5 × 49 / UCAD HH 2784

217 Frankreich / 1845–1850 / Satinierter Grund. Handdruck, 10 Farben / 61 × 50 / 54 × 47,5 / UCAD HH 757 / Paris, 1967, Nr. 303

218 Frankreich / 1845–1850 / Matter Grund. Handdruck, 19 Farben / 70 × 49 / 64 × 47 / BF 31

219 Frankreich / 1845–1850 / Geglätteter Grund. Handdruck, 21 Farben / 48 × 49 / BF 156

220 Victor POTERLET / Manufaktur MAR-CHAND / 1848 / Matter Grund. Handdruck, 6 Farben / 69,5 × 47 / 54 × 47 / Vorderseite beschriftet: »Poterlet-Marchand 1848« / UCAD HH 761 / Paris, 1967, Nr. 181

221 Frankreich / 1850 / Satinierter Grund. Handdruck, 8 Farben / 61 × 52 / BF 20

222 Manufaktur RIOTTOT et PACON / Um 1850 / Satinierter Grund. Handdruck, 18 Farben / 69 × 50,5 / Auf der Vorderseite Stempel: »Riottot et Pacon« / UCAD HH 917 / Paris, 1967, Nr. 206

213

212

214

216

215

217

218

219

221

220

222

Figures en médaillons

223 MADER et HAUTOT L'AINE ? / 1810–1820 / Fond mat. Imp. pl. 5 coul. / 175 × 47 / Verso, manuscrit: «D'après Mader et Hautot l'Aîné» / UCAD HH 102 / Paris, 1967, n° 268

224 France / 1810–1820 / Fond mat. Imp. pl. 5 coul. / 139 × 47 / UCAD HH 101 / Paris, 1967, n° 267

225 Manufacture ZUBER / 1828 / Fond mat. irisé. Impression taille douce 1 couleur / 70 × 46,5 / 39,5 × 47 / UCAD HH 849

226 France / 1830–1835 / Fond satin. Imp. pl. 15 coul. Irisés / 82 × 48,5 / UCAD HH 2791

227 France / 1835–1840 / Fond satin. Imp. pl. 7 coul. Irisés / 57 × 49 / UCAD 29553 / SEGUIN 1968, p. 7 / Paris, 1967, n° 337

228 France / 1840–1850 / Fond satin. Imp. pl. 22 coul. Irisé / 136 × 50 / UCAD 48945

229 Manufacture RIOTTOT et PACON / 1840–1845 / Fond mat. imp. pl. 18 coul. / 70 × 50 / 56,5 × 47 / Recto, tampon «Riottot et Pacon» / UCAD HH 880 / Paris, 1967, n° 208

230 France / 1840–1845 / Fond mat. Imp. pl. 8 coul. Irisés / 56 × 51 / UCAD HH 130

231 France / 1840–1845 / Fond satin. Imp. pl. 14 coul. Irisé / 61 × 50 / UCAD HH 778

232 France / 1840–1845 / Fond satin. Imp. pl. 14 coul. / 94 × 50,5 / UCAD HH 2786

Figures in Medallions

223 MADER et HAUTOT L'AINE? / 1810–1820 / Matt ground. Block-print 5 col. / 175 × 47 / Verso, inscribed: 'D' après Mader et Hautot l'Aîné'. / UCAD HH 102 / Paris, 1967, n° 268

224 France / 1810–1820 / Matt ground. Block-print 5 col. / 139 × 47 / UCAD HH 101 / Paris, 1967, n° 267

225 Manufacture ZUBER / 1828 / Matt *irisé* ground. Metal engr. 1 col. / 70 × 46,5 / 39,5 × 47 / UCAD HH 849

226 France / 1830–1835 / Satin ground. Block-print 15 col. *Irisé* / 82 × 48,5 / UCAD HH 2791

227 France / 1835–1840 / Satin ground. Block-print 7 col. *Irisé* / 57 × 49 / UCAD 29553 / SEGUIN, 1968, p. 7 / Paris, 1967, n° 337

228 France / 1840–1845 / Satin ground. Block-print 22 col. *Irisé* / 136 × 50 / UCAD 48945

229 Manufacture RIOTTOT et PACON / 1840–1845 / Matt ground. Block-print 18 col. / 70 × 50 / 56,5 × 47 / Recto, stamped: 'Riottot et Pacon' / UCAD HH 880 / Paris, 1967, n° 208

230 France / 1840–1845 / Matt ground. Block-print 8 col. *Irisé* / 56 × 51 / UCAD HH 130

231 France / 1840–1845 / Satin ground. Block-print 14 col. *Irisé* / 61 × 50 / UCAD HH 778

232 France / 1840–1845 / Satin ground. Block-print 14 col. / 94 × 50,5 / UCAD HH 2786

Figuren in Medaillons

223 MADER und HAUTOT L'AINE? / 1810–1820 / Matter Grund. Handdruck, 5 Farben / 175 × 47 / Rückseitig beschriftet: »D' après Mader et Hautot l'Aîné« / UCAD HH 102 / Paris, 1967, Nr. 268

224 Frankreich / 1810–1820 / Matter Grund. Handdruck, 5 Farben / 139 × 47 / UCAD HH 101 / Paris, 1967, Nr. 267

225 Manufaktur ZUBER / 1828 / Matter, irisierter Grund. Druck mittels Kupferstichwalze, 1 Farbe / 70 × 46,5 / 39,5 × 47 / UCAD HH 849

226 Frankreich / 1830–1835 / Satinierter Grund. Handdruck, 15 Farben. Irisiert / 82 × 48,5 / UCAD HH 2791

227 Frankreich / 1835–1840 / Satinierter Grund. Handdruck, 7 Farben. Irisiert / 57 × 49 / UCAD 29553 / SEGUIN, 1968, S. 7 / Paris, 1967, Nr. 337

228 Frankreich / 1840–1845 / Satinierter Grund. Handdruck, 22 Farben. Irisiert / 136 × 50 / UCAD 48945

229 Manufaktur RIOTTOT et PACON / 1840–1845 / Matter Grund. Handdruck, 18 Farben / 70 × 50 / 56,5 × 47 / Vorderseite Stempel: »Riottot et Pacon« / UCAD HH 880 / Paris, 1967, Nr. 208

230 Frankreich / 1840–1845 / Matter Grund. Handdruck, 8 Farben. Irisiert / 56 × 51 / UCAD HH 130

231 Frankreich / 1840–1845 / Satinierter Grund. Handdruck, 14 Farben. Irisiert / 61 × 50 / UCAD HH 778

232 Frankreich / 1840–1845 / Satinierter Grund. Handdruck, 14 Farben / 94 × 50,5 / UCAD HH 2786

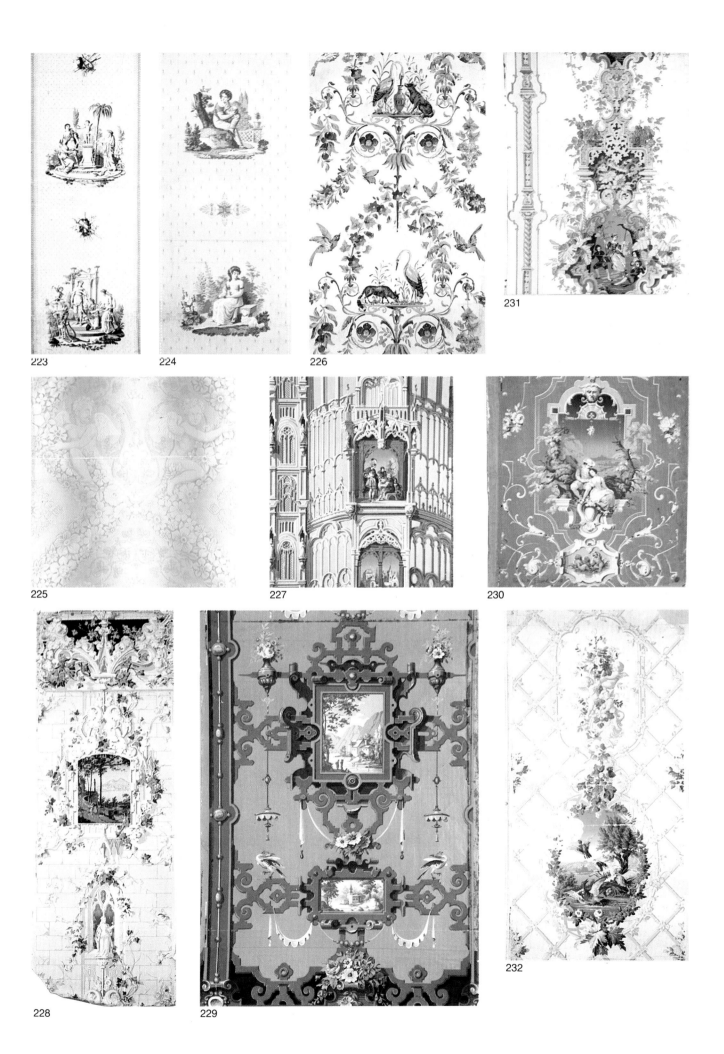

223

224

226

231

225

227

230

228

229

232

233 Hippolyte HENRY ? / Manufacture RIOTTOT et PACON / 1840–1845 / Fond mat. Imp. pl. 11 coul. / 60 × 50 / 57 × 47 / Recto, tampon «Riottot et Pacon». Verso, manuscrit: «Henry, 3.405 Hélène 1.50» / BF 359

234 Hippolyte HENRY ? / 1840–1845 / Fond mat. Imp. pl. 23 coul. / 75 × 50 / 62 × 47 / Verso, manuscrit: «Henry. 2443 Citron mat 2,50» / BF 361

235 WAGNER / 1840–1845 / Fond lissé. Imp. pl. 7 coul. Feuille d'or / 58 × 49 / Verso, manuscrit: «Wagner» / BF 357

236 Victor POTERLET / 1840–1845 / Fond mat. Imp. pl. 16 coul. / 95 × 50 / 95 × 48 / Verso, manuscrit: «Poterlet» / BF 442

237 France / 1840–1845 / Fond satin. Imp. pl. 16 coul. / 64,5 × 50 / BF 111

238 Henri CARRE / 1840–1845 / Fond satin. Imp. pl. 26 coul. / 137 × 49 / 96 × 47 / Verso, manuscrit: «Henry Carré» / BF 555

231 Victor POTERLET / 1845 env. / Fond satin. Imp. pl. 14 coul. / 105 × 47 / 97 × 47 / UCAD HH 476 A / Paris, 1967, n° 315

240 Victor POTERLET / 1845 env. / Fond satin. Imp. pl. 7 coul. / 90 × 51 / UCAD HH 476 B / Paris, 1967, n° 316

241 France / 1845 env. / Fond satin. Imp. pl. 18 coul. Irisé / 86 × 50 / UCAD HH 476 C

242 France / 1845–1850 / Fond mat. Imp. pl. 14 coul. Irisé / 128 × 56 / UCAD 48 946

243 Hippolyte HENRY / Manufacture RIOTTOT / Fond satin. Imp. pl. 21 coul. / 220 × 52 / 93 × 48 / Recto, tampon: «J. R.». Verso, manuscrit: «Henry (Hippolyte) chez Riottot» / BF 471

233 Hippolyte HENRY? / Manufacture RIOTTOT et PACON / 1840–1845 / Matt ground. Block-print 11 col. / 60 × 50 / 57 × 47 / Recto, stamped: 'Riottot et Pacon'. / Verso, inscribed: 'Henry 3.405 Hélène 1.50'. / BF 359

234 Hippolyte HENRY? / 1840–1845 / Matt ground. Block-print 23 col. / 75 × 50 / 62 × 47 / Verso, inscribed: 'Henry. 2443 Citron mat 2,50' / BF 361

235 WAGNER / 1840–1845 / Smooth ground. Block-print 7 col. Gold leaf / 58 × 49 / Verso, inscribed: 'Wagner' / BF 357

236 Victor POTERLET / 1840–1845 / Matt ground. Block-print 16 col. / 95 × 50 / 95 × 48 / Verso, inscribed: 'Poterlet' / BF 442

237 France / 1840–1845 / Satin ground. Block-print 16 col. / 64,5 × 50 / BF 111

238 Henri CARRE / 1840–1845 / Satin ground. Block-print 26 col. / 137 × 49 / 96 × 47 / Verso, inscribed: 'Henry Carré' / BF 555

239 Victor POTERLET / 1845 env. / Satin ground. Block-print 14 col. / 105 × 47 / 97 × 47 / UCAD HH 476 A / Paris, 1967, n° 315

240 Victor POTERLET / 1845 env. / Satin ground. Block-print 7 col. / 90 × 51 / UCAD HH 476 B / Paris, 1967, n° 316

241 France / 1845 env. / Satin ground. Block-print 18 col. *Irisé* / 86 × 50 / UCAD HH 476 C

242 France / 1845–1850 / Matt ground. Block-print 14 col. *Irisé* / 128 × 56 / UCAD 48946

243 Hippolyte HENRY / Manufacture RIOTTOT / Satin ground. Block-print 21 col. / 220 × 52 / 93 × 48 / Recto, stamped: 'J. R.'. / Verso, inscribed: 'Henry (Hippolyte) chez Riottot'. / BF 471

233 Hippolyte HENRY? / Manufaktur RIOTTOT et PACON / 1840–1845 / Matter Grund. Handdruck, 11 Farben / 60 × 50 / 57 × 47 / Vorderseite Stempel: »Riottot et Pacon«. Rückseitig beschriftet: »Henry, 3.405 Hélène 1.50« / BF 359

234 Hippolyte HENRY? / 1840–1845 / Matter Grund. Handdruck, 23 Farben / 75 × 50 / 62 × 47 / Rückseitig beschriftet: »Henry. 2443 Citron mat 2,50« / BF 361

235 WAGNER / 1840–1845 / Geglätteter Grund. Handdruck, 7 Farben. Blattgold / 58 × 49 / Rückseitig beschriftet: »Wagner« / BF 357

236 Victor POTERLET / 1840–1845 / Matter Grund. Handdruck, 16 Farben / 95 × 50 / 95 × 48 / Rückseitig beschriftet: »Poterlet« / BF 442

237 Frankreich / 1840–1845 / Satinierter Grund. Handdruck, 16 Farben / 64,5 × 50 / BF 111

238 Henri CARRE / 1840–1845 / Satinierter Grund. Handdruck, 26 Farben / 137 × 49 / 96 × 47 / Rückseitig beschriftet: »Henry Carré« / BF 555

239 Victor POTERLET / Um 1845 / Satinierter Grund. Handdruck, 14 Farben / 105 × 47 / 97 × 47 / UCAD HH 476 A / Paris, 1967, Nr. 315

240 Victor POTERLET / Um 1845 / Satinierter Grund. Handdruck, 7 Farben / 90 × 51 / UCAD HH 476 B / Paris, 1967, Nr. 316

241 Frankreich / Um 1845 / Satinierter Grund. Handdruck, 18 Farben. Irisiert / 86 × 50 / UCAD HH 476 C

242 Frankreich / 1845–1850 / Matter Grund. Handdruck, 14 Farben. Irisiert / 128 × 56 / UCAD 48946

243 Hippolyte HENRY / Manufaktur RIOTTOT / Satinierter Grund. Handdruck, 21 Farben / 220 × 52 / 93 × 48 / Vorderseite Stempel: »J. R.«. Rückseitig beschriftet: »Henry (Hippolyte) chez Riottot« / BF 471

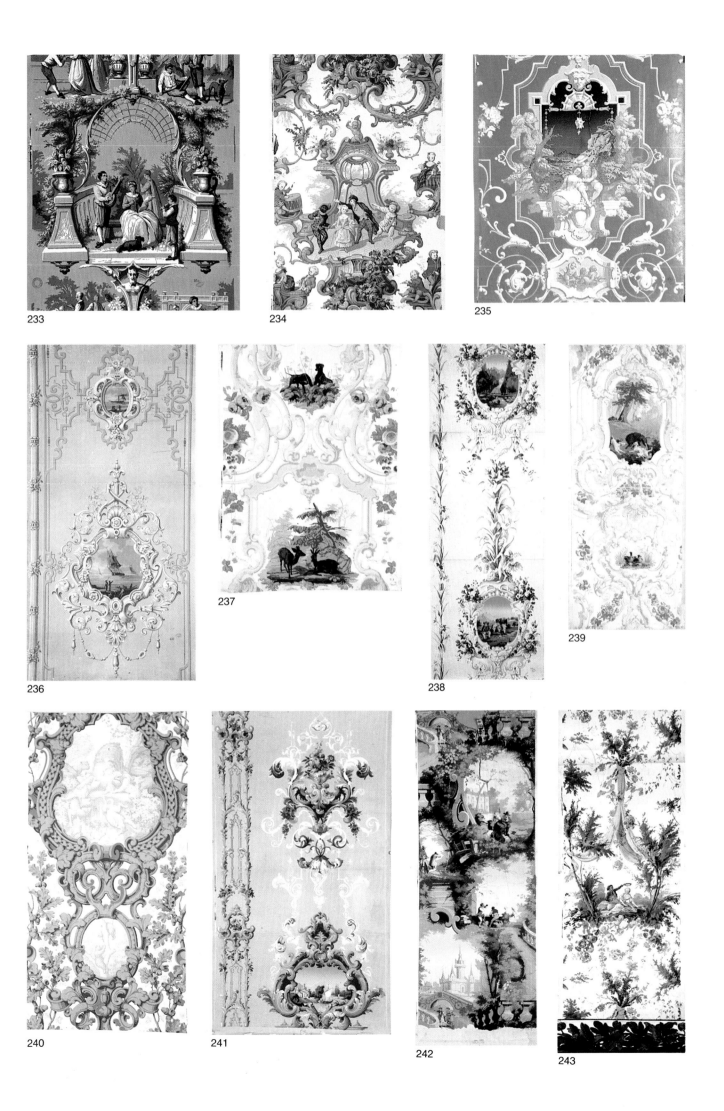

233

234

235

236

237

238

239

240

241

242

243

Bordures

Borders

Bordüren

Fleurs et feuilles

244 Manufactur JACQUEMART et BENARD / 1800–1805 / Fond mat. Imp. pl. 12 coul. / 22 × 34 / 22 × 27 / UCAD HH 315

245 Manufacture JACQUEMART et BENARD / 1800–1805 / Fond mat. Imp. pl. 13 coul. / 26,5 × 55,5 / 26 × 53,5 / UCAD HH 337

246 Joseph Laurent MALAINE ? / Manufacture ZUBER ? / 1800–1805 / Fond mat. Imp. pl. 15 coul. / 20 × 66 / 18 × 53,5 / Recto, manuscrit: «Zuber père ler Malaine» / UCAD HH 2639

247 Manufacture JACQUEMART et BENARD / 1800–1810 / Fond mat. Imp. pl. 11 coul. Veloutage et repiquage / 26,5 × 54,5 / UCAD HH 324

248 Manufacture JACQUEMART et BENARD / 1800–1810 / Fond satin. Imp. pl. 5 coul. / 14 × 29,5 / 14 × 21 / UCAD HH 366

249 Manufacture JACQUEMART et BENARD / 1805–1810 / Fond mat. Imp. pl. 11 coul. Veloutage et repiquage / 27,5 × 55 / 27,5 × 54 / UCAD HH 330

250 France / 1810–1815 / Fond mat. Dessin original 9 coul. / 28 × 51 / 22,5 × 23,5 / UCAD HH 2565

251 France / 1810–1815 / Fond mat. Dessin original 8 coul. / 33 × 52,5 / 46,5 × 31,5 / UCAD HH 2566

252 France / 1810–1815 / Fond mat. Imp. pl. 6 coul. / 18,5 × 49 / 11,5 × 11,5 / UCAD HH 2567

253 Manufacture DUFOUR / 1810–1815 / Fond mat. Imp. pl. 21 coul. / 57 × 69 / BF 1414

254 Manufacture DUFOUR ? / 1810–1815 / Fond mat. Imp. pl. 23 coul. / 55 × 75 / 55 × 54 / BF 1415

255 France / 1810–1820 / Fond mat. Imp. pl. 3 coul. Veloutage et repiquage / 23 × 41 / UCAD HH 2393

256 France / 1810–1820 / Fond satin. Dessin original 10 coul. / 16,5 × 49 / 15,5 × 16 / UCAD HH 2607

Flowers and Leaves

244 Manufacture JACQUEMART et BENARD / 1800–1805 / Matt ground. Block-print 12 col. / 22 × 34 / 22 × 27 / UCAD HH 315

245 Manufacture JACQUEMART et BENARD / 1800–1805 / Matt ground. Block-print 13 col. / 26,5 × 55,5 / 26 × 53,5 / UCAD HH 337

246 Joseph Laurent MALAINE? / Manufacture ZUBER? / 1800–1805 / Matt ground. Block-print 15 col. / 20 × 66 / 18 × 53,5 / Recto, inscribed: 'Zuber Père ler Malaine' / UCAD HH 2639

247 Manufacture JACQUEMART et BENARD / 1800–1810 / Matt ground. Block-print 11 col. Flocking and over-printing / 26,5 × 54,5 / UCAD HH 324

248 Manufacture JACQUEMART et BENARD / 1800–1810 / Satin ground. Block-print 5 col. / 14 × 29,5 / 14 × 21 / UCAD HH 366

249 Manufacture JACQUEMART et BENARD / 1805–1810 / Matt ground. Block-print 11 col. Flocking and over-printing / 27,5 × 55 / 27,5 × 54 / UCAD HH 330

250 France / 1810–1815 / Matt ground. Original design 9 col. / 28 × 51 / 22,5 × 23,5 / UCAD HH 2565

251 France / 1810–1815 / Matt ground. Original design 8 col. / 33 × 52,5 / 46,5 × 31,5 / UCAD HH 2566

252 France / 1810–1815 / Matt ground. Block-print 6 col. / 18,5 × 49 / 11,5 × 11,5 / UCAD HH 2567

253 Manufacture DUFOUR / 1810–1815 / Matt ground. Block-print 21 col. / 57 × 69 / BF 1414

254 Manufacture DUFOUR? / 1810–1815 / Matt ground. Block-print 23 col. / 55 × 75 / 55 × 54 / BF 1415

255 France / 1810–1820 / Matt ground. Block-print 3 col. Flocking and over-printing / 23 × 41 / UCAD HH 2393

256 France / 1810–1820 / Satin ground. Original design 10 col. / 16,5 × 49 / 15,5 × 16 / UCAD HH 2607

Blumen und Blätter

244 Manufaktur JACQUEMART et BENARD / 1800–1805 / Matter Grund. Handdruck, 12 Farben / 22 × 34 / 22 × 27 / UCAD HH 315

245 Manufaktur JACQUEMART et BENARD / 1800–1805 / Matter Grund. Handdruck, 13 Farben / 26,5 × 55,5 / 26 × 53,5 / UCAD HH 337

246 Joseph-Laurent MALAINE? / Manufaktur ZUBER? / 1800–1805 / Matter Grund. Handdruck, 15 Farben / 20 × 66 / 18 × 53,5 / Vorderseite beschriftet: »Zuber père ler Malaine« / UCAD HH 2639

247 Manufaktur JACQUEMART et BENARD / 1800–1810 / Matter Grund. Handdruck, 11 Farben. Veloutiert und repiquiert / 26,5 × 54,5 / UCAD HH 324

248 Manufaktur JACQUEMART et BENARD / 1800–1810 / Satinierter Grund. Handdruck, 5 Farben / 14 × 29,5 / 14 × 21 / UCAD HH 366

249 Manufaktur JACQUEMART et BENARD / 1805–1810 / Matter Grund. Handdruck, 11 Farben. Veloutiert und repiquiert / 27,5 × 55 / 27,5 × 54 / UCAD HH 330

250 Frankreich / 1810–1815 / Matter Grund. Originalentwurf, 9 Farben / 28 × 51 / 22,5 × 23,5 / UCAD HH 2565

251 Frankreich / 1810–1815 / Matter Grund. Originalentwurf, 8 Farben / 33 × 52,5 / 46,5 × 31,5 / UCAD HH 2566

252 Frankreich / 1810–1815 / Matter Grund. Handdruck, 6 Farben / 18,5 × 49 / 11,5 × 11,5 / UCAD HH 2567

253 Manufaktur DUFOUR / 1810–1815 / Matter Grund. Handdruck, 21 Farben / 57 × 69 / BF 1414

254 Manufaktur DUFOUR ? / 1810–1815 / Matter Grund. Handdruck, 23 Farben / 55 × 75 / 55 × 54 / BF 1415

255 Frankreich / 1810–1820 / Matter Grund. Handdruck, 3 Farben. Veloutiert und repiquiert / 23 × 41 / UCAD HH 2393

256 Frankreich / 1810–1820 / Satinierter Grund. Originalentwurf, 10 Farben / 16,5 × 49 / 15,5 × 16 / UCAD HH 2607

244

246

245

247

248

249

253

251

254

252

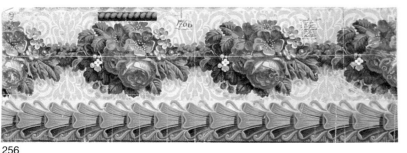

256

255

250

257 France / 1810–1820 / Fond mat. Dessin original 12 coul. / 25,5 × 48 / 23,5 × 23,5 / UCAD HH 2626

258 France / 1810–1820 / Fond mat. Imp. pl. 23 coul. Veloutage et repiquage / 37 × 46 / UCAD HH 2651

259 France / 1810–1820 / Imp. pl. 12 coul. / 22,5 × 47 / 22,5 × 23,5 / UCAD HH 2652

260 Manufacture ZUBER / 1815 / Fond mat. Imp. pl. 13 coul. / 38 × 50 / 38 × 36 / MISE 980 PP 33 / Archives ZUBER, n° 1453

261 France / 1815 / Fond satin Imp. pl. 10 coul. Veloutage et repiquage / 48 × 66 / 25 × 48 / UCAD HH 2713

262 France / 1815–1820 / Fond mat. Imp. pl. 9 coul. / 54,5 × 63,5 / Verso manuscrit: «1609» / UCAD HH 938 A / Paris, 1967, n° 274

263 France / 1815–1825 / Fond mat. Imp. pl. 21 coul. / 43 × 63 / 43 × 63 / BF 457

264 Manufacture ZUBER / 1820 / Fond satin. Imp. pl. 24 coul. Veloutage et repiquage / 27 × 49 / 27 × 49 / MISE 980 PP 35 / Archives ZUBER n° 1830

265 Manufacture ZUBER ? / 1820 env. / Fond mat. Imp. pl. 11 coul. Veloutage et repiquage / 32 × 59 / 32 × 47 / UCAD HH 2759

266 MERY / 1820 / Fond mat. Imp. pl. 15 coul. / 17 × 52 / 16,5 × 47 / Recto, manuscrit: «Vas . . . (?) Méry Del. 1820» / UCAD HH 2649

267 France / 1820 env. / Fond mat. Imp. pl. 8 coul. Veloutage et repiquage / 26 × 45 / 26 × 27 / UCAD HH 2424

268 France / 1820 env. / Fond mat. Imp. pl. 9 coul. Veloutage et repiquage / 24 × 46 / UCAD HH 2426

269 France / 1820 env. / Fond mat. Imp. pl. 9 coul. Veloutage et repiquage / 24 × 47 / 23,5 × 47 / UCAD HH 2428

257 France / 1810–1820 / Matt ground. Original design 12 col. / 25,5 × 48 / 23,5 × 23,5 / UCAD HH 2626

258 France / 1810–1820 / Matt ground. Block-print 23 col. Flocking and over-printing / 37 × 46 / UCAD HH 2651

259 France / 1810–1820 / Block-print 12 col. / 22,5 × 47 / 22,5 × 23,5 / UCAD HH 2652

260 Manufacture ZUBER / 1815 / Matt ground. Block-print 13 col. / 38 × 50 / 38 × 36 / MISE 980 PP 33 / Archives ZUBER, n° 1453

261 France / 1815 / Satin ground. Block-print 10 col. Flocking and over-printing / 48 × 66 / 25 × 48 / UCAD HH 2713

262 France / 1815–1820 / Matt ground. Block-print 9 col. / 54,5 × 63,5 / Verso, inscribed: '1609' / UCAD HH 938 A / Paris, 1967, n° 274

263 France / 1815–1825 / Matt ground. Block-print 21 col. / 43 × 63 / 43 × 63 / BF 457

264 Manufacture ZUBER / 1820 / Satin ground; Block-print 24 col. Flocking and over-printing / 27 × 49 / 27 × 49 / MISE 980 PP 35 / Archives ZUBER n° 1830

265 Manufacture ZUBER? / 1820 env. / Matt ground. Block-print 11 col. Flocking and over-printing / 32 × 59 / 32 × 47 / UCAD HH 2759

266 MERY / 1820 / Matt ground. Block-print 15 col. / 17 × 52 / 16,5 × 47 / Recto, inscribed: 'Vas . . . (?) Méry Del. 1820' / UCAD HH 2649

267 France / 1820 env. / Matt ground. Block-print 8 col. Flocking and over-printing / 26 × 45 / 26 × 27 / UCAD HH 2424

268 France / 1820 env. / Matt ground. Block-print 9 col. Flocking and over-printing / 24 × 46 / UCAD HH 2426

269 France / 1820 env. / Matt ground. Block-print 9 col. Flocking and over-printing / 24 × 47 / 23,5 × 47 / UCAD HH 2428

257 Frankreich / 1810–1820 / Matter Grund. Originalentwurf, 12 Farben / 25,5 × 48 / 23,5 × 23,5 / UCAD HH 2626

258 Frankreich / 1810–1820 / Matter Grund. Handdruck, 23 Farben. Veloutiert und repiquiert / 37 × 46 / UCAD HH 2651

259 Frankreich / 1810–1820 / Handdruck, 12 Farben / 22,5 × 47 / 22,5 × 23,5 / UCAD HH 2652

260 Manufaktur ZUBER / 1815 / Matter Grund. Handdruck, 13 Farben / 38 × 50 / 38 × 36 / MISE 980 PP 33 / Archives Zuber Nr. 1453

261 Frankreich / 1815 / Satinierter Grund. Handdruck, 10 Farben. Veloutiert und repiquiert / 48 × 66 / 25 × 48 / UCAD HH 2713

262 Frankreich / 1815–1820 / Matter Grund. Handdruck, 9 Farben / 54,5 × 63,5 / Rückseitig beschriftet: »1609« / UCAD HH 938 A / Paris, 1967, Nr. 274

263 Frankreich / 1815–1820 / Matter Grund. Handdruck, 21 Farben / 43 × 63 / 43 × 63 / BF 457

264 Manufaktur ZUBER / 1820 / Satinierter Grund. Handdruck, 24 Farben. Veloutiert und repiquiert / 27 × 49 / 27 × 49 / MISE 980 PP 35 / Archives Zuber Nr. 1830

265 Manufaktur ZUBER ? / Um 1820 / Matter Grund. Handdruck, 11 Farben. Veloutiert und repiquiert / 32 × 59 / 32 × 47 / UCAD HH 2759

266 MERY / 1820 / Matter Grund. Handdruck, 15 Farben / 17 × 52 / 16,5 × 47 / Vorderseite beschriftet: »Vas . . . (?) Méry Del. 1820« / UCAD HH 2649

267 Frankreich / Um 1820 / Matter Grund. Handdruck, 8 Farben. Veloutiert und repiquiert / 26 × 45 / 26 × 27 / UCAD HH 2424

268 Frankreich / Um 1820 / Matter Grund. Handdruck, 9 Farben. Veloutiert und repiquiert / 24 × 46 / UCAD HH 2426

269 Frankreich / Um 1820 / Matter Grund. Handdruck, 9 Farben. Veloutiert und repiquiert / 24 × 47 / 23,5 × 47 / UCAD HH 2428

257

259

258

260

261

265

262

266

268

263

264

267

269

270 France / 1820 env. / Fond mat. Imp. pl. 8 coul. Veloutage et repiquage / 24 × 48 / UCAD HH 2431

271 France / 1820 env. / Fond mat. Imp. pl. 13 coul. Veloutage et repiquage / 25 × 38 / 23,5 × 37,5 / UCAD HH 2434

272 France / 1820 env. / Fond satin. Imp. pl. 9 coul. / 18 × 38 / 17 × 26,5 / UCAD HH 2444

273 France / 1820–1825 / Fond mat. Imp. pl. 7 coul. Irisé, Veloutage et repiquage / 27 × 48 / 23,5 × 48 / UCAD HH 2423

274 France / 1820–1825 / Fond mat. Imp. pl. 3 coul. Veloutage et repiquage / 16 × 47 / 15,5 × 15,5 / UCAD HH 2450

275 France / 1820–1825 / Fond satin. Imp. pl. 13 coul. / 16 × 52 / 16 × 46,5 / UCAD HH 2460

276 France / 1820–1825 / Fond satin. Imp. pl. 15 coul. Veloutage et repiquage / 23 × 48 / UCAD HH 2466

277 France / 1820–1825 / Fond satin. Imp. pl. 11 coul. / 25 × 49 / 23 × 47 / UCAD HH 2479

278 France / 1820–1830 / Fond satin. Imp. pl. 3 coul. Veloutage et repiquage / 24 × 48 / UCAD HH 2399

279 France / 1820–1830 / Fond satin. Imp. pl. 28 coul. Poudre dorée, veloutage et repiquage / 26 × 45 / UCAD HH 2435

280 France / 1820–1825 / Fond satin. Dessin original 11 coul. / 23,5 × 50 / 23,5 × 24 / UCAD HH 2527

281 Manufacture JACQUEMART et BENARD / 1822 / Fond mat. Imp. pl. 13 coul. Veloutage et repiquage / 56 × 82 / 27 × 53 / Verso, manuscrit: «4809–1822» / UCAD HH 2716

282 Manufacture JACQUEMART et BENARD / 1825 / Fond mat. Imp. pl. 24 coul. Veloutage et repiquage / 56 × 103 / 37 × 26 / Verso, manuscrit: «1825», «5535 imprimé chez Jacquemart en 1825» / UCAD HH 2717

283 France / 1825–1830 / Fond satin. Imp. pl. 8 coul. Veloutate et repiquage / 23 × 42 / UCAD HH 2396

284 KUPFER / Manufacture ZUBER / 1826 / Imp. pl. 16 coul. Veloutage et repiquage / 48 × 47 / MISE 826 2289 A et B PP / Archives Zuber n° 2289

270 France / 1820 env. / Matt ground. Block-print 8 col. Flocking and overprinting / 24 × 48 / UCAD HH 2431

271 France / 1820 env. / Matt ground. Block-print 13 col. Flocking and over-printing / 25 × 38 / 23,5 × 37,5 / UCAD HH 2434

272 France / 1820 env. / Satin ground. Block-print 9 col. / 18 × 38 / 17 × 26,5 / UCAD HH 2444

273 France / 1820–1825 / Matt ground. Block-print 7 col. Irisé, flocking and over-printing / 27 × 48 / 23,5 × 48 / UCAD HH 2423

274 France / 1820–1825 / Matt ground. Block-print 3 col. Flocking and over-printing / 16 × 47 / 15,5 × 15,5 / UCAD HH 2450

275 France / 1820–1825 / Satin ground. Block-print 13 col. / 16 × 52 / 16 × 46,5 / UCAD HH 2460

276 France / 1820–1825 / Satin ground. Block-print 15 col. Flocking and over-printing / 23 × 48 / UCAD HH 2466

277 France / 1820–1825/ Satin ground. Block-print 11 col. / 25 × 49 / 23 × 47 / UCAD HH 2479

278 France / 1820–1830 / Satin ground. Block-print 3 col. Flocking and over-printing / 24 × 48 / UCAD HH 2399

279 France / 1820–1830 / Satin ground. Block-print 28 col. Gold dust, flocking and over-printing / 26 × 45 / UCAD HH 2435

280 France / 1820–1825 / Satin ground. Original design 11 col. / 23,5 × 50 / 23,5 × 24 / UCAD HH 2527

281 Manufacture JACQUEMART et BENARD / 1822 / Matt ground. Block-print 13 col. Flocking and over-printing / 56 × 82 / 27 × 53 / Verso, inscribed: '4809–1822' / UCAD HH 2716

282 Manufacture JACQUEMART et BENARD / 1825 / Matt ground. Block-print 24 col. Flocking and over-printing / 56 × 103 / 37 × 26 / Verso, inscribed: '1825', '5535 imprimé chez Jacquemart en 1825' / UCAD HH 2717

283 France / 1825–1830 / Satin ground. Block-print 8 col. Flocking and over-printing / 23 × 42 / UCAD HH 2396

284 KUPFER / Manufacture ZUBER / 1826 / Block-print 16 col. Flocking and over-printing / 48 × 47 / MISE 826 2289 A and B PP / Archives Zuber n° 2289

270 Frankreich / Um 1820 / Matter Grund. Handdruck, 8 Farben. Veloutiert und repiquiert / 24 × 48 / UCAD HH 2431

271 Frankreich / Um 1820 / Matter Grund. Handdruck, 13 Farben. Veloutiert und repiquiert / 25 × 38 / 23,5 × 37,5 / UCAD HH 2434

272 Frankreich / Um 1820 / Satinierter Grund. Handdruck, 9 Farben / 18 × 38 / 17 × 26,5 / UCAD HH 2444

273 Frankreich / 1820–1825 / Matter Grund. Handdruck, 7 Farben. Irisiert, veloutiert und repiquiert / 27 × 48 / 23,5 × 48 / UCAD HH 2423

274 Frankreich / 1820–1825 / Matter Grund. Handdruck, 3 Farben. Veloutiert und repiquiert / 16 × 47 / 15,5 × 15,5 / UCAD HH 2450

275 Frankreich / 1820–1825 / Satinierter Grund. Handdruck, 13 Farben / 16 × 52 / 16 × 46,5 / UCAD HH 2460

276 Frankreich / 1820–1825 / Satinierter Grund. Handdruck, 15 Farben. Veloutiert und repiquiert / 23 × 48 / UCAD HH 2466

277 Frankreich / 1820–1825 / Satinierter Grund. Handdruck, 11 Farben / 25 × 49 / 23 × 47 / UCAD HH 2479

278 Frankreich / 1820–1830 / Satinierter Grund. Handdruck, 3 Farben. Veloutiert und repiquiert / 24 × 48 / UCAD 2399

279 Frankreich / 1820–1830 / Satinierter Grund. Handdruck, 28 Farben. Goldstaub. Veloutiert und repiquiert / 26 × 45 / UCAD HH 2435

280 Frankreich / 1820–1825 / Satinierter Grund. Originalentwurf, 11 Farben / 23,5 × 50 / 23,5 × 24 / UCAD HH 2527

281 Manufaktur JACQUEMART et BENARD / 1822 / Matter Grund. Handdruck, 13 Farben. Veloutiert und repiquiert / 56 × 82 / 27 × 53 / Rückseitig beschriftet: »4809–1822« / UCAD HH 2716

282 Manufaktur JACQUEMART et BENARD / 1825 / Matter Grund. Handdruck, 24 Farben. Veloutiert und repiquiert / 56 × 103 / 37 × 26 / Rückseitig beschriftet: »1825«, »5535 imprimé chez Jacquemart en 1825« / UCAD HH 2717

283 Frankreich / 1825–1830 / Satinierter Grund. Handdruck, 8 Farben. Veloutiert und repiquiert / 23 × 42 / UCAD HH 2396

284 KUPFER / Manufaktur ZUBER / 1826 / Handdruck, 16 Farben. Veloutiert und repiquiert / 48 × 47 / MISE 826 2289 A und B PP / Archives Zuber Nr. 2289

270

271

272

274

275

273

278

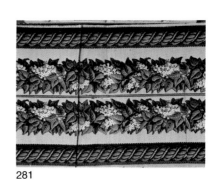

281

276

280

277

282

279

283

284

285 Joseph Laurent MALAINE / Manufacture ZUBER / 1826 / Imp. pl. 29 coul. Veloutage et repiquage / 23,5 × 48 / MISE 826 2357 PP / Archives Zuber n° 2357

286 Manufacture ZUBER / 1828 / Fond taille douce. Imp. pl. 9 coul. Veloutage et repiquage / 22 × 47,5 / 22 × 23,5 / MISE 980 PP 65 / Archives Zuber TD 65

287 TERNE / Manufacture ZUBER / 1829 / Imp. pl. 14 coul. Irisés / 25 × 51 / 24 × 51 / MISE 829 2777 PP / Archives Zuber n° 2777

288 Manufacture ZUBER / 1830 / Fond taille douce. Imp. pl. 4 coul. Veloutage et repiquage / 23 × 47 / 23 × 23,5 / MISE 980 PP 67 / Archives Zuber TD 67

289 France / 1830 env. / Fond mat. Imp. pl. 20 coul. Veloutage et repiquage / 47 × 68,5 / 40 × 64,5 / UCAD HH 951

Fruits

290 Joseph-Laurent MALAINE ? / Manufacture ZUBER ? / 1800–1805 / Fond mat. Imp. pl. 16 coul. / 27 × 66 / 26 × 54,5 / Recto, manuscrit: «Zuber père 1er Malaine» / UCAD HH 2640

291 Joseph-Laurent MALAINE ? / Manufacture ZUBER ? / 1800–1805 / Fond mat. Imp. pl. 16 coul. / 24 × 66 / 24 × 54 / Recto, manuscrit: »Zuber père. Malaine» / UCAD HH 2655

292 France / 1800–1805 / Fond mat. Imp. pl. 4 coul. Veloutage / 19 × 48 / 18 × 22 / UCAD HH 2667

293 Manufacture JACQUEMART et BENARD / 1800–1810 / Fond mat. Imp. pl. 11 coul. Veloutage et repiquage / 26 × 31 / UCAD HH 440

294 Manufacture JACQUEMART et BENARD / 1800–1810 / Fond mat. Imp. pl. 10 coul. / 37,5 × 56 / 37,5 × 56 / UCAD HH 334

295 Manufacture JACQUEMART et BENARD / 1800–1810 / Fond mat. Imp. pl. 6 coul. / 13,5 × 27 / 13,5 × 27 / UCAD HH 367

285 Joseph Laurent MALAINE / Manufacture ZUBER / 1826 / Block-print 29 col. Flocking and over-printing / 23,5 × 48 / MISE 826 2357 PP / Archives Zuber n° 2357

286 Manufacture ZUBER / 1828 / Metal engraved ground. Block-print 9 col. Flocking and over-printing / 22 × 47,5 / 22 × 23,5 / MISE 980 PP 65 / Archives Zuber n° TD 65

287 TERNE / Manufacture ZUBER / 1829 / Block-print 13 col. *Irisé* / 25 × 51 / 24 × 51 / MISE 829 2777 PP / Archives Zuber n° 2777

288 Manufacture ZUBER / 1830 / Metal engraved ground. Block-print 4 col. Flocking and over-printing / 23 × 47 / 23 × 23,5 / MISE 980 PP 67 / Archives Zuber n° TD67

289 France / 1830 env. / Matt ground. Block-print 20 col. Flocking and over-printing / 47 × 68,5 / 40 × 64,5 / UCAD HH 951

Fruit

290 Joseph-Laurent MALAINE? / Manufacture ZUBER? / 1800–1805 / Matt ground. Block-print 16 col. / 27 × 66 / 26 × 54,5 / Recto, inscribed: 'Zuber père ler Malaine' / UCAD HH 2640

291 Joseph-Laurent MALAINE? / Manufacture ZUBER? / 1800–1805 / Matt ground. Block-print 16 col. / 24 × 66 / 24 × 54 / Recto, inscribed: 'Zuber père. Malaine' / UCAD HH 2655

292 France / 1800–1805 / Matt ground. Block-print 4 col. Flocking / 19 × 48 / 18 × 22 / / UCAD HH 2667

293 Manufacture JACQUEMART et BENARD / 1800–1810 / Matt ground. Block-print 11 col. Flocking and over-printing / 26 × 31 / UCAD HH 440

294 Manufacture JACQUEMART et BENARD / 1800–1810 / Matt ground. Block-print 10 col. / 37,5 × 56 / 37,5 × 56 / UCAD HH 334

295 Manufacture JACQUEMART et BENARD / 1800–1810 / Matt ground. Block-print 6 col. / 13,5 × 27 / 13,5 × 27 / UCAD HH 367

285 Joseph-Laurent MALAINE / Manufaktur ZUBER / 1826 / Handdruck, 29 Farben. Veloutiert und repiquiert / 23,5 × 48 / MISE 826 2357 PP / Archives Zuber Nr. 2357

286 Manufaktur ZUBER / 1828 / Kupferstich-Grund. Handdruck, 9 Farben. Veloutiert und repiquiert / 22 × 47,5 / 22 × 23,5 / MISE 980 PP 65 / Archives Zuber Nr. TD 65

287 TERNE / Manufaktur ZUBER / 1829 / Handdruck, 14 Farben. Irisiert / 25 × 51 / 24 × 51 / MISE 829 2777 PP / Archives Zuber Nr. 2777

288 Manufaktur ZUBER / 1830 / Kupferstich-Grund. Handdruck, 4 Farben. Veloutiert und repiquiert / 23 × 47 / 23 × 23,5 / MISE 980 PP 67 / Archives Zuber Nr. TD 67

289 Frankreich / Um 1830 / Matter Grund. Handdruck, 20 Farben. Veloutiert und repiquiert / 47 × 68,5 / 40 × 64,5 / UCAD HH 951

Früchte

290 Joseph-Laurent MALAINE ? / Manufaktur ZUBER ? / 1800–1805 / Matter Grund. Handdruck, 16 Farben / 27 × 66 / 26 × 54,5 / Vorderseite beschriftet: »Zuber père ler Malaine« / UCAD HH 2640

291 Joseph-Laurent MALAINE ? / Manufaktur ZUBER ? / 1800–1805 / Matter Grund. Handdruck, 16 Farben / 24 × 66 / 24 × 54 / Vorderseite beschriftet: »Zuber père. Malaine« / UCAD HH 2655

292 Frankreich / 1800–1805 / Matter Grund. Handdruck, 4 Farben. Veloutiert / 19 × 48 / 18 × 22 / UCAD HH 2667

293 Manufaktur JACQUEMART et BENARD / 1800–1810 / Matter Grund. Handdruck, 11 Farben. Veloutiert und repiquiert / 26 × 31 / UCAD HH 440

294 Manufaktur JACQUEMART et BENARD / 1800–1810 / Matter Grund. Handdruck, 10 Farben / 37,5 × 56 / 37,5 × 56 / UCAD HH 334

295 Manufaktur JACQUEMART et BENARD / 1800–1810 / Matter Grund. Handdruck, 6 Farben / 13,5 × 27 / 13,5 × 27 / UCAD HH 367

285

287

286

289

288

294

290

291

293

292

295

Feuillages

296 France / 1805–1810 / Fond mat. Dessin original 3 coul. / 37 × 53 / 23,5 × 47,5 / UCAD HH 2534

297 France / 1810 env. / Fond mat. Dessin original 6 coul. / 27 × 49 / 23,5 × 23,5 / UCAD HH 2562

298 France / 1815–1820 / Fond mat. Imp. pl. 8 coul. Veloutage et repiquage / 25 × 44 / 25 × 26,5 / UCAD HH 2420

299 France / 1815–1820 / Fond satin. Dessin original 8 coul. / 24,5 × 52 / 23,5 × 16 / UCAD HH 2596

300 France / 1820–1825 / Fond mat. Imp. pl. 3 coul. Veloutage et repiquage / 23 × 48 / UCAD HH 2402 B

301 France / 1820–1825 / Fond satin. Imp. pl. 3 coul. Veloutage et repiquage / 24 × 49 / UCAD HH 2407

302 France / 1820–1825 / Fond mat. Imp. pl. 4 coul. Veloutage et repiquage / 18 × 46 / 17,5 × 24 / UCAD HH 2443

303 France / 1820–1825 / Fond satin. Imp. pl. 6 coul. Veloutage et repiquage / 48 × 58 / 24 × 48 / UCAD HH 2714

304 Manufacture ZUBER / 1828 / Fond satin. Imp. pl. 6 coul. Irisé, Veloutage et repiquage / 34 × 48 / 33 × 48 / UCAD 29827 / Paris, 1967, N° 245

305 Manufacture ZUBER / 1828 / Fond satin. Imp. taille douce 1 coul. Imp. pl. 3 coul. Veloutage et repiquage / 92 × 47 / 37 × 47 / UCAD 29824 / Paris, 1967, N° 247

Stucs végétaux

306 France / 1800–1805 / Fond mat. Imp. pl. 4 coul. / 36 × 58 / 17 × 17 / UCAD HH 2666

307 Manufacture JACQUEMART et BENARD / 1800–1810 / Fond mat. Imp. pl. 5 coul. / 28 × 55 / 27,5 × 55 / UCAD HH 326

308 Manufacture JACQUEMART et BENARD / 1800–1810 / Fond mat. Imp. pl. 4 coul. / 22 × 38 / 6 × 18,5 / UCAD HH 356

309 Manufacture JACQUEMART et BENARD / 1800–1810 / Fond mat. Imp. pl. 7 coul. / 26,5 × 38 / 18 × 5 / UCAD HH 357 A

310 Manufacture JACQUEMART et BENARD / 1800–1810 / Fond mat. Imp. pl. 7 coul. / 25,5 × 32,5 / UCAD HH 460

Foliage

296 France / 1805–1810 / Matt ground. Original design 3 col. / 37 × 53 / 23,5 × 47,5 / UCAD HH 2534

297 France / 1810 env. Matt ground. Original design 6 col. / 27 × 49 / 23,5 × 23,5 / UCAD HH 2562

298 France / 1815–1820 / Matt ground. Block-print 8 col. Flocking and over-printing / 25 × 44 / 25 × 26,5 / UCAD HH 2420

299 France / 1815–1820 / Satin ground. Original design 8 col. / 24,5 × 52 / 23,5 × 16 / UCAD HH 2596

300 France / 1820–1825 / Matt ground. Block-print 3 col. Flocking and over-printing / 23 × 48 / UCAD HH 2402 B

301 France / 1820–1825 / Satin ground. Block-print 3 col. Flocking and over-printing / 24 × 49 / UCAD HH 2407

302 France / 1820–1825 / Matt ground. Block-print 4 col. Flocking and over-printing / 18 × 46 / 17,5 × 24 / UCAD HH 2443

303 France / 1820–1825 / Satin ground. Block-print 6 col. Flocking and over-printing / 48 × 58 / 24 × 48 / UCAD HH 2714

304 Manufacture ZUBER / 1828 / Satin ground. Block-print 6 col. *Irisé*, flocking and over-printing / 34 × 48 / 33 × 48 / UCAD 29827 / Paris, 1967, N° 245

305 Manufacture ZUBER / 1828 / Satin ground. Metal engr. 1 col. Block-print 3 col. Flocking and over-printing / 92 × 47 / 37 × 47 / UCAD 29824 / Paris, 1967, N° 247

Plant Stucco

306 France / 1800–1805 / Matt ground. Block-print 4 col. / 36 × 58 / 17 × 17 / UCAD HH 2666

307 Manufacture JACQUEMART et BENARD / 1800–1810 / Matt ground. Block-print 5 col. / 28 × 55 / 27,5 × 55 / UCAD HH 326

308 Manufacture JACQUEMART et BENARD / 1800–1810 / Matt ground. Block-print 4 col. / 22 × 38 / 6 × 18,5 / UCAD HH 356

309 Manufacture JACQUEMART et BENARD / 1800–1810 / Matt ground. Block-print 7 col. / 26,5 × 38 / 18 × 5 / UCAD HH 357 A

310 Manufacture JACQUEMART et BENARD / 1800–1810 / Matt ground. Block-print 7 col. / 25,5 × 32,5 / UCAD HH 460

Blattwerk

296 Frankreich / 1805–1810 / Matter Grund. Originalentwurf, 3 Farben / 37 × 53 / 23,5 × 47,5 / UCAD HH 2534

297 Frankreich / Um 1810 / Matter Grund. Originalentwurf, 6 Farben / 27 × 49 / 23,5 × 23,5 / UCAD HH 2562

298 Frankreich / 1815–1820 / Matter Grund. Handdruck, 8 Farben. Veloutiert und repiquiert / 25 × 44 / 25 × 26,5 / UCAD HH 2420

299 Frankreich / 1815–1820 / Satinierter Grund. Originalentwurf, 8 Farben / 24,5 × 52 / 23,5 × 16 / UCAD HH 2596

300 Frankreich / 1820–1825 / Matter Grund. Handdruck, 3 Farben. Veloutiert und repiquiert / 23 × 48 / UCAD HH 2402 B

301 Frankreich / 1820–1825 / Satinierter Grund. Handdruck, 3 Farben. Veloutiert und repiquiert / 24 × 49 / UCAD HH 2407

302 Frankreich / 1820–1825 / Matter Grund. Handdruck, 4 Farben. Veloutiert und repiquiert / 18 × 46 / 17,5 × 24 / UCAD HH 2443

303 Frankreich / 1820–1825 / Satinierter Grund. Handdruck, 6 Farben. Veloutiert und repiquiert / 48 × 58 / 24 × 48 / UCAD HH 2714

304 Manufaktur ZUBER / 1828 / Satinierter Grund. Handdruck, 6 Farben. Irisiert, veloutiert und repiquiert / 34 × 48 / 33 × 48 / UCAD 29827 / Paris, 1967, Nr. 245

305 Manufaktur ZUBER / 1828 / Satinierter Grund. Druck mittels Kupferstichwalze, 1 Farbe. Handdruck, 3 Farben. Veloutiert und repiquiert / 92 × 47 / 37 × 47 / UCAD 29824 / Paris, 1967, Nr. 247

Pflanzlicher Stuck

306 Frankreich / 1800–1805 / Matter Grund. Handdruck, 4 Farben / 36 × 58 / 17 × 17 / UCAD HH 2666

307 Manufaktur JACQUEMART et BENARD / 1800–1810 / Matter Grund. Handdruck, 5 Farben / 28 × 55 / 27,5 × 55 / UCAD HH 326

308 Manufaktur JACQUEMART et BENARD / 1800–1810 / Matter Grund. Handdruck, 4 Farben / 22 × 38 / 6 × 18,5 / UCAD HH 356

309 Manufaktur JACQUEMART et BENARD / 1800–1810 / Matter Grund. Handdruck, 7 Farben / 26,5 × 38 / 18 × 5 / UCAD HH 357 A

310 Manufaktur JACQUEMART et BENARD / 1800–1810 / Matter Grund. Handdruck, 7 Farben / 25,5 × 32,5 / UCAD HH 460

296

297

301

299

298

300

306

304

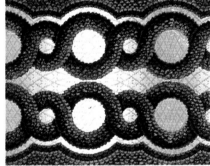

303

305

302

307

308

310

309

311 France / 1800–1810 / Fond mat. Imp. pl. 11 coul. / 9,5 × 28,5 / 8 × 24 / UCAD HH 2515

312 France / 1800–1810 / Fond mat. Dessin original 5 coul. / 25,5 × 34,5 / 12 × 7,5 / UCAD HH 2547

313 France / 1800–1810 / Fond mat. Dessin original 5 coul. / 14,5 × 48 / 12,5 × 8 / UCAD HH 2558

314 France / 1800–1810 / Fond mat. Dessin original 7 coul. / 25 × 47 / 23 × 47 / UCAD HH 2597

315 Manufacture MADER ? / 1800–1810 / Fond mat. Imp. pl. 10 coul. / 27,5 × 59 / 13 × 13 / Recto manuscrit: «Mader» / UCAD HH 2659

316 France / 1810 env. / Fond mat Dessin original 5 coul. / 28 × 46,5 / 26 × 46 / UCAD HH 2638

317 France / 1810–1815 / Fond mat. Imp. pl. 8 coul. Veloutage et repiquage / 24 × 42 / UCAD HH 2394

318 France / 1810–1815 / Fond mat. Imp. pl. 11 coul. Veloutage et repiquage / 26 × 49 / UCAD HH 2414

319 France / 1810–1815 / Fond mat. Imp. pl. 6 coul. Veloutage / 24 × 47 / 23,5 × 26,5 / UCAD HH 2415

320 France / 1810–1815 / Fond mat. Imp. pl. 5 coul. / 11 × 44 / 11 × 3,7 / UCAD HH 2471

321 France / 1810–1815 / Fond mat. Imp. pl. 8 coul. / 14 × 35 / 13,5 × 17,5 / UCAD HH 2475

322 France / 1810–1820 / Fond satin. Imp. pl. 2 coul. Veloutage et repiquage / 24 × 48 / UCAD HH 2398

323 France / 1810–1815 / Fond mat. Dessin original 7 coul. / 50 × 53 / 46,5 × 46,5 / Recto, manuscrit: «2019. Réduire l'ombre portée de la guirlande, réduire l'ombre portée de la cimaise» / UCAD HH 2734

324 France / 1810–1815 / Fond mat. Imp. pl. 5 coul. / 46,5 × 68 / 46,5 × 59 / UCAD HH 2737

325 France / 1810–1820 / Fond satin. Dessin original 6 coul. / 48,5 × 37 / 48 × 24 / UCAD HH 2622

311 France / 1800–1810 / Matt ground. Block-print 11 col. / 9,5 × 28,5 / 8 × 24 / UCAD HH 2515

312 France / 1800–1810 / Matt ground. Original design 5 col. / 25,5 × 34,5 / 12 × 7,5 / UCAD HH 2547

313 France / 1800–1810 / Matt ground. Original design 5 col. / 14,5 × 48 / 12,5 × 8 / UCAD HH 2558

314 France / 1800–1810 / Matt ground. Original design 7 col. / 25 × 47 / 23 × 47 / UCAD HH 2597

315 Manufacture MADER? / 1800–1810 / Matt ground. Block-print 10 col. / 27,5 × 59 / 13 × 13 / Recto, inscribed: 'Mader' / UCAD HH 2659

316 France / 1810 env. / Matt ground. Original design 5 col. / 28 × 46,5 / 26 × 46 / UCAD HH 2638

317 France / 1810–1815 / Matt ground. Block-print 8 col. Flocking and over-printing / 24 × 42 / UCAD HH 2394

318 France / 1810–1815 / Matt ground. Block-print 11 col. Flocking and over-printing / 26 × 49 / UCAD HH 2414

319 France / 1810–1815 / Matt ground. Block-print 6 col. Flocking / 24 × 47 / 23,5 × 26,5 / UCAD HH 2415

320 France / 1810–1815 / Matt ground. Block-print 5 col. / 11 × 44 / 11 × 3,7 / UCAD HH 2471

321 France / 1810–1815 / Matt ground. Block-print 8 col. / 14 × 35 / 13,5 × 17,5 / UCAD HH 2475

322 France / 1810–1820 / Satin ground. Block-print 2 col. Flocking and over-printing / 24 × 48 / UCAD HH 2398

323 France / 1810–1815 / Matt ground. Original design 7 col. / 50 × 53 / 46,5 × 46,5 / Recto, inscribed: '2019. Réduire l'ombre portée de la guirlande, réduire l'ombre portée de la cimaise'. / UCAD HH 2734

324 France / 1810–1815 / Matt ground. Block-print 5 col. / 46,5 × 68 / 46,5 × 59 / UCAD HH 2737

325 France / 1810–1820 / Satin ground. Original design 6 col. / 48,5 × 37 / 48 × 24 / UCAD HH 2622

311 Frankreich / 1800–1810 / Matter Grund. Handdruck, 11 Farben / 9,5 × 28,5 / 8 × 24 / UCAD HH 2515

312 Frankreich / 1800–1810 / Matter Grund. Originalentwurf, 5 Farben / 25,5 × 34,5 / 12 × 7,5 / UCAD HH 2547

313 Frankreich / 1800–1810 / Matter Grund. Originalentwurf, 5 Farben / 14,5 × 48 / 12,5 × 8 / UCAD HH 2558

314 Frankreich / 1800–1810 / Matter Grund. Originalentwurf, 7 Farben / 25 × 47 / 23 × 47 / UCAD HH 2597

315 Manufaktur MADER ? / 1800–1810 / Matter Grund. Handdruck, 10 Farben / 27,5 × 59 / 13 × 13 / Vorderseite beschriftet: »Mader« / UCAD HH 2659

316 Frankreich / Um 1810 / Matter Grund. Handdruck, 5 Farben / 28 × 46,5 / 26 × 46 / UCAD HH 2638

317 Frankreich / 1810–1815 / Matter Grund. Handdruck, 8 Farben. Veloutiert und repiquiert / 24 × 42 / UCAD HH 2394

318 Frankreich / 1810–1815 / Matter Grund. Handdruck, 11 Farben. Veloutiert und repiquiert / 26 × 49 / UCAD HH 2414

319 Frankreich / 1810–1815 / Matter Grund. Handdruck, 6 Farben. Veloutiert / 24 × 47 / 23,5 × 26,5 / UCAD HH 2415

320 Frankreich / 1810–1815 / Matter Grund. Handdruck, 5 Farben / 11 × 44 / 11 × 3,7 / UCAD HH 2471

321 Frankreich / 1810–1815 / Matter Grund. Handdruck, 8 Farben / 14 × 35 / 13,5 × 17,5 / UCAD HH 2475

322 Frankreich / 1810–1820 / Satinierter Grund. Handdruck, 2 Farben. Veloutiert und repiquiert / 24 × 48 / UCAD HH 2398

323 Frankreich / 1810–1815 / Matter Grund. Originalentwurf, 7 Farben / 50 × 53 / 46,5 × 46,5 / Vorderseite beschriftet: »2019. Réduire l'ombre portée de la guirlande, réduire l'ombre portée de la cimaise« / UCAD HH 2734

324 Frankreich / 1810–1815 / Matter Grund. Handdruck, 5 Farben / 46,5 × 68 / 46,5 × 59 / UCAD HH 2737

325 Frankreich / 1810–1820 / Satinierter Grund. Originalentwurf, 6 Farben / 48,5 × 37 / 48 × 24 / UCAD HH 2622

311

313

312

317

315

314

316

318

319

320

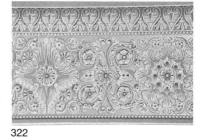

321

322

323

324

325

326 France / 1815 env. / Fond mat. Imp. pl. 6 coul. / 26 × 34 / 26 × 24,5 / UCAD HH 2438

327 France / 1815–1820 / Fond mat. Imp. pl. 11 coul. Veloutage et repiquage / 23 × 40 / UCAD HH 2395

328 France / 1815–1820 / Fond mat. Imp. pl. 11 coul. Feuille d'argent, veloutage et repiquage / 26 × 45 / UCAD HH 2411

329 France / 1815–1820 / Fond satin. Imp. pl. 3 coul. Veloutage et repiquage / 27 × 48 / 27 × 23,5 / UCAD HH 2417

330 France / 1815–1820 / Fond mat. Imp. pl. 12 coul. Veloutage / 48 × 27 / 27 × 13,5 / UCAD HH 2418

331 France / 1815–1820 / Fond mat. Imp. pl. 9 coul. / 27 × 45 / 26 × 24 / UCAD HH 2419

332 France / 1815–1820 / Fond mat. Imp. pl. 3 coul. Veloutage et repiquage / 22 × 45 / UCAD HH 2436

333 France / 1815–1820 / Fond mat. Imp. pl. 8 coul. Veloutage et repiquage / 25 × 39 / 25 × 6,5 / UCAD HH 2437

334 France / 1815–1820 / Fond mat. Imp. pl. 10 coul. Veloutage et repiquage / 14 × 43 / 13 × 18 / UCAD HH 2452

335 France / 1815–1820 / Fond satin. Imp. pl. 1 coul. / 33 × 54 / 32 × 54 / UCAD HH 2454

336 France / 1815–1820 / Fond mat Imp. pl. 7 coul. / 22 × 49 / 22 × 38 / UCAD HH 2469

337 France / 1820 env. / Fond mat. Imp. pl. 8 coul. Feuille d'argent, veloutage et repiquage / 13 × 38 / 13 × 3,8 / UCAD HH 2462

338 France/ 1820–1825 / Fond mat. Imp. pl. 4 coul. / 18 × 51 / UCAD HH 2446

339 LAPEYRE / Manufacture ZUBER / 1826 / Fond mat. Imp. pl. 7 coul. / 23 × 35 / 23 × 23,5 / MISE 826 2309 PP / Archives ZUBER, n° 2309

340 TERNE / Manufacture ZUBER / 1832 / Fond mat. Imp. pl. 5 coul. / 50 × 50 / A: 33 × 50. B: 15,5 × 50 / MISE 2797 / Archives Zuber, n° 2797

341 France / 1850 env. / Fond mat. Imp. pl. 7 coul. Poudre d'or et feuille d'or / A: 94 × 70. B: 96 × 67. C 93 × 68 / UCAD HH 2774 ABC

326 France / 1815 env. / Matt ground. Block-print 6 col. / 26 × 34 / 26 × 24,5 / UCAD HH 2438

327 France / 1815–1820 / Matt ground. Block-print 11 col. Flocking and over-printing / 23 × 40 / UCAD HH 2395

328 France / 1815–1820 / Matt ground. Block-print 11 col. Silver leaf, flocking and over-printing / 26 × 45 / UCAD HH 2411

329 France / 1815–1820 / Satin ground. Block-print 3 col. Flocking and over-printing / 27 × 48 / 27 × 23,5 / UCAD HH 2417

330 France / 1815–1820 / Matt ground. Block-print 12 col. Flocking / 48 × 27 / 27 × 13,5 / UCAD HH 2418

331 France / 1815–1820 / Matt ground. Block-print 9 col. / 27 × 45 / 26 × 24 / UCAD HH 2419

332 France / 1815–1820 / Matt ground. Block-print 3 col. Flocking and over-printing / 22 × 45 / UCAD HH 2436

333 France / 1815–1820 / Matt ground. Block-print 8 col. Flocking and over-printing / 25 × 39 / 25 × 6,5 / UCAD HH 2437

334 France / 1815–1820 / Matt ground. Block-print 10 col. Flocking and over-printing / 14 × 43 / 13 × 18 / UCAD HH 2452

335 France / 1815–1820 / Satin ground. Block-print 1 col. / 33 × 54 / 32 × 54 / UCAD HH 2454

336 France / 1815–1820 / Matt ground. Block-print 7 col. / 22 × 49 / 22 × 38 / UCAD HH 2469

337 France / 1820 env. / Matt ground. Block-print 8 col. Silver leaf, flocking and over-printing / 13 × 38 / 13 × 3,8 / UCAD HH 2462

338 France / 1820–1825 / Matt ground. Block-print 4 col. / 18 × 51 / UCAD HH 2446

339 LAPEYRE / Manufacture ZUBER / 1826 / Matt ground. Block-print 7 col. / 23 × 35 / 23 × 23,5 / MISE 826 2309 PP / Archives Zuber, n° 2309

340 TERNE / Manufacture ZUBER / 1832 / Matt ground. Block-print 5 col. / 50 × 50 / A: 33 × 50. B: 15,5 × 50 / MISE 2797 / Archives Zuber, n° 2797

341 France / 1850 env. / Matt ground. Block-print 7 col. Gold dust and gold leaf / A: 94 × 70. B: 96 × 67. C: 93 × 68 / UCAD HH 2774 ABC

326 Frankreich / Um 1815 / Matter Grund. Handdruck, 6 Farben / 26 × 34 / 26 × 24,5 / UCAD HH 2438

327 Frankreich / 1815–1820 / Matter Grund. Handdruck, 11 Farben. Veloutiert und repiquiert / 23 × 40 / UCAD HH 2395

328 Frankreich / 1815–1820 / Matter Grund. Handdruck, 11 Farben. Blattsilber. Veloutiert und repiquiert / 26 × 45 / UCAD HH 2411

329 Frankreich / 1815–1820 / Satinierter Grund. Handdruck, 3 Farben. Veloutiert und repiquiert / 27 × 48 / 27 × 23,5 / UCAD HH 2417

330 Frankreich / 1815–1820 / Matter Grund. Handdruck, 12 Farben. Veloutiert / 48 × 27 / 27 × 13,5 / UCAD HH 2418

331 Frankreich / 1815–1820 / Matter Grund. Handdruck, 9 Farben / 27 × 45 / 26 × 24 / UCAD HH 2419

332 Frankreich / 1815–1820 / Matter Grund. Handdruck, 3 Farben. Veloutiert und repiquiert / 22 × 45 / UCAD HH 2436

333 Frankreich / 1815–1820 / Matter Grund. Handdruck, 8 Farben. Veloutiert und repiquiert / 25 × 39 / 25 × 6,5 / UCAD HH 2437

334 Frankreich / 1815–1820 / Matter Grund. Handdruck, 10 Farben. Veloutiert und repiquiert / 14 × 43 / 13 × 18 / UCAD HH 2452

335 Frankreich / 1815–1820 / Satinierter Grund. Handdruck, 1 Farbe / 33 × 54 / 32 × 54 / UCAD HH 2454

336 Frankreich / 1815–1820 / Matter Grund. Handdruck, 7 Farben / 22 × 49 / 22 × 38 / UCAD HH 2469

337 Frankreich / Um 1820 / Matter Grund. Handdruck, 8 Farben. Blattsilber. Veloutiert und repiquiert / 13 × 38 / 13 × 3,8 / UCAD HH 2462

338 Frankreich / 1820–1825 / Matter Grund. Handdruck, 4 Farben / 18 × 51 / UCAD HH 2446

339 LAPEYRE / Manufaktur ZUBER / 1826 / Matter Grund. Handdruck, 7 Farben / 23 × 35 / 23 × 23,5 / MISE 826 2309 PP / Archives Zuber Nr. 2309

340 TERNE / Manufaktur ZUBER / 1832 / Matter Grund. Handdruck, 5 Farben / 50 × 50 / A: 33 × 50. B: 15,5 × 50 / MISE 2797 / Archives Zuber Nr. 2797

341 Frankreich / Um 1850 / Matter Grund. Handdruck, 7 Farben. Goldstaub und Blattgold / A: 94 × 70. B: 96 × 67. C: 93 × 68 / UCAD HH 2774 A, B, C

326

327

328

329

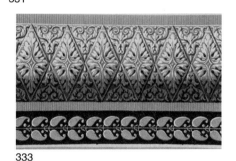

331

330

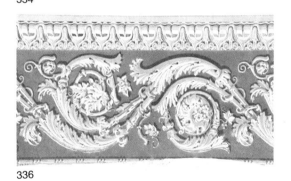

332

333

335

334

338

336

337

339

340

341

Corniches

342 France / 1805–1810 / Fond mat. Imp. pl. 8 coul. / 46 × 48 / 48 × 7 / UCAD HH 2709

343 France / 1810 env. / Fond mat. Imp. pl. 9 coul. / 40 × 47 / 40 × 12 / UCAD HH 2710

344 France / 1815 env. / Fond mat. Imp. pl. 5 coul. / 47 × 65 / UCAD HH 2708

Ballustrades

345 France / 1825–1830 / Fond mat. Imp. pl. 3 coul. / 50 × 68 / 46 × 11,5 / UCAD HH 956

346 Manufacture JACQUEMART et BENARD / 1830 / Fond mat. Imp. pl. 8 coul. / 56 × 82 / 51,5 × 12,5 / Verso, manuscrit: «6019 (1830) J. & B. (Jacquemart) » / UCAD HH 2776

Gothique

347 France / 1820–1825 / Fond satin. Imp. pl. 6 coul. Veloutage et repiquage / 47 × 47 / 47 × 23,5 / UCAD HH 2485

348 ZIPELIUS / Manufacture ZUBER / 1833 / Fond mat. Imp. pl. 7 coul. Poudre dorée, veloutage et repiquage / 54 × 40 / 47 × 23,5 / Mise 980 PP 668 / Archives ZUBER, n° 2887

349 ZIPELIUS / Manufacture ZUBER / 1842 / Fond lissé. Imp. pl. 9 coul. Veloutage et repiquage / 25 × 63 / 21,5 × 54 / MISE 980 PP 672 / Archives ZUBER, n° 3571

Stucs rocaille

350 France / 1840–1845 / Fond mat. Imp. pl. 8 coul. Veloutage et repiquage / 25,5 × 54,5 / 25,5 × 25,5 / UCAD HH 2727

351 France / 1840–1850 / Imp. pl. 7 coul. Veloutage et repiquage / 27 × 53 / 26 × 46,5 / UCAD HH 2724

352 France / 1845 env. / Fond satin. Imp. pl. 4 coul. Poudre dorée, veloutage et repiquage / 15 × 48 / 15 × 47 / UCAD HH 2730

353 France / 1845 env. / Fond lissé. Imp. pl. 9 coul. Veloutage et repiquage / 52 × 17 / 16 × 13,5 / UCAD HH 2726

354 France / 1845 env. / Imp. pl. 11 coul. Poudre dorée, veloutage et repiquage / 50 × 70 / 47 × 32 / UCAD HH 2731

Cornices

342 France / 1805–1810 / Matt ground. Block-print 8 col. / 46 × 48 / 48 × 7 / UCAD HH 2709

343 France / 1810 env. / Matt ground. Block-print 9 col. / 40 × 47 / 40 × 12 / UCAD HH 2710

344 France / 1815 env. / Matt ground. Block-print 5 col. / 47 × 65 / UCAD HH 2708

Balustrades

345 France / 1825–1830 / Matt ground. Block-print 3 col. / 50 × 68 / 46 × 11,5 / UCAD HH 956

346 Manufacture JACQUEMART et BENARD / 1830 / Matt ground. Block-print 8 col. / 56 × 82 / 51,5 × 12,5 / Verso, inscribed: '6019 (1830) J. & B. (Jacquemart)' / UCAD HH 2776

Gothic Designs

347 France / 1820–1825 / Satin ground. Block-print 6 col. Flocking and over-printing / 47 × 47 / 47 × 23,5 / UCAD HH 2485

348 ZIPELIUS / Manufacture ZUBER / 1833 / Matt ground. Block-print 7 col. Gold dust, flocking and over-printing / 54 × 40 / 47 × 23,5 / MISE 980 PP 668 / Archives Zuber, n° 2887

349 ZIPELIUS / Manufacture ZUBER / 1842 / Smooth ground. Block-print 9 col. Flocking and over-printing / 25 × 63 / 21,5 × 54 / MISE 980 PP 672 / Archives Zuber, n° 3571

Rocaille Stucco

350 France / 1840–1845 / Matt ground. Block-print 8 col. Flocking and over-printing / 25,5 × 54,5 / 25,5 × 25,5 / UCAD HH 2727

351 France / 1840–1850 / Block-print 7 col. Flocking and over-printing / 27 × 53 / 26 × 46,5 / UCAD HH 2724

352 France / 1845 env. / Satin ground. Block-print 4 col. Gold dust, flocking and over-printing / 15 × 48 / 15 × 47 / UCAD HH 2730

353 France / 1845 env. / Smooth ground. Block-print 9 col. Flocking and over-printing / 52 × 17 / 16 × 13,5 / UCAD HH 2726

354 France / 1845 env. / Block-print 11 col. Gold dust, flocking and over-printing / 50 × 70 / 47 × 32 / UCAD HH 2731

Gesimse

342 Frankreich / 1805–1810 / Matter Grund. Handdruck, 8 Farben / 46 × 48 / 48 × 7 / UCAD HH 2709

343 Frankreich / Um 1810 / Matter Grund. Handdruck, 9 Farben / 40 × 47 / 40 × 12 / UCAD HH 2710

344 Frankreich / Um 1815 / Matter Grund. Handdruck, 5 Farben / 47 × 65 / UCAD HH 2708

Balustraden

345 Frankreich / 1825–1830 / Matter Grund. Handdruck, 3 Farben / 50 × 68 / 46 × 11,5 / UCAD HH 956

346 Manufaktur JACQUEMART et BENARD / 1830 / Matter Grund. Handdruck, 8 Farben / 56 × 82 / 51,5 × 12,5 / Rückseitig beschriftet: »6019 (1830) J. & B. (Jacquemart)« / UCAD HH 2776

Gotische Muster

347 Frankreich / 1820–1825 / Satinierter Grund. Handdruck, 6 Farben. Veloutiert und repiquiert / 47 × 47 / 47 × 23,5 / UCAD HH 2485

348 ZIPELIUS / Manufaktur ZUBER / 1833 / Matter Grund. Handdruck, 7 Farben. Goldstaub. Veloutiert und repiquiert / 54 × 40 / 47 × 23,5 / MISE 980 PP 668 / Archives Zuber Nr. 2887

349 ZIPELIUS / Manufaktur ZUBER / 1842 / Geglätteter Grund. Handdruck, 9 Farben. Veloutiert und repiquiert / 25 × 63 / 21,5 × 54 / MISE 980 PP 672 / Archives Zuber Nr. 3571

Rocaille-Stuck

350 Frankreich / 1840–1845 / Matter Grund. Handdruck, 8 Farben. Veloutiert und repiquiert / 25,5 × 54,5 / 25,5 × 25,5 / UCAD HH 2727

351 Frankreich / 1840–1850 / Handdruck, 7 Farben. Veloutiert und repiquiert / 27 × 53 / 26 × 46,5 / UCAD HH 2724

352 Frankreich / Um 1845 / Satinierter Grund. Handdruck, 4 Farben. Goldstaub. Veloutiert und repiquiert / 15 × 48 / 15 × 47 / UCAD HH 2730

353 Frankreich / Um 1845 / Geglätteter Grund. Handdruck, 9 Farben. Veloutiert und repiquiert / 52 × 17 / 16 × 13,5 / UCAD HH 2726

354 Frankreich / Um 1845 / Handdruck, 11 Farben. Goldstaub. Veloutiert und repiquiert / 50 × 70 / 47 × 32 / UCAD HH 2731

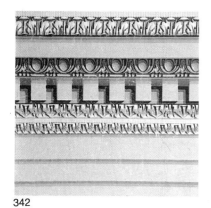

342

343

344

345

346

347

349

348

351

352

350

354

353

Cabochons

355 Manufacture JACQUEMART et BE-NARD? / 1825? / Fond satin. Imp. pl. 14 coul. / 28 × 67,5 / 26 × 53,5 / UCAD HH 2739

356 France / 1830–1840 / Fond satin. Imp. pl. 7 coul. Veloutage et repiquage / 23 × 47 / UCAD HH 2397

357 France / 1840 env. / Fond mat. Imp. pl. 22 coul. Irisés. / 50 × 220 / 44,5 × 213 / UCAD 29670

358 France / 1840 env. / Fond satin. Imp. pl. 27 coul. / 64 × 106 / 64 × 106 / UCAD 29696 / Paris, 1967, n° 283

359 France / 1840–1845 / Fond mat. Imp. pl. 8 coul. / 49 × 60 / 47 × 47,5 / UCAD HH 131

360 Martin POLISCH / 1840–1845 / Fond mat. Imp. pl. 27 coul. Poudre dorée, veloutage et re-piquage / 70 × 53 / BF. 363

Plumes

361 Manufacture JACQUEMART et BENARD / 1800–1810 / Fond mat. Imp. pl. 11 coul. / 11 × 29 / 11 × 8 / UCAD HH 409

362 LAGRENEE / Manufacture ZUBER / 1827 / Imp. pl. 23 coul. Veloutage et repiquage / 31,5 × 48,5 / MISE 827 2363 PP / Archives Zu-ber n° 2363

363 LAPEYRE / Manufacture ZUBER / 1827 / Fond mat. Imp. pl. 15 coul. / 25,5 × 36 / 23,5 × 23,5 / MISE 829 2769 PP / Archives Zu-ber n° 2769

364 France / 1830–1840 / Fond mat. Imp. pl. 4 coul. Veloutage et repiquage / 25 × 48 / UCAD HH 2385

365 France / 1830 env. / Fond mat. Imp. pl. 17 coul. Poudre dorée, veloutage et repiquage / 54 × 56,5 / 54 × 54 / UCAD HH 948

Bois

366 Manufacture JACQUEMART et BENARD / 1836 / Fond façon bois, satin. Imp. pl. 2 coul. / 50 × 82 / 46,5 × 61,5 / Verso, manuscrit: «Imi-tation de bois imprimé chez Jacquemart vers 1836» / UCAD HH 2718

Brass Nails

355 Manufacture JACQUEMART et BE-NARD? / 1825? / Satin ground. Block-print 14 col. / 28 × 67,5 / 26 × 53,5 / UCAD HH 2739

356 France / 1830–1840 / Satin ground. Block-print 7 col. Flocking and over-printing / 23 × 47 / UCAD HH 2397

357 France / 1840 env. / Matt ground. Block-print 22 col. *Irisé* / 50 × 220 / 44,5 × 213 / UCAD 29670

358 France / 1840 env. / Satin ground. Block-print 27 col. / 64 × 106 / 64 × 106 / UCAD 29696 / Paris, 1967, n° 283

359 France / 1840–1845 / Matt ground. Block-print 8 col. / 49 × 60 / 47 × 47,5 / UCAD HH 131

360 Martin POLISCH / 1840–1845 / Matt ground. Block-print 27 col. Gold dust, flocking and over-printing / 70 × 53 / BF 363

Feathers

361 Manufacture JACQUEMART et BENARD / 1800–1810 / Matt ground. Block-print 11 col. / 11 × 29 / 11 × 8 / UCAD HH 409

362 LAGRENEE / Manufacture ZUBER / 1827 / Block-print 23 col. Flocking and over-print-ing / 31,5 × 48,5 / MISE 827 2363 PP / Ar-chives Zuber n° 2363

363 LAPEYRE / Manufacture ZUBER / 1827 / Matt ground. Block-print 15 col. / 25,5 × 36 / 23,5 × 23,5 / MISE 829 2769 PP / Archives Zu-ber n° 2769

364 France / 1830–1840 / Matt ground. Block-print 4 col. Flocking and over-printing / 25 × 48 / UCAD HH 2385

365 France / 1830 env. / Matt ground. Block-print 17 col. Gold dust, flocking and over-print-ing / 54 × 56,5 / 54 × 54 / UCAD HH 948

Wood

366 Manufacture JACQUEMART et BENARD / 1836 / Imitation wood, satin ground, Block-print 2 col. / 50 × 82 / 46,5 × 61,5 / Verso, in-scribed: 'Imitation de bois imprimé chez Jacquemart vers 1836' / UCAD HH 2718

Cabochons

355 Manufaktur JACQUEMART et BENARD ? / 1825 ? / Satinierter Grund. Handdruck, 14 Farben / 28 × 67,5 / 26 × 53,5 / UCAD HH 2739

356 Frankreich / 1830–1840 / Satinierter Grund. Handdruck, 7 Farben. Veloutiert und repiquiert / 23 × 47 / UCAD HH 2397

357 Frankreich / Um 1840 / Matter Grund. Handdruck, 22 Farben. Irisiert / 50 × 220 / 44,5 × 213 / UCAD 29670

358 Frankreich / Um 1840 / Satinierter Grund. Handdruck, 27 Farben / 64 × 106 / 64 × 106 / UCAD 29696 / Paris, 1967, Nr. 283

359 Frankreich / 1840–1845 / Matter Grund. Handdruck, 8 Farben / 49 × 60 / 47 × 47,5 / UCAD HH 131

360 Martin POLISCH / 1840–1845 / Matter Grund. Handdruck, 27 Farben. Goldstaub. Ve-loutiert und repiquiert / 70 × 53 / BF 363

Federn

361 Manufaktur JACQUEMART et BENARD / 1800–1810 / Matter Grund. Handdruck, 11 Farben / 11 × 29 / 11 × 8 / UCAD HH 409

362 LAGRENEE / Manufaktur ZUBER / 1827 / Handdruck, 23 Farben. Veloutiert und repi-quiert / 31,5 × 48,5 / MISE 827 2363 PP / Ar-chives Zuber Nr. 2363

363 LAPEYRE / Manufaktur ZUBER / 1827 / Matter Grund. Handdruck, 15 Farben / 25,5 × 36 / 23,5 × 23,5 / MISE 829 2769 PP / Archi-ves Zuber Nr. 2769

364 Frankreich / 1830–1840 / Matter Grund. Handdruck, 4 Farben. Veloutiert und repi-quiert / 25 × 48 / UCAD HH 2385

365 Frankreich / Um 1830 / Matter Grund. Handdruck, 17 Farben. Goldstaub. Veloutiert und repiquiert / 54 × 56,5 / 54 × 54 / UCAD HH 948

Holzimitation

366 Manufaktur JACQUEMART et BENARD / 1836 / Satinierter, holzartiger Grund. Hand-druck, 2 Farben / 50 × 82 / 46,5 × 61,5 / Rück-seitig beschriftet: »Imitation de bois imprimé chez Jacquemart vers 1836« / UCAD HH 2718

355

360

356

357

358

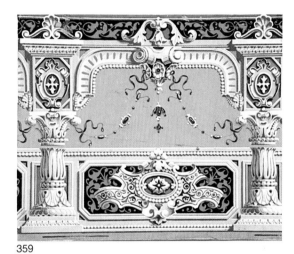

359

361

362

363

364

365

366

Géométriques

367 France / 1800–1810 / Fond mat. Dessin original 6 coul. / 19 × 42 / 12,5 × 13 / UCAD HH 2604

368 FRANCE / 1800–1810 / Fond mat. Imp. pl. 2 coul. Veloutage / 12 × 39 / 11,5 × 13,5 / UCAD HH 2668

369 France / 1810 env. / Fond mat. Dessin original 4 coul. Tissu satin collé/ 26,5 × 50 / 23,5 × 23,5 / UCAD HH 2531

370 France / 1820 env. / Fond mat. Imp. pl. 1 coul. Veloutage / 12 × 46 / 12 × 1,5 / UCAD HH 2480

371 TERNE et KÜPFER / Manufacture ZUBER / 1828 / Fond taille douce. Imp. pl. 4 coul. Veloutage et repiquage / 28,5 × 41 / 22,5 × 8 / MISE 828 2537 PP / Archives Zuber n° 2537

372 France / 1840–1845 / Fond satin. Imp. pl. 3 coul. Veloutage et poudre d'or. Gauffrage pointe de diamants / 12 × 67 / 12 × 36,5 / UCAD HH 2725

373 France / 1840–1845 / Fond mat. Imp. pl. 2 coul. Veloutage et poudre d'or. Gauffrage en pointe de diamants / 15 × 54 / 15 × 23,5 / UCAD HH 2733

Rubans et cordelettes

374 France / 1800–1805 / Fond satin. Imp. pl. 6 coul. Veloutage et repiquage / 25 × 66 / 25 × 8 / UCAD HH 2677 A

375 Manufacture JACQUEMART et BENARD / 1800–1805 / Fond mat. Imp. pl. 12 coul. / 55 × 42 / 27 × 42 / UCAD HH 340

376 Manufacture JACQUEMART et BENARD / 1800–1810 / Fond mat. Imp. pl. 11 coul. / 26,5 × 56 / UCAD HH 332 A

377 Manufacture JACQUEMART et BENARD / 1800–1810 / Fond satin. Dessin original 10 coul. / 31 × 24 / UCAD HH 394

378 France / 1805–1810 / Fond satin. Dessin original 7 coul. / 30 × 47 / 22,5 × 12 / UCAD HH 2600

Geometric Designs

367 France / 1800–1810 / Matt ground. Original design 6 col. / 19 × 42 / 12,5 × 13 / UCAD HH 2604

368 FRANCE / 1800–1810 / Matt ground. Block-print 2 col. Flocking / 12 × 39 / 11,5 × 13,5 / UCAD HH 2668

369 France / 1810 env. / Matt ground. Original design 4 col. Satin fabric collage / 26,5 × 50 / 23,5 × 23,5 / UCAD HH 2531

370 France / 1820 env. / Matt ground. Block-print 1 col. Flocking / 12 × 46 / 12 × 1,5 / UCAD HH 2480

371 TERNE et KUPFER / Manufacture ZUBER / 1828 / Metal engraved ground. Block-print 4 col. Flocking and over-printing / 28,5 × 41 / 22,5 × 8 / MISE 828 2537 PP / Archives Zuber n° 2537

372 France / 1840–1845 / Satin ground. Block-print 3 col. Flocking, gold dust and light embossing in diamond point / 12 × 67 / 12 × 36,5 / UCAD HH 2725

373 France / 1840–1845 / Matt ground. Block-print 2 col. Flocking, gold dust and light embossing in diamond point / 15 × 54 / 15 × 23,5 / UCAD HH 2733

Ribbons and Cording

374 France / 1800–1805 / Satin ground. Block-print 6 col. Flocking and over-printing / 25 × 66 / 25 × 8 / UCAD HH 2677 A

375 Manufacture JACQUEMART et BENARD / 1800–1805 / Matt ground. Block-print 12 col. / 55 × 42 / 27 × 42 / UCAD HH 340

376 Manufacture JACQUEMART et BENARD / 1800–1810 / Matt ground. Block-print 11 col. / 26,5 × 56 / UCAD HH 332 A

377 Manufacture JACQUEMART et BENARD / 1800–1810 / Satin ground. Original design 10 col. / 31 × 24 / UCAD HH 394

378 France / 1805–1810 / Satin ground. Original design 7 col. /30 × 47 / 22,5 × 12 / UCAD HH 2600

Geometrische Muster

367 Frankreich / 1800–1810 / Matter Grund. Originalentwurf, 6 Farben / 19 × 42 / 12,5 × 13 / UCAD HH 2604

368 Frankreich / 1800–1810 / Matter Grund. Handdruck, 2 Farben. Veloutiert / 12 × 39 / 11,5 × 13,5 / UCAD HH 2668

369 Frankreich / Um 1810 / Matter Grund. Originalentwurf, 4 Farben. Aufgeklebtes Satingewebe / 26,5 × 50 / 23,5 × 23,5 / UCAD HH 2531

370 Frankreich / Um 1820 / Matter Grund. Handdruck, 1 Farbe. Veloutiert / 12 × 46 / 12 × 1,5 / UCAD HH 2480

371 TERNE und KUPFER / Manufaktur ZUBER / 1828 / Kupferstich-Grund. Handdruck, 4 Farben. Veloutiert und repiquiert / 28,5 × 41 / 22,5 × 8 / MISE 828 2537 PP / Archives Zuber Nr. 2537

372 Frankreich / 1840–1845 / Satinierter Grund. Handdruck, 3 Farben. Veloutiert und Goldstaub. »Pointe de diamant«-Gaufrierung / 12 × 67 / 12 × 36,5 / UCAD HH 2725

373 Frankreich / 1840–1845 / Matter Grund. Handdruck, 2 Farben. Veloutiert und Goldstaub. »Pointe de diamant«-Gaufrierung / 15 - × 54 / 15 × 23,5 / UCAD HH 2733

Bänder und Schnüre

374 Frankreich / 1800–1805 / Satinierter Grund. Handdruck, 6 Farben. Veloutiert und repiquiert / 25 × 66 / 25 × 8 / UCAD HH 2677 A

375 Manufaktur JACQUEMART et BENARD / 1800–1805 / Matter Grund. Handdruck, 12 Farben / 55 × 42 / 27 × 42 / UCAD HH 340

376 Manufaktur JACQUEMART et BENARD / 1800–1810 / Matter Grund. Handdruck, 11 Farben / 26,5 × 56 / UCAD HH 332 A

377 Manufaktur JACQUEMART et BENARD / 1800–1810 / Satinierter Grund. Originalentwurf, 10 Farben / 31 × 24 / UCAD HH 394

378 Frankreich / 1805–1810 / Satinierter Grund. Originalentwurf, 7 Farben / 30 × 47 / 22,5 × 12 / UCAD HH 2600

367

368

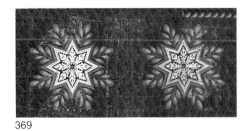

369

371

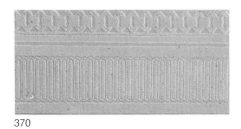

370

372

375

373

374

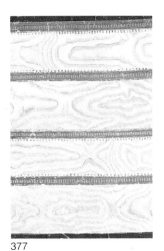

377

376

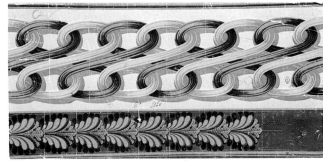

378

379 France / 1810 env. / Fond mat. Dessin original 8 coul. / 13 × 47 / 12 × 23 / UCAD HH 2631

380 France / 1810–1815 / Fond satin. Dessin original 9 coul. / 27,5 × 50,5 / 23,5 × 11,5 / UCAD HH 2578 B

381 France / 1810–1815 / Fond mat. Imp. pl. 5 coul. / 26,5 × 65 / 26 × 54 / UCAD HH 2674

382 France / 1820–1825 / Fond satin irisé. Imp. pl. 5 coul. Veloutage et repiquage / 24 × 49 / 24 × 24 / UCAD HH 2519

383 France / 1815–1820 / Fond mat. Imp. pl. 4 coul. Veloutage et repiquage / 24 × 46 / UCAD HH 2389

384 France / 1815–1820 / Fond mat. Imp. pl. 3 coul. Veloutage et repiquage / 24 × 47 / 22,5 × 47,5 / UCAD HH 2416

385 France / 1815–1825 / Fond mat. Imp. pl. 3 coul. Veloutage et repiquage / 15,5 × 41 / 15,5 × 23,5 / UCAD HH 2453

386 France / 1820–1825 / Fond mat. Imp. pl. 9 coul. / 13 × 50 / 12 × 13,5 / UCAD HH 2467

387 France / 1820–1825 / Fond mat. Imp. pl. 3 coul. / 12 × 46 / 10,5 × 12 / UCAD HH 2473

388 France / 1820–1825 / Fond mat. Imp. pl. 7 coul. Veloutage et repiquage / 12,5 × 42 / 12,5 × 15 / UCAD HH 2477

389 Manufacture ZUBER / 1829 / Fond mat. Imp. pl. 8 coul. Veloutage / 30 × 49 / 11,5 × 4,5 / MISE 829 2581 PP / Archives ZUBER N° 2581

390 A. MERII / France / 1829 / Fond mat. Dessin original 12 coul. / 36 × 52 / 22,5 × 23,5 / Recto, manuscrit: «A. Mérii, rue de Montreuil 49 le 27 Juillet 1829» / UCAD HH 2619

379 France / 1810 env. / Matt ground. Original design 8 col. / 13 × 47 / 12 × 23 / UCAD HH 2631

380 France / 1810–1815 / Satin ground. Original design 9 col. / 27,5 × 50,5 / 23,5 × 11,5 / UCAD HH 2578 B

381 France / 1810–1815 / Matt ground. Block-print 5 col. / 26,5 × 65 / 26 × 54 / UCAD HH 2674

382 France / 1820–1825 / Satin *irisé* ground. Block-print 5 col. Flocking and over-printing / 24 × 49 / 24 × 24 / UCAD HH 2519

383 France / 1815–1820 / Matt ground. Block-print 4 col. Flocking and over-printing / 24 × 46 / UCAD HH 2389

384 France / 1815–1820 / Matt ground. Block-print 3 col. Flocking and over-printing / 24 × 47 / 22,5 × 47,5 / UCAD HH 2416

385 France / 1815–1825 / Matt ground. Block-print 3 col. Flocking and over-printing / 15,5 × 41 / 15,5 × 23,5 / UCAD HH 2453

386 France / 1820–1825 / Matt ground. Block-print 9 col. / 13 × 50 / 12 × 13,5 / UCAD HH 2467

387 France / 1820–1825 / Matt ground. Block-print 3 col. / 12 × 46 / 10,5 × 12 / UCAD HH 2473

388 France / 1820–1825 / Matt ground. Block-print 7 col. Flocking and over-printing / 12,5 × 42 / 12,5 × 15 / UCAD HH 2477

389 Manufacture ZUBER / 1829 / Matt ground. Block-print 8 col. Flocking / 30 × 49 / 11,5 × 4,5 / MISE 829 2581 PP / Archives Zuber N° 2581

390 A. MERII / France / 1829 / Matt ground. Original design 12 col. / 36 × 52 / 22,5 × 23,5 / Recto, inscribed: 'A. Mérii, rue de Montreuil 49 le 27 Juillet 1829' / UCAD HH 2619

379 Frankreich / Um 1810 / Matter Grund. Originalentwurf, 8 Farben / 13 × 47 / 12 × 23 / UCAD HH 2631

380 Frankreich / 1810–1815 / Satinierter Grund. Originalentwurf, 9 Farben / 27,5 × 50,5 / 23,5 × 11,5 / UCAD HH 2578 B

381 Frankreich / 1810–1815 / Matter Grund. Handdruck, 5 Farben / 26,5 × 65 / 26 × 54 / UCAD HH 2674

382 Frankreich / 1820–1825 / Satinierter, irisierter Grund. Handdruck, 5 Farben. Veloutiert und repiquiert / 24 × 49 / 24 × 24 / UCAD HH 2519

383 Frankreich / 1815–1820 / Matter Grund. Handdruck, 4 Farben. Veloutiert und repiquiert / 24 × 46 / UCAD HH 2389

384 Frankreich / 1815–1820 / Matter Grund. Handdruck, 3 Farben. Veloutiert und repiquiert / 24 × 47 / 22,5 × 47,5 / UCAD HH 2416

385 Frankreich / 1815–1825 / Matter Grund. Handdruck, 3 Farben. Veloutiert und repiquiert / 15,5 × 41 / 15,5 × 23,5 / UCAD HH 2453

386 Frankreich / 1820–1825 / Matter Grund. Handdruck, 9 Farben / 13 × 50 / 12 × 13,5 / UCAD HH 2467

387 Frankreich / 1820–1825 / Matter Grund. Handdruck, 3 Farben / 12 × 46 / 10,5 × 12 / UCAD HH 2473

388 Frankreich / 1820–1825 / Matter Grund. Handdruck, 7 Farben. Veloutiert und repiquiert / 12,5 × 42 / 12,5 × 15 / UCAD HH 2477

389 Manufaktur ZUBER / 1829 / Matter Grund. Handdruck, 8 Farben. Veloutiert / 30 × 49 / 11,5 × 4,5 / MISE 829 2581 PP / Archives Zuber Nr. 2581

390 A. MERII / 1829 / Matter Grund. Originalentwurf, 12 Farben / 36 × 52 / 22,5 × 23,5 / Vorderseite beschriftet: »A. Mérii, rue de Montreuil 49 le 27 juillet 1829« / UCAD HH 2619

379

381

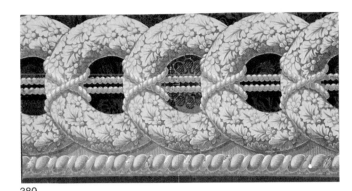

380

382

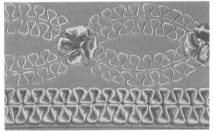

383

384

389

386

385

387

388

390

Draperies

391 France / 1800 env. / Fond mat. Imp. pl. 8 coul. Veloutage / 28 × 62 / UCAD HH 2698

392 France / 1800–1805 / Fond satin. Imp. pl. 8 coul. / 47 × 66 / A: 34 × 24. B 12 × 23,5 / UCAD HH 2700 A et B

393 Manufacture JACQUEMART et BENARD / 1805–1810 / Fond mat. Imp. pl. 13 coul. / 53 × 58,5 / 52,5 × 53 / UCAD HH 342

394 Manufacture JACQUEMART et BENARD / 1805–1810 / Fond mat. Imp. pl. 17 coul. / 48,5 × 53 / 47 × 53 / UCAD HH 345

395 Manufacture JACQUEMART et BENARD / 1805–1810 / Fond mat. Dessin original 10 coul. / 46 × 55 / 45 × 53 / UCAD HH 351

396 Manufacture JACQUEMART et BENARD / 1805–1810 / Fond mat. Dessin original 10 coul. / 56,5 × 55 / 47 × 48 / UCAD HH 353

397 France / 1805–1810 / Fond mat. Imp. pl. 7 coul. / 48 × 66 / A: 35 × 48. B: 13 × 24 / UCAD HH 2702 A et B

398 France / 1805–1815 / Fond mat. Imp. pl. 11 coul. / 45 × 96 / 24 × 48,5 / UCAD 36 807

399 Manufacture DUFOUR / 1812 env. / Fond mat. Imp. pl. 20 coul. Veloutage et repiquage / 112 × 62 / 54 × 45 / B: 591 / Paris, 1967, n° 116

400 Manufacture DUFOUR / 1812 env. / Fond mat. Imp. pl. 23 coul. Veloutage et repiquage / 55 × 67 / 53 × 54 / UCAD HH 949

401 Manufacture JACQUEMART et BENARD / 1810–1815 / Fond mat. Imp. pl. 26 coul. / 53 × 44 / 53 × 44 / UCAD HH 344

402 France / 1810–1815 / Fond mat. Imp. pl. 8 coul. / 51 × 110 / 48,5 × 48 / UCAD 29 757

403 France / 1810–1815 / Fond mat. Imp. pl. 14 coul. / 57 × 109 / 53,5 × 53,5 / UCAD 36 813

404 France / 1810–1815 / Fond mat. Imp. pl. 18 coul. Veloutage et repiquage / 54 × 109 / 54 × 54 / UCAD 29 806 / FOURNY, 1967, p. 67 n° 10 / Paris, 1967, n° 269

Draperies

391 France / 1800 env. / Matt ground. Block-print 8 col. Flocking / 28 × 62 / UCAD HH 2698

392 France / 1800–1805 / Satin ground. Block-print 8 col. / 47 × 66 / A: 34 × 24. B: 12 × 23,5 / UCAD HH 2700 A and B

393 Manufacture JACQUEMART et BENARD / 1805–1810 / Matt ground. Block-print 13 col. / 53 × 58,5 / 52,5 × 53 / UCAD HH 342

394 Manufacture JACQUEMART et BENARD / 1805–1810 / Matt-ground. Block-print 17 col. / 48,5 × 53 / 47 × 53 / UCAD HH 345

395 Manufacture JACQUEMART et BENARD / 1805–1810 / Matt ground. Original design 10 col. / 46 × 55 / 45 × 53 / UCAD HH 351

396 Manufacture JACQUEMART et BENARD / 1805–1810 / Matt ground. Original design 10 col. / 56,5 × 55 / 47 × 48 / UCAD HH 353

397 France / 1805–1810 / Matt ground. Block-print 7 col. / 48 × 66 / A: 35 × 48. B: 13 × 24 / UCAD HH 2702 A and B

398 France / 1805–1815 / Matt ground. Block-print 11 col. / 45 × 96 / 24 × 48,5 / UCAD 36807

399 Manufacture DUFOUR / 1812 env. / Matt ground. Block-print 20 col. Flocking and over-printing / 112 × 62 / 54 × 45 / BF 591 / Paris, 1967, N° 116

400 Manufacture DUFOUR / 1812 env. / Matt ground. Block-print 23 col. Flocking and over-printing / 55 × 67 / 53 × 54 / UCAD HH 949

401 Manufacture JACQUEMART et BENARD / 1810–1815 / Matt ground. Block-print 26 col. / 53 × 44 / 53 × 44 / UCAD HH 344

402 France / 1810–1815 / Matt ground. Block-print 8 col. / 51 × 110 / 48,5 × 48 / UCAD 29757

403 France / 1810–1815 / Matt ground. Block-print 14 col. / 57 × 109 / 53,5 × 53,5 / UCAD 36813

404 France / 1810–1815 / Matt ground. Block-print 18 col. Flocking and over-printing / 54 × 109 / 54 × 54 / UCAD 29806 / FOURNY, 1967, p. 67 N° 10 / Paris, 1967, N° 269

Draperien

391 Frankreich / Um 1800 / Matter Grund. Handdruck, 8 Farben. Veloutiert / 28 × 62 / UCAD HH 2698

392 Frankreich / 1800–1805 / Satinierter Grund. Handdruck, 8 Farben / 47 × 66 / A: 34 × 24. B: 12 × 23,5 / UCAD HH 2700 A und B

393 Manufaktur JACQUEMART et BENARD / 1805–1810 / Matter Grund. Handdruck, 13 Farben / 53 × 58,5 / 52,5 × 53 / UCAD HH 342

394 Manufaktur JACQUEMART et BENARD / 1805–1810 / Matter Grund. Handdruck, 17 Farben / 48,5 × 53 / 47 × 53 / UCAD HH 345

395 Manufaktur JACQUEMART et BENARD / 1805–1810 / Matter Grund. Originalentwurf, 10 Farben / 46 × 55 / 45 × 53 / UCAD HH 351

396 Manufaktur JACQUEMART et BENARD / 1805–1810 / Matter Grund. Originalentwurf, 10 Farben / 56,5 × 55 / 47 × 48 / UCAD HH 353

397 Frankreich / 1805–1810 / Matter Grund. Handdruck, 7 Farben / 48 × 66 / A: 35 × 48. B: 13 × 24 / UCAD HH 2702 A und B

398 Frankreich / 1805–1815 / Matter Grund. Handdruck, 11 Farben / 45 × 96 / 24 × 48,5 / UCAD 36807

399 Manufaktur DUFOUR / Um 1812 / Matter Grund. Handdruck, 20 Farben. Veloutiert und repiquiert / 112 × 62 / 54 × 45 / BF 591 / Paris, 1967, Nr. 116

400 Manufaktur DUFOUR / Um 1812 / Matter Grund. Handdruck, 23 Farben. Veloutiert und repiquiert / 55 × 67 / 53 × 54 / UCAD HH 949

401 Manufaktur JACQUEMART et BENARD / 1810–1815 / Matter Grund. Handdruck, 26 Farben / 53 × 44 / 53 × 44 / UCAD HH 344

402 Frankreich / 1810–1815 / Matter Grund. Handdruck, 8 Farben / 51 × 110 / 48,5 × 48 / UCAD 29757

403 Frankreich / 1810–1815 / Matter Grund. Handdruck, 14 Farben / 57 × 109 / 53,5 × 53,5 / UCAD 36813

404 Frankreich / 1810–1815 / Matter Grund. Handdruck, 18 Farben. Veloutiert und repiquiert / 54 × 109 / 54 × 54 / UCAD 29806 / FOURNY, 1967, S. 67 Nr. 10 / Paris, 1967, Nr. 269

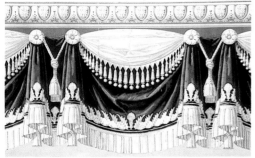

404

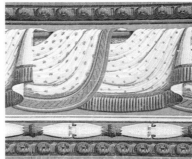

392

397

393

394

395

396

398

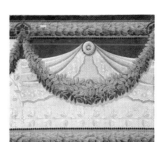

400

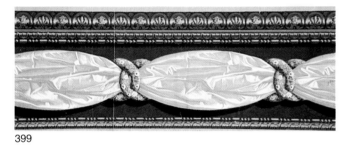

399

401

402

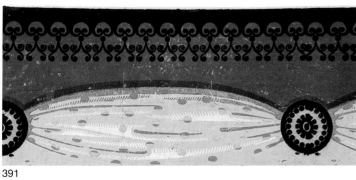

391

403

405 France / 1810–1815 / Fond mat. Imp. pl. 10 coul. / 48 × 66 / UCAD HH 2703 A et B

406 France / 1810–1815 / Fond mat. Imp. pl. 12 coul. Veloutage / 54 × 70 / 53 × 53 / UCAD HH 1989

407 France / 1810–1815 / Fond satin. Imp. pl. 12 coul. / 51 × 68 / UCAD HH 947

408 France / 1810–1820 / Fond satin. Imp. pl. 11 coul. Feuille d'or, veloutage et repiquage / 49,5 × 70 / 49 × 46,5 / UCAD HH 955

409 France / 1815 env. / Fond mat. Imp. pl. 13 coul. / 54,5 × 62 / 54 × 53 / UCAD HH 2740

410 France / 1815 env. / Fond mat. Imp. pl. 13 coul. / 51 × 69 / 43 × 54 / UCAD HH 2754

411 France / 1815–1820 / Fond mat. Dessin original 18 coul. / 55 × 59 / 54 × 54 / BF 1570

412 France / 1815–1820 / Fond mat. Dessin original 6 coul. / 16,5 × 47,5 / 11,5 × 23,5 / UCAD HH 2559

413 France / 1815–1820 / Fond satin. Imp. pl. 15 coul. / 48,5 × 62 / 40 × 53,5 / UCAD HH 2742

414 France / 1815–1820 / Fond mat. Imp. pl. 14 coul. / 47 × 66 / A: 47,5 × 66. B. 48 × 66 / UCAD HH 2704 A et B

415 France / 1820 env. / Fond satin. Dessin original 10 coul. / 32 × 49 / 31 × 16 / UCAD HH 2544

416 France / 1820–1825 / Fond mat. Dessin original 6 coul. / 30,5 × 51,5 / 23,5 × 23,5 / UCAD HH 2588

417 France / 1820–1825 / Fond mat. Dessin original 12 coul. / 25,5 × 48,5 / 23 × 11,5 / UCAD HH 2615

405 France / 1810–1815 / Matt ground. Block-print 10 col. / 48 × 66 / UCAD HH 2703 A and B

406 France / 1810–1815 / Matt ground. Block-print 12 col. Flocking / 54 × 70 / 53 × 53 / UCAD HH 1989

407 France / 1810–1815 / Satin ground. Block-print 12 col. / 51 × 68 / UCAD HH 947

408 France / 1810–1820 / Satin ground. Block-print 11 col. Gold leaf, flocking and over-printing / 49,5 × 70 / 49 × 46,5 / UCAD HH 955

409 France / 1815 env. / Matt ground. Block-print 13 col. / 54,5 × 62 / 54 × 53 / UCAD HH 2740

410 France / 1815 env. / Matt ground. Block-print 13 col. / 51 × 69 / 43 × 54 / UCAD HH 2754

411 France / 1815–1820 / Matt ground. Original design 18 col. / 55 × 59 / 54 × 54 / BF 1570

412 France / 1815–1820 / Matt ground. Original design 6 col. / 16,5 × 47,5 / 11,5 × 23,5 / UCAD HH 2559

413 France / 1815–1820 / Satin ground. Block-print 15 col. / 48,5 × 62 / 40 × 53,5 / UCAD HH 2742

414 France / 1815–1820 / Matt ground. Block-print 14 col. / 47 × 66 / A: 47,5 × 66. B: 48 × 66 / UCAD HH 2704 A and B

415 France / 1820 env. / Satin ground. Original design 10 col. / 32 × 49 / 31 × 16 / UCAD HH 2544

416 France / 1820–1825 / Matt ground. Original design 6 col. / 30,5 × 51,5 / 23,5 × 23,5 / UCAD HH 2588

417 France / 1820–1825 / Matt ground. Original design 12 col. / 25,5 × 48,5 / 23 × 11,5 / UCAD HH 2615

405 Frankreich / 1810–1815 / Matter Grund. Handdruck, 10 Farben / 48 × 66 / UCAD HH 2703 A und B

406 Frankreich / 1810–1815 / Matter Grund. Handdruck, 12 Farben. Veloutiert / 54 × 70 / 53 × 53 / UCAD HH 1989

407 Frankreich / 1810–1815 / Satinierter Grund. Handdruck, 12 Farben / 51 × 68 / UCAD HH 947

408 Frankreich / 1810–1820 / Satinierter Grund. Handdruck, 11 Farben. Blattgold. Veloutiert und repiquiert / 49,5 × 70 / 49 × 46,5 / UCAD HH 955

409 Frankreich / Um 1815 / Matter Grund. Handdruck, 13 Farben / 54,5 × 62 / 54 × 53 / UCAD HH 2740

410 Frankreich / Um 1815 / Matter Grund. Handdruck, 13 Farben / 51 × 69 / 43 × 54 / UCAD HH 2754

411 Frankreich / 1815–1820 / Matter Grund. Originalentwurf, 18 Farben / 55 × 59 / 54 × 54 / BF 1570

412 Frankreich / 1815–1820 / Matter Grund. Originalentwurf, 6 Farben / 16,5 × 47,5 / 11,5 × 23,5 / UCAD HH 2559

413 Frankreich / 1815–1820 / Satinierter Grund. Handdruck, 15 Farben / 48,5 × 62 / 40 × 53,5 / UCAD HH 2742

414 Frankreich / 1815–1820 / Matter Grund. Handdruck, 14 Farben / 47 × 66 / A: 47,5 × 66. B: 48 × 66 / UCAD HH 2704 A und B

415 Frankreich / Um 1820 / Satinierter Grund. Originalentwurf, 10 Farben / 32 × 49 / 31 × 16 / UCAD HH 2544

416 Frankreich / 1820–1825 / Matter Grund. Originalentwurf, 6 Farben / 30,5 × 51,5 / 23,5 × 23,5 / UCAD HH 2588

417 Frankreich / 1820–1825 / Matter Grund. Originalentwurf, 12 Farben / 25,5 × 48,5 / 23 × 11,5 / UCAD HH 2615

405

406

407

408

409

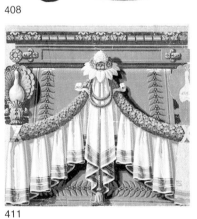

410

411

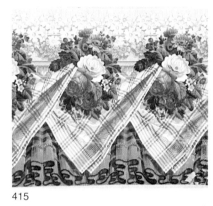

413

415

412

414

416

417

418 France / 1820–1825 / Fond mat. Imp. pl. 11 coul. / 19 × 50 / 16,5 × 42,5 / UCAD HH 2630

419 France / 1820–1825 / Fond satin. Imp. pl. 14 coul. / 49 × 47,5 / A: 26 × 24. B: 21 × 24 / UCAD HH 2743 A B

420 France / 1820–1825 / Fond mat. Dessin original 11 coul. / 52 × 53 / A: 33,5 × 47,5. B: 13,5 × 47,5 / UCAD HH 2756 A B

421 France / 1820–1830 / Fond mat. Imp. pl. 22 coul. Veloutage et repiquage / 51 × 97 / 47 × 47 / BF 535

422 France / 1820–1830 / Fond mat. Imp. pl. 15 coul. Veloutage / 58 × 115 / 54 × 54 / UCAD 29 750 / Paris, 1967, n° 270

423 France / 1825 env. / Fond mat. Imp. pl. 17 coul. / 56,5 × 120 / 56,5 × 48 / UCAD 29 759 / Paris, 1967, H.C.

424 France / 1825–1830 / Fond mat. Imp. pl. 16 coul. / 34 × 50 / UCAD HH 115 / Paris, 1967, n° 266

425 M. Y.? (MERY?) / Manufacture ZUBER / 1826 / Fond mat. Imp. pl. 10 coul. / 47 × 45 MISE 826 2353 a PP / Archives Zuber n° 2353

426 Mry? (MERY?) / Manufacture ZUBER / 1826 / Fond mat. Imp. pl. 14 coul. Veloutage et repiquage / 47 × 47,5 / 47,5 × 47,5 / MISE 826 2365 b PP / Archives ZUBER n° 2365

427 LAPEYRE / Manufacture ZUBER / 1826 / Fond mat. Imp. pl. 22 coul. Veloutage et repiquage / 49 × 69 / 49 × 70 / MISE 826 2375 PP / Archives ZUBER n° 2375

428 France / 1830–1835 / Fond mat. Imp. pl. 16 coul. / 50 × 54 / 48 × 46,5 / UCAD HH 2741 A B

429 Manufacture RIOTTOT / 1840 env. / Fond mat. Imp. pl. 11 coul. Veloutage et repiquage / 53 × 67 / 53 × 53 / UCAD HH 953

430 Manufacture RIOTTOT / 1840 env. / Fond mat. Imp. pl. 14 coul. Veloutage et repiquage / 54 × 68 / 53,5 × 53,5 / UCAD HH 954

418 France / 1820–1825 / Matt ground. Block-print 11 col. / 19 × 50 / 16,5 × 42,5 / UCAD HH 2630

419 France / 1820–1825 / Satin ground. Block-print 14 col. / 49 × 47,5 / A: 26 × 24. B: 21 × 24 / UCAD HH 2743 A B

420 France / 1820–1825 / Matt ground. Original design 11 col. / 52 × 53 / A: 33,5 × 47,5. B: 13,5 × 47,5 / UCAD HH 2756 A B

421 France / 1820–1830 / Matt ground. Block-print 22 col. Flocking and over-printing / 51 × 97 / 47 × 47 / BF 535

422 France / 1820–1830 / Matt ground. Block-print 15 col. Flocking / 58 × 115 / 54 × 54 / UCAD 29 750 / Paris, 1967, n° 270

423 France / 1825 env. / Matt ground. Block-print 17 col. / 56,5 × 120 / 56,5 × 48 / UCAD 29 759 / Paris, 1967, H. C.

424 France / 1825–1830 / Matt ground. Block-print 16 col. / 34 × 50 / UCAD HH 115 / Paris, 1967, n° 266

425 M. Y.? (MERY?) / Manufacture ZUBER / 1826 / Matt ground. Block-print 10 col. / 47 × 45 / MISE 826 2353 a PP / Archives Zuber n° 2353

426 Mry? (MERY?) / Manufacture ZUBER / 1826 / Matt ground. Block-print 14 col. Flocking and over-printing / 47 × 47,5 / 47,5 × 47,5 / MISE 826 2365 b PP / Archives Zuber n° 2365

427 LAPEYRE / Manufacture ZUBER / 1826 / Matt ground. Block-print 22 col. Flocking and over-printing / 49 × 69 / 49 × 70 / MISE 826 2375 PP / Archives Zuber n° 2375

428 France / 1830–1835 / Matt ground. Block-print 16 col. / 50 × 54 / 48 × 46,5 / UCAD HH 2741 A B

429 Manufacture RIOTTOT / 1840 env. / Matt ground. Block-print 11 col. Flocking and over-printing / 53 × 67 / 53 × 53 / UCAD HH 953

430 Manufacture RIOTTOT / 1840 env. / Matt ground. Block-print 14 col. Flocking and over-printing / 54 × 68 / 53,5 × 53,5 / UCAD HH 954

418 Frankreich / 1820–1825 / Matter Grund. Handdruck, 11 Farben / 19 × 50 / 16,5 × 42,5 / UCAD HH 2630

419 Frankreich / 1820–1825 / Satinierter Grund. Handdruck, 14 Farben / 49 × 47,5 / A: 26 × 24. B: 21 × 24 / UCAD HH 2743 A und B

420 Frankreich / 1820–1825 / Matter Grund. Originalentwurf, 11 Farben / 52 × 53 / A: 33,5 × 47,5. B: 13,5 × 47,5 / UCAD HH 2756 A und B

421 Frankreich / 1820–1830 / Matter Grund. Handdruck, 22 Farben. Veloutiert und repiquiert / 51 × 97 / 47 × 47 / BF 535

422 Frankreich / 1820–1830 / Matter Grund. Handdruck, 15 Farben. Veloutiert / 58 × 115 / 54 × 54 / UCAD 29 750 / Paris, 1967, Nr. 270

423 Frankreich / Um 1825 / Matter Grund. Handdruck, 17 Farben / 56,5 × 120 / 56,5 × 48 / UCAD 29 759 / Paris, 1967 (nicht im Katalog)

424 Frankreich / 1825–1830 / Matter Grund. Handdruck, 16 Farben / 34 × 50 / UCAD HH 115 / Paris, 1967, Nr. 266

425 M.Y. ? (MERY ?) / Manufaktur ZUBER / 1826 / Matter Grund. Handdruck, 10 Farben / 47 × 45 / MISE 826 2353 a PP / Archives Zuber Nr. 2353

426 MRY ? (MERY?) / Manufaktur ZUBER / 1826 / Matter Grund. Handdruck, 14 Farben. Veloutiert und repiquiert / 47 × 47,5 / 47,5 × 47,5 / MISE 826 2365 b PP / Archives Zuber Nr. 2365

427 LAPEYRE / Manufaktur ZUBER / 1826 / Matter Grund. Handdruck, 22 Farben. Veloutiert und repiquiert / 49 × 69 / 49 × 70 / MISE 826 2375 PP / Archives Zuber Nr. 2375

428 Frankreich / 1830–1835 / Matter Grund. Handdruck, 16 Farben / 50 × 54 / 48 × 46,5 / UCAD HH 2741 A und B

429 Manufaktur RIOTTOT / Um 1840 / Matter Grund. Handdruck, 11 Farben. Veloutiert und repiquiert / 53 × 67 / 53 × 53 / UCAD HH 953

430 Manufaktur RIOTTOT / Um 1840 / Matter Grund. Handdruck, 14 Farben. Veloutiert und repiquiert / 54 × 68 / 53,5 × 53,5 / UCAD HH 954

Hommes et animaux

431 France / 1800–1805 / Fond mat. Imp. pl. 7 coul. / 27,5 × 63 / 27,5 × 117 / UCAD HH 2695 A

432 Manufacture JACQUEMART et BENARD / 1800–1805 / Fond satin. Imp. pl. 10 coul. / 28 × 54 / 28 × 54 / UCAD HH 336

People and Animals

431 France / 1800–1805 / Matt ground. Block-print 7 col. / 27,5 × 63 / 27,5 × 117 / UCAD HH 2695 A

432 Manufacture JACQUEMART et BENARD / 1800–1805 / Satin ground. Block-print 10 col. / 28 × 54 / 28 × 54 / UCAD HH 336

Menschen und Tiere

431 Frankreich / 1800–1805 / Matter Grund. Handdruck, 7 Farben / 27,5 × 63 / 27,5 × 117 / UCAD HH 2695 A

432 Manufaktur JACQUEMART et BENARD / 1800–1805 / Satinierter Grund. Handdruck, 10 Farben / 28 × 54 / 28 × 54 / UCAD HH 336

418

422

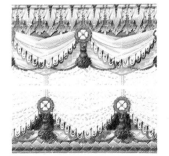

419

420

423

424

429

427

430

421

425

426

428

431

432

433 France / 1800–1805 / Fond mat. Imp. pl. 11 coul. / 67 × 108 / 67 × 107 / MISE 980 pp 810-1

434 France / 1800–1805 / Fond mat. Imp. pl. 11 coul. / 67 × 67 / MISE 980 pp 813-1

435 France / 1800–1805 / Fond mat. Imp. pl. 8 coul. / 57 × 110 / UCAD 29755

436 France / 1800–1810 / Fond mat. Dessin original 4 coul. / 25,5 × 51 / 24 × 47 / UCAD HH 2517

437 Manufacture JACQUEMART et BENARD / 1800–1810 / Fond mat. Imp. pl. 16 coul. / 55 × 53 / 55 × 53 / UCAD HH 323

438 Manufacture JACQUEMART et BENARD / 1800–1810 / Fond satin. Imp. pl. 10 coul. / 55 × 81 / UCAD HH 316

439 France / 1815–1820 / Fond mat. Imp. pl. 17 coul. / 57 × 110 / UCAD 29754 / AMIC et BRUNHAMMER, 1967, p. 46 n° 2 / Paris, 1967, n° 270

440 Manufacture ZUBER / 1815–1820 / Fond mat. Imp. pl. 19 coul. Veloutage et repiquage / 52 × 53 / UCAD HH 103 / Paris, 1967, n° 246

441 POLISCH d'après HUET / Manufacture DAUPTAIN ou RIOTTOT ? / 1837 / Fond satin. Imp. pl. 26 coul. / 65,5 × 155 / UCAD 29762 / RIOUX de MAILLOU, s. d., p. 354

442 POLISCH d'après HUET / Manufacture RIOTTOT / 1835–1840 / Fond satin. Imp. pl. 31 coul. / 53,5 × 69 / Recto, manuscrit «Composition de Huet, arrangement de POLISCH, fabrique RIOTTOT» / UCAD 29763

443 POLISCH d'après HUET / Manufacture RIOTTOT / 1835–1840 / Fond mat. Imp. pl. 38 coul. / 63,7 × 132 / UCAD 29761

444 France / 1835–1840 / Fond satin. Imp. pl. 38 coul. / 54 × 70 / UCAD 29764

433 France / 1800–1805 / Matt ground. Block-print 11 col. / 67 × 108 / 67 × 107 / MISE 980 pp 810-1

434 France / 1800–1805 / Matt ground. Block-print 11 col. / 67 × 67 / MISE 980 pp 813-1

435 France / 1800–1805 / Matt ground. Block-print 8 col. / 57 × 110 / UCAD 29755

436 France / 1800–1810 / Matt ground. Original design 4 col. / 25,5 × 51 / 24 × 47 / UCAD HH 2517

437 Manufacture JACQUEMART et BENARD / 1800–1810 / Matt ground. Block-print 16 col. / 55 × 53 / 55 × 53 / UCAD HH 323

438 Manufacture JACQUEMART et BENARD / 1800–1810 / Satin ground. Block-print 10 col. / 55 × 81 / UCAD HH 316

439 France / 1815–1820 / Matt ground. Block-print 17 col. / 57 × 110 / UCAD 29754 / AMIC et BRUNHAMMER, 1967, p. 46 N° 2/ Paris, 1967, N° 270

440 Manufacture ZUBER / 1815–1820 / Matt ground. Block-print 19 col. Flocking and overprinting / 52 × 53 / UCAD HH 103 / Paris, 1967, N° 246

441 POLISCH after HUET / Manufacture DAUPTAIN or RIOTTOT? / 1837 / Satin ground. Block-print 26 col. / 65,5 × 155 / UCAD 29762 / RIOUX de MAILLOU, n. d., p. 354

442 POLISCH after HUET / Manufacture RIOTTOT / 1835–1840 / Satin ground. Block-print 31 col. / 53,5 × 69 / Recto, inscribed: 'Composition de Huet, arrangement de POLISCH, fabrique RIOTTOT' / UCAD 29763

443 POLISCH after HUET / Manufacture RIOTTOT / 1835–1840 / Matt ground. Block-print 38 col. / 63,7 × 132 / UCAD 29761

444 France / 1835–1840 / Satin ground. Block-print 38 col. / 54 × 70 / UCAD 29764

433 Frankreich / 1800–1805 / Matter Grund. Handdruck, 11 Farben / 67 × 108 / 67 × 107 / MISE 980 PP 810-1

434 Frankreich / 1800–1805 / Matter Grund. Handdruck, 11 Farben / 67 × 67 / MISE 980 PP 813-1

435 Frankreich / 1800–1805 / Matter Grund. Handdruck, 8 Farben / 57 × 110 / UCAD 29755

436 Frankreich / 1800–1810 / Matter Grund. Originalentwurf, 4 Farben / 25,5 × 51 / 24 × 47 / UCAD HH 2517

437 Manufaktur JACQUEMART et BENARD / 1800–1810 / Matter Grund. Handdruck, 16 Farben / 55 × 53 / 55 × 53 / UCAD HH 323

438 Manufaktur JACQUEMART et BENARD / 1800–1810 / Satinierter Grund. Handdruck, 10 Farben / 55 × 81 / UCAD HH 316

439 Frankreich / 1815–1820 / Matter Grund. Handdruck, 17 Farben / 57 × 110 / UCAD 29754 / AMIC und BRUNHAMMER, 1967, S. 46 Nr. 2 / Paris, 1967, Nr. 270

440 Manufaktur ZUBER / 1815–1820 / Matter Grund. Handdruck, 19 Farben. Veloutiert und repiquiert / 52 × 53 / UCAD HH 103 / Paris, 1967, Nr. 246

441 POLISCH nach HUET / Manufaktur DAUPTAIN oder RIOTTOT ? / 1837 / Satinierter Grund. Handdruck, 26 Farben / 65,5 × 155 / UCAD 29762 / RIOUX de MAILLOU, o. J., S. 354

442 POLISCH nach HUET / Manufaktur RIOTTOT / 1835–1840 / Satinierter Grund. Handdruck, 31 Farben / 53,5 × 69 / Vorderseite beschriftet: »Composition de Huet, arrangement de POLISCH, fabrique RIOTTOT« / UCAD 29763

443 POLISCH nach HUET / Manufaktur RIOTTOT / 1835–1840 / Matter Grund. Handdruck, 38 Farben / 63,7 × 132 / UCAD 29761

444 Frankreich / 1835–1840 / Satinierter Grund. Handdruck, 38 Farben / 54 × 70 / UCAD 29764

433

434

436

437

438

440

435

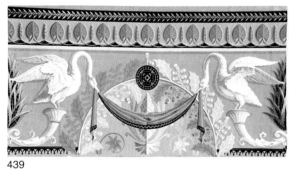

439

441

443

442

444

Amours, renommées, guirlandes, cornes d'abondance

445 Manufacture JACQUEMART et BENARD / 1800 env. / Fond mat. Imp. pl. 13 coul. / 57 × 110 / UCAD 29751 CLOUZOT et FOLLOT, 1935, p. 89. AMIC et BRUNHAMMER, 1967, p. 41 n° 1 / Paris, 1967, n° 153

446 France / 1800–1805 / Fond mat. Imp. pl. 12 coul. / 58 × 110 / UCAD 29756

447 France / 1805–1810 / Fond mat. Imp. pl. 14 coul. / 58 × 94 / 50 × 54 / UCAD 36812

448 Manufacture ZUBER / 1810 / Fond mat. Imp. pl. 20 coul. / 53 × 54 / UCAD HH 104 / Paris, 1967, n° 249

449 Xavier MADER? / Manufacture DUFOUR ? / 1810 env. / Fond mat. Imp. pl. 20 coul. Poudre dorée / 50 × 126 / UCAD 29572 A / Paris, 1967, n° 263

450 Xavier MADER ? / Manufacture DUFOUR ? / 1810 env. / Fond mat. Imp. pl. 20 coul. Poudre dorée / 50 × 110 / UCAD 29572 B / Paris, 1967, n° 263

451 France / 1810 env. / Fond satin. Imp. pl. 9 coul. Poudre dorée / 55 × 120 / UCAD HH 109 / Paris, 1967, n° 262

452 Manufacture JACQUEMART et BENARD / 1810 env. / Fond mat. Imp. pl. 17 coul. / 57 × 135 / UCAD HH 105 / Paris, 1967, n° 156

453 France / 1810 env. / Fond satin. Imp. pl. 8 coul. / 56 × 144 / UCAD 29752

454 France / 1810 env. / Fond mat. Imp. pl. 11 coul. / 58 × 96 / UCAD 29760

455 Xavier MADER ? / Manufacture DUFOUR / 1810 env. / Fond mat. Imp. pl. 16 coul. / 56 × 85 / 53,5 × 56 / BF 1454

456 Xavier MADER / Manufacture DUFOUR / 1810 env. / Fond mat. Imp. pl. 6 coul. / 58 × 144 / 50 × 106 / BF 1457

Putti, Attendant Spirits, Garlands, Horns of Plenty

445 Manufacture JACQUEMART et BENARD / 1800 env. / Matt ground. Block-print 13 col. / 57 × 110 / UCAD 29751 / CLOUZOT et FOLLOT, 1935, p. 89. AMIC et BRUNHAMMER, 1967, p. 41 N° 1 / Paris, 1967, N° 153

446 France / 1800–1805 / Matt ground. Block-print 12 col. / 58 × 110 / UCAD 29756

447 France / 1805–1810 / Matt ground. Block-print 14 col. / 58 × 94 / 50 × 54 / UCAD 36812

448 Manufacture ZUBER / 1810 / Matt ground. Block-print 20 col. / 53 × 54 / UCAD HH 104 / Paris, 1967, N° 249

449 Xavier MADER? / Manufacture DUFOUR? / 1810 env. / Matt ground. Block-print 20 col. Gold dust / 50 × 126 / UCAD 29572 A / Paris, 1967, N° 263

450 Xavier MADER? / Manufacture DUFOUR? / 1810 env. / Matt ground. Block-print 20 col. Gold dust / 50 × 110 / UCAD 29572 B / Paris, 1967, N° 263

451 France / 1810 env. / Satin ground. Block-print 9 col. Gold dust / 55 × 120 / UCAD HH 109 / Paris, 1967, N° 262

452 Manufacture JACQUEMART et BENARD / 1810 env. / Matt ground. Block-print 17 col. / 57 × 135 / UCAD HH 105 / Paris, 1967, N° 156

453 France / 1810 env. / Satin ground. Block-print 8 col. / 56 × 144 / UCAD 29752

454 France / 1810 env. / Matt ground. Block-print 11 col. / 58 × 96 / UCAD 29760

455 Xavier MADER? / Manufacture DUFOUR / 1810 env. / Matt ground. Block-print 16 col. / 56 × 85 / 53,5 × 56 / BF 1454

456 Xavier MADER / Manufacture DUFOUR / 1810 env. / Matt ground. Block-print 6 col. / 58 × 144 / 50 × 106 / BF 1457

Putten, Genien, Girlanden, Füllhörner

445 Manufaktur JACQUEMART et BENARD / Um 1800 / Matter Grund. Handdruck, 13 Farben / 57 × 110 / UCAD 29751 / CLOUZOT und FOLLOT, 1935, S. 89. AMIC und BRUNHAMMER, 1967, S. 41 Nr. 1 / Paris, 1967, Nr. 153

446 Frankreich / 1800–1805 / Matter Grund. Handdruck, 12 Farben / 58 × 110 / UCAD 29756

447 Frankreich / 1805–1810 / Matter Grund. Handdruck, 14 Farben / 58 × 94 / 50 × 54 / UCAD 36812

448 Manufaktur ZUBER / 1810 / Matter Grund. Handdruck, 20 Farben / 53 × 54 / UCAD HH 104 / Paris, 1967, Nr. 249

449 Xavier MADER ? / Manufaktur DUFOUR ? / Um 1810 / Matter Grund. Handdruck, 20 Farben. Goldstaub / 50 × 126 / UCAD 29572 A / Paris, 1967, Nr. 263

450 Xavier MADER ? / Manufaktur DUFOUR ? / Um 1810 / Matter Grund. Handdruck, 20 Farben. Goldstaub / 50 × 110 / UCAD 29572 B / Paris, 1967, Nr. 263

451 Frankreich / Um 1810 / Satinierter Grund. Handdruck, 9 Farben. Goldstaub / 55 × 120 / UCAD HH 109 / Paris, 1967, Nr. 262

452 Manufaktur JACQUEMART et BENARD / Um 1810 / Matter Grund. Handdruck, 17 Farben / 57 × 135 / UCAD HH 105 / Paris, 1967, Nr. 156

453 Frankreich / Um 1810 / Satinierter Grund. Handdruck, 8 Farben / 56 × 144 / UCAD 29752

454 Frankreich / Um 1810 / Matter Grund. Handdruck, 11 Farben / 58 × 96 / UCAD 29760

455 Xavier MADER ? / Manufaktur DUFOUR ? / Um 1810 / Matter Grund. Handdruck, 16 Farben / 56 × 85 / 53,5 × 56 / BF 1454

456 Xavier MADER / Manufaktur DEFOUR / Um 1810 / Matter Grund. Handdruck, 6 Farben / 58 × 144 / 50 × 106 / BF 1457

445

446

447

449

450

451

452

453

454

455

448

456

457 Manufacture DUFOUR / 1810 env. / Fond mat. Dessin original 11 coul. / 53 × 136 / 54 × 130 / BF 1465

458 France / 1810–1815 / Fond mat. Imp. pl. 5 coul. / 21 × 90 / 21 × 81 / UCAD HH 2746

459 France / 1810–1820 / Fond mat. Imp. pl. 17 coul. / 55,5 × 97 / 48,5 × 97 / Recto, manuscrit: «3327 frise fond bleu impérial teinté d'or et gris. 26,-. 3328 talon du haut teinté d'or 11,- 3329 talon du bas teinté d'or 11,-» / UCAD HH 2780

460 France / 1810–1820 / Fond mat. Imp. pl. 13 coul. / 57 × 120 / 54 × 54 / UCAD HH 2781

461 France / 1815–1820 / Fond mat. Imp. pl. 19 coul. / 68 × 46 / MISE 980 pp 823–1

457 Manufacture DUFOUR / 1810 env. / Matt ground. Original design 11 col. / 53 × 136 / 54 × 130 / BF 1465

458 France / 1810–1815 / Matt ground. Block-print 5 col. / 21 × 90 / 21 × 81 / UCAD HH 2746

459 France / 1810–1820 / Matt ground. Block-print 17 col. / 55,5 × 97 / 48,5 × 97 / Recto, inscribed: '3327 frise fond bleu impérial / teinté d'or et gris. 26,–3328 talon du haut / teinté d'or 11,–3329 talon du bas teinté d'or 11,–' / UCAD HH 2780

460 France / 1810–1820 / Matt ground. Block-print 13 col. / 57 × 120 / 54 × 54 / UCAD HH 2781

461 France / 1815–1820 / Matt ground. Block-print 19 col. / 68 × 46 / MISE 980 pp 823–1

457 Manufaktur DUFOUR / Um 1810 / Matter Grund. Originalentwurf, 11 Farben / 53 × 136 / 54 × 130 / BF 1465

458 Frankreich / 1810–1815 / Matter Grund. Handdruck, 5 Farben / 21 × 90 / 21 × 81 / UCAD HH 2746

459 Frankreich / 1810–1820 / Matter Grund. Handdruck, 17 Farben / 55,5 × 97 / 48,5 × 97 / Vorderseite beschriftet: »3327 frise fond bleu impérial teinté d'or et gris. 26,- 3328 talon du haut teinté d'or 11,- 3329 talon du bas teinté d'or 11,-« / UCAD HH 2780

460 Frankreich / 1810–1820 / Matter Grund. Handdruck, 13 Farben / 57 × 120 / 54 × 54 / UCAD HH 2781

461 Frankreich / 1815–1820 / Matter Grund. Handdruck, 19 Farben / 68 × 46 / MISE 980 PP 823-1

Figures en médaillons

462 Manufacture JACQUEMART et BENARD / 1800–1805 / Fond mat. Imp. pl. 9 coul. Feuille d'or / 55 × 43 / UCAD HH 303

463 Manufacture JACQUEMART et BENARD / 1800–1805 / Fond mat. Imp. pl. 4 coul. / 49 × 43 / UCAD HH 307

464 Manufacture JACQUEMART et BENARD / 1800–1805 / Fond mat. Dessin original 8 coul. / 53,5 × 77 / 53,5 × 63,5 / UCAD HH 306

465 Manufacture JACQUEMART et BENARD / 1800–1805 / Fond mat. Imp. pl. 18 coul. / 56 × 48 / UCAD HH 305

466 Manufacture JACQUEMART et BENARD / 1800–1810 / Fond mat. Imp. pl. 12 coul. / 54 × 53 / UCAD HH 308

467 Manufacture JACQUEMART et BENARD / 1800–1810 / Fond satin. Imp. pl. 18 coul. / 54 × 42 / UCAD HH 331

Figures in Medallions

462 Manufacture JACQUEMART et BENARD / 1800–1805 / Matt ground. Block-print 9 col. Gold dust / 55 × 43 / UCAD HH 303

463 Manufacture JACQUEMART et BENARD / 1800–1805 / Matt ground. Block-print 4 col. / 49 × 43 / UCAD HH 307

464 Manufacture JACQUEMART et BENARD / 1800–1805 / Matt ground. Original design 8 col. / 53,5 × 77 / 53,5 × 63,5 / UCAD HH 306

465 Manufacture JACQUEMART et BENARD / 1800–1805 / Matt ground. Block-print 18 col. / 56 × 48 / UCAD HH 305

466 Manufacture JACQUEMART et BENARD / 1800–1810 / Matt ground. Block-print 12 col. / 54 × 53 / UCAD HH 308

467 Manufacture JACQUEMART et BENARD / 1800–1810 / Satin ground. Block-print 18 col. / 54 × 42 / UCAD HH 331

Figuren in Medaillons

462 Manufaktur JACQUEMART et BENARD / 1800–1805 / Matter Grund. Handdruck, 9 Farben. Blattgold / 55 × 43 / UCAD HH 303

463 Manufaktur JACQUEMART et BENARD / 1800–1805 / Matter Grund. Handdruck, 4 Farben / 49 × 43 / UCAD HH 307

464 Manufaktur JACQUEMART et BENARD / 1800–1805 / Matter Grund. Originalentwurf, 8 Farben / 53,5 × 77 / 53,5 × 63,5 / UCAD HH 306

465 Manufaktur JACQUEMART et BENARD / 1800–1805 / Matter Grund. Handdruck, 18 Farben / 56 × 48 / UCAD HH 305

466 Manufaktur JACQUEMART et BENARD / 1800–1810 / Matter Grund. Handdruck, 12 Farben / 54 × 53 / UCAD HH 308

467 Manufaktur JACQUEMART et BENARD / 1800–1810 / Satinierter Grund. Handdruck, 18 Farben / 54 × 42 / UCAD HH 331

457

458

461

460

459

462

464

463

466

467

465

468 France / 1805–1810 / Fond satin. Dessin original 7 coul./ 53 × 70 / 52 × 68,5 / UCAD HH 2738

469 France / 1805–1810 / Fond mat. Imp. pl.9 coul. / 20 × 55 / UCAD HH 2747 B

470 France / 1810–1815 / Fond mat. Imp. pl. 13 coul. / 54 × 105 / UCAD HH 1744 A

471 France / 1810–1815 / Fond mat. Imp. pl. 20 coul. / 62,5 × 100 / 62,5 × 64 / UCAD 2736

472 Xavier MADER ? / Manufacture DUFOUR ? / 1825 env. / Fond mat. Imp. pl. 6 coul. / 64 × 134 / UCAD 29565 A

473 Xavier MADER ? / Manufacture DUFOUR ? / 1825 env. / Fond mat. Imp. pl. 6 coul. / 64 × 52 / UCAD 29565 B

474 Xavier MADER ? / Manufacture DUFOUR ? / 1825 env. / Fond mat. Imp. pl. 6 coul. / 64 × 53 / UCAD 29565 C

475 Xavier MADER ? / Manufacture DUFOUR ? / 1825 env. / Fond mat. Imp. pl. 6 coul. / 64 × 53 / UCAD 29565 D

476 Xavier MADER ? / Manufacture DUFOUR ? / 1825 env. / Fond mat. Imp. pl. 6 coul. / 65 × 208 / BF 1483

477 France / 1840 env. / Fond satin. Imp. pl. 14 coul. Veloutage et repiquage / 57 × 88 / 17 × 45 / BF 528

478 France / 1840 env. / Fond mat. Imp. pl. 4 coul. / 51,5 × 107 / UCAD HH 2782

479 France / 1840 env. / Fond mat. Imp. pl. 8 coul. / 77 × 111 / UCAD HH 2783

468 France / 1805–1810 / Satin ground. Original design 7 col. / 53 × 70 / 52 × 68,5 / UCAD HH 2738

469 France / 1805–1810 / Matt ground. Block-print 9 col. / 20 × 55 / UCAD HH 2747 B

470 France / 1810–1815 / Matt ground. Block-print 13 col. / 54 × 105 / UCAD HH 1744 A

471 France / 1810–1815 / Matt ground. Block-print 20 col. / 62,5 × 100 / 62,5 × 64 / UCAD 2736

472 Xavier MADER? / Manufacture DUFOUR? / 1825 env. / Matt ground. Block-print 6 col. / 64 × 134 / UCAD 29565 A

473 Xavier MADER? / Manufacture DUFOUR? / 1825 env. / Matt ground. Block-print 6 col. / 64 × 52 / UCAD 29565 B

474 Xavier MADER? / Manufacture DUFOUR? / 1825 / Matt ground. Block-print 6 col. / 64 × 53 / UCAD 29565 C

475 Xavier MADER? / Manufacture DUFOUR? / 1825 / Matt ground. Block-print 6 col. / 64 × 53 / UCAD 29565 D

476 Xavier MADER? / Manufacture DUFOUR? / 1825 / Matt ground. Block-print 6 col. / 65 × 208 / BF 1483

477 France / 1840 env. / Satin ground. Block-print 14 col. Flocking and over-printing / 57 × 88 / 17 × 45 / BF 528

478 France / 1840 env. / Matt ground. Block-print 4 col. / 51,5 × 107 / UCAD HH 2782

479 France / 1840 env. / Matt ground. Block-print 8 col. / 77 × 111 / UCAD HH 2783

468 Frankreich / 1805–1810 / Satinierter Grund. Originalentwurf, 7 Farben / 53 × 70 / 52 × 68,5 / UCAD HH 2738

469 Frankreich / 1805–1810 / Matter Grund. Handdruck, 9 Farben / 20 × 55 / UCAD HH 2747 B

470 Frankreich / 1810–1815 / Matter Grund. Handdruck, 13 Farben / 54 × 105 / UCAD HH 1744 A

471 Frankreich / 1810–1815 / Matter Grund. Handdruck, 20 Farben / 62,5 × 100 / 62,5 × 64 / UCAD 2736

472 Xavier MADER ? / Manufaktur DUFOUR ? / Um 1825 / Matter Grund. Handdruck, 6 Farben / 64 × 134 / UCAD 29565 A

473 Xavier MADER ? / Manufaktur DUFOUR ? / Um 1825 / Matter Grund. Handdruck, 6 Farben / 64 × 52 / UCAD 29565 B

474 Xavier MADER ? / Manufaktur DUFOUR ? / Um 1825 / Matter Grund. Handdruck, 6 Farben / 64 × 53 / UCAD 29565 C

475 Xavier MADER ? / Manufaktur DUFOUR ? / Um 1825 / Matter Grund. Handdruck 6 Farben / 64 × 53 / UCAD 29565 D

476 Xavier MADER ? / Manufaktur DUFOUR ? / Um 1825 / Matter Grund. Handdruck, 6 Farben / 65 × 208 / BF 1483

477 Frankreich / Um 1840 / Satinierter Grund. Handdruck, 14 Farben. Veloutiert und repiquiert / 57 × 88 / 17 × 45 / BF 528

478 Frankreich / Um 1840 / Matter Grund. Handdruck, 4 Farben / 51,5 × 107 / UCAD I II I 2782

479 Frankreich / Um 1840 / Matter Grund. Handdruck, 8 Farben / 77 × 111 / UCAD HH 2783

468

469

470

473

476

474

475

472

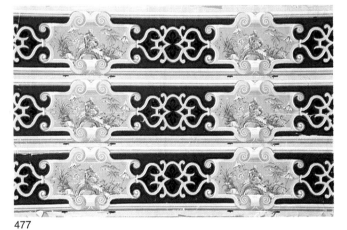

477

471

478

479

Figures seules en frise

480 France / 1805–1810 / Fond mat. Imp. pl. 9 coul. / 57 × 127 / UCAD HH 107 A / Paris, 1967, n° 260 – Paris, 1973, n° 330

481 France / 1805–1810 / Fond mat. Imp. pl. 9 coul. / 57 × 163 / UCAD HH 107 B / Paris, 1967, n° 260 – Paris, 1973, n° 330

482 France / 1805–1810 / Fond mat. Imp. pl. 9 coul. / 53 × 118/ UCAD HH 2748 A

483 France / 1805–1810 / Fond mat. Imp. pl. 9 coul. / 53 × 118 / UCAD HH 2748 B

484 France / 1805–1810 / Fond mat. Imp. pl. 9 coul. / 54 × 132 / UCAD HH 2748 C

485 France / 1805–1810 / Fond mat. Imp. pl. 9 coul. / 54 × 129 / UCAD HH 2748 D

486 France / 1805–1810 / Fond mat. Imp. pl. 8 coul. / 45 × 97 / UCAD HH 2749 A

487 France / 1805–1810 / Fond mat. Imp. pl. 8 coul. / 45 × 96 / UCAD HH 2749 B

488 France / 1805–1810 / Fond mat. Imp. pl. 8 coul. / 45 × 92 / UCAD HH 2749 C

489 France / 1805–1810 / Fond mat. Imp. pl. 8 coul. / 45 × 93 / UCAD HH 2749 D

490 France / 1805–1810 / Fond mat. Imp. pl. 10 coul. / 43 × 65 / MISE 980 PP 822–1

491 France / 1805–1810 / Fond mat. Imp. pl. 11 coul. / 53 × 63 / MISE 980 PP 823–1

492 France / 1805–1810 / Fond mat. Imp. pl. 10 coul. / 52 × 67 / MISE 980 PP 825–1

493 France / 1805–1810 / Fond mat. Imp. pl. 7 coul. / 54 × 66 / MISE 980 PP 826–1

494 France / 1805–1810 / Fond mat. Imp. pl. 7 coul. / 53 × 91 / MISE 980 PP 827–1

Single Figures in Friezes

480 France / 1805–1810 / Matt ground. Block-print 9 col. / 57 × 127 / UCAD HH 107 A / Paris, 1967, N° 260 – Paris, 1973, N° 330

481 France / 1805–1810 / Matt ground. Block-print 9 col. / 57 × 163 / UCAD HH 107 B / Paris, 1967, N° 260 – Paris, 1973, N° 330

482 France / 1805–1810 / Matt ground. Block-print 9 col. / 53 × 118 / UCAD HH 2748 A

483 France / 1805–1810 / Matt ground. Block-print 9 col. / 53 × 118 / UCAD HH 2748 B

484 France / 1805–1810 / Matt ground. Block-print 9 col. / 54 × 132 / UCAD HH 2748 C

485 France / 1805–1810 / Matt ground. Block-print 9 col. / 54 × 129 / UCAD HH 2748 D

486 France / 1805–1810 / Matt ground. Block-print 8 col. / 45 × 97 / UCAD HH 2749 A

487 France / 1805–1810 / Matt ground. Block-print 8 col. / 45 × 96 / UCAD HH 2749 B

488 France / 1805–1810 / Matt ground. Block-print 8 col. / 45 × 92 / UCAD HH 2749 C

489 France / 1805–1810 / Matt ground. Block-print 8 col. / 45 × 93 / UCAD HH 2749 D

490 France / 1805–1810 / Matt ground. Block-print 10 col. / 43 × 65 / MISE 980 PP 822–1

491 France / 1805–1810 / Matt ground. Block-print 11 col. / 53 × 63 / MISE 980 PP 823–1

492 France / 1805–1810 / Matt ground. Block-print 10 col. / 52 × 67 / MISE 980 PP 825–1

493 France / 1805–1810 / Matt ground. Block-print 7 col. / 54 × 66 / MISE 980 PP 826–1

494 France / 1805–1810 / Matt ground. Block-print 7 col. / 53 × 91 / MISE 980 PP 827–1

Figurenfriese

480 Frankreich / 1805–1810 / Matter Grund. Handdruck, 9 Farben / 57 × 127 / UCAD HH 107 A / Paris, 1967, Nr. 260 – Paris, 1973, Nr. 330

481 Frankreich / 1805–1810 / Matter Grund. Handdruck, 9 Farben / 57 × 163 / UCAD HH 107 B / Paris 1967, Nr. 260 – Paris, 1973, Nr. 330

482 Frankreich / 1805–1810 / Matter Grund. Handdruck, 9 Farben / 53 × 118 / UCAD HH 2748 A

483 Frankreich / 1805–1810 / Matter Grund. Handdruck, 9 Farben / 53 × 118 / UCAD HH 2748 B

484 Frankreich / 1805–1810 / Matter Grund. Handdruck, 9 Farben / 54 × 132 / UCAD HH 2748 C

485 Frankeich / 1805–1810 / Matter Grund. Handdruck, 9 Farben / 54 × 129 / UCAD HH 2748 D

486 Frankreich / 1805–1810 / Matter Grund. Handdruck, 8 Farben / 45 × 97 / UCAD HH 2749 A

487 Frankreich / 1805–1810 / Matter Grund. Handdruck, 8 Farben / 45 × 96 / UCAD HH 2749 B

488 Frankreich / 1805–1810 / Matter Grund. Handdruck, 8 Farben / 45 × 92 / UCAD HH 2749 C

489 Frankreich / 1805–1810 / Matter Grund. Handdruck, 8 Farben / 45 × 93 / UCAD HH 2749 D

490 Frankreich / 1805–1810 / Matter Grund. Handdruck, 10 Farben / 43 × 65 / MISE 980 PP 822-1

491 Frankreich / 1805–1810 / Matter Grund. Handdruck, 11 Farben / 53 × 63 / MISE 980 PP 823-1

492 Frankreich / 1805–1810 / Matter Grund. Handdruck, 10 Farben / 52 × 67 / MISE 980 PP 825-1

493 Frankreich / 1805–1810 / Matter Grund. Handdruck, 7 Farben / 56 × 66 / MISE 980 PP 826-1

494 Frankreich / 1805–1810 / Matter Grund. Handdruck, 7 Farben / 53 × 91 / MISE 980 PP 827-1

480

481

482

483

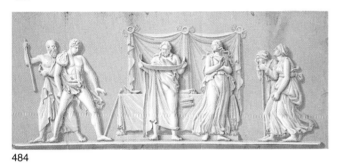

484

485

486

487

488

489

490

491

492

493

494

Panneaux décoratifs et intermédiaires

Decorative and Intermediary Panels

Dekorative Panneaus und Einsatzstücke

Panneaux intermédiaires

495 Joseph-Laurent MALAINE / Manufacture ZUBER / 1800 env. / Fond mat. Imp. pl. 45 coul. / 100 × 53 / UCAD 29589 A / Paris, 1967, n° 240

496 Joseph-Laurent MALAINE / Manufacture ZUBER / 1800 env. / Fond mat. Imp. pl. 45 coul. / 100 × 53 / UCAD 29589 B / Paris, 1967, n° 240

497 MADER Père / Manufacture DUFOUR / 1812 / Fond mat. Imp. pl. 11 coul. Feuille d'or, veloutage, repiquage / 274 × 55 / BF 1471 / Paris, 1967, n° 118

498 MADER Père / Manufacture DUFOUR / 1812 / Fond mat. Imp. pl. 5 coul. Feuille d'or, veloutage, repiquage / UCAD 29570 / Paris, 1967, n° 118

499 France / 1820 env. / Fond mat. Imp. pl. 7 coul. Poudre dorée / 167 × 62 / UCAD HH 2772 A

500 France / 1820 env. / Fond mat. Imp. pl. 10 coul. / 168 × 64 / UCAD HH 2772 B

501–506 MADER Père / 1825 / Fond mat. Imp. pl. 10 coul. / UCAD 29583 ABCDEF / CLOUZOT et FOLLOT, 1935, p. 204–205 / Paris, 1967, n° 57

507 MADER / 1825 env. / Fond mat. Imp. pl. 21 coul. / UCAD 29823 / Paris, 1967, n° 175

508 Eugène THIBAUDIER / 1825 env. / Fond mat. Imp. pl. 7 coul. / 203 × 51 / BF 1485

509 Eugène THIBAUDIER / 1825 env. / Fond mat. Imp. pl. 7 coul. / 200 × 50 / Verso: tampon E-T / BF : 1486

Intermediary Panels

495 Joseph-Laurent MALAINE / Manufacture ZUBER / 1800 env. / Matt ground. Block-print 45 col. / 100 × 53 / UCAD 29589 A / Paris, 1967, N° 240

496 Joseph-Laurent MALAINE / Manufacture ZUBER / 1800 env. / Matt ground. Block-print 45 col. / 100 × 53 / UCAD 29589 B / Paris, 1967, N° 240

497 MADER Père / Manufacture DUFOUR / 1812 / Matt ground. Block-print 11 col. Gold leaf, flocking and over-printing / 274 × 55 / BF 1471 / Paris, 1967, N° 118

498 MADER Père / Manufacture DUFOUR / 1812 / Matt ground. Block-print 5 col. Gold leaf, flocking and over-printing / UCAD 29570 / Paris, 1967, N° 118

499 France / 1820 env. / Matt ground. Block-print 7 col. Gold dust / 167 × 62 / UCAD HH 2772 A

500 France / 1820 env. / Matt ground. Block-print 10 col. / 168 × 64 / UCAD HH 2772 B

501–506 MADER Père / 1825 / Matt ground. Block-print 10 col. / UCAD 29583 ABCDEF / CLOUZOT et FOLLOT, 1935, p. 204–205 / Paris, 1967, N° 57

507 MADER / 1825 env. / Matt ground. Block-print 21 col. / UCAD 29823 / Paris, 1967, N° 175

508 Eugène THIBAUDIER / 1825 env. / Matt ground. Block-print 7 col. / 203 × 51 / BF 1485

509 Eugène THIBAUDIER / 1825 env. / Matt ground. Block-print 7 col. / 200 × 50 / Verso, stamped: 'E–T' / BF 1486

Einsatzstücke

495 Joseph-Laurent MALAINE / Manufaktur ZUBER / Um 1800 / Matter Grund. Handdruck, 45 Farben / 100 × 53 / UCAD 29589 A / Paris, 1967, Nr. 240

496 Joseph-Laurent MALAINE / Manufaktur ZUBER / Um 1800 / Matter Grund. Handdruck, 45 Farben / 100 × 53 / UCAD 29589 B / Paris, 1967, Nr. 240

497 MADER Père / Manufaktur DUFOUR / 1812 / Matter Grund. Handdruck, 11 Farben. Blattgold. Veloutiert und repiquiert / 274 × 55 / BF 1471 / Paris, 1967, Nr. 118

498 MADER Père / Manufaktur DUFOUR / 1812 / Matter Grund. Handdruck, 5 Farben. Blattgold. Veloutiert und repiquiert / UCAD 29570 / Paris, 1967, Nr. 118

499 Frankreich / Um 1820 / Matter Grund. Handdruck, 7 Farben. Goldstaub / 167 × 62 / UCAD HH 2772 A

500 Frankreich / Um 1820 / Matter Grund. Handdruck, 10 Farben / 168 × 64 / UCAD HH 2772 B

501–506 MADER Père / 1825 / Matter Grund. Handdruck, 10 Farben / UCAD 29583 A, B, C, D, E, F / CLOUZOT und FOLLOT, 1935, S. 204–205 / Paris, 1967, Nr. 57

507 MADER / Um 1825 / Matter Grund. Handdruck, 21 Farben / UCAD 29823 / Paris, 1967, Nr. 175

508 Eugène THIBAUDIER / Um 1825 / Matter Grund. Handdruck, 7 Farben / 203 × 51 / BF 1485

509 Eugène THIBAUDIER / Um 1825 / Matter Grund. Handdruck, 7 Farben / 200 × 50 / Rückseitig Stempel: »E-T« / BF 1486

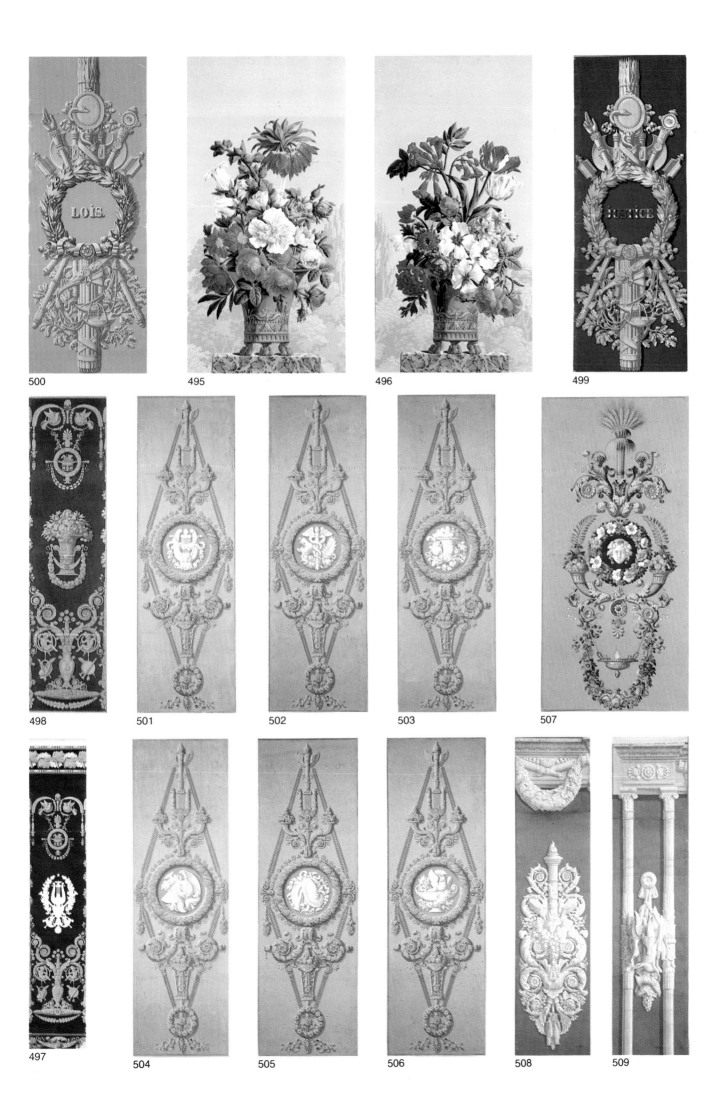

500

495

496

499

498

501

502

503

507

497

504

505

506

508

509

510 Manufacture Amable LEROY / 1833 / Fond satin, peigné. Imp. pl. 2 coul. / 227 × 56 / UCAD H 116 / Paris, 1900, p. 34 n° 141; Paris, 1967, n° 137

511 Manufacture JACQUEMART et BENARD / 1834 / Fond satin. Imp. pl. 4 coul. / 160 × 56 / Verso: «6460. Décor et coins imprimés chez JACQUEMART en 1834» / UCAD HH 1027 A

512 France / 1830–1840 / Fond mat. Imp. pl. 33 coul. / 153 × 53 / BF 2130

513 France / 1840–1845 / Fond mat. Imp. pl. 29 coul. / 170 × 54 / BF 473

514 Martin POLISCH / Manufacture DESFOSSE et KARTH / 1840–1845 / Fond mat. Imp. pl. 23 coul. / 201 × 66 / BF 715

515 Martin POLISCH / Manufacture DESFOSSE et KARTH / 1840–1845 / Fond mat. Imp. pl. 33 coul. / 204 × 66 / BF 716

516 Martin POLISCH / Manufacture DESFOSSE et KARTH / 1840–1845 / Fond mat. Imp. pl. 24 coul. / 195 × 63 / BF 714

510 Manufacture Amable LEROY / 1833 / Satin ground, painted. Block-print 2 col. / 227 × 56 / UCAD HH 116 / Paris, 1900, p. 34 N° 141; Paris, 1967, N° 137

511 Manufacture JACQUEMART et BENARD / 1834 / Satin ground. Block-print 4 col. / 160 × 56 / Verso, inscribed: '6460. Décor et coins imprimés chez JACQUEMART en 1834' / UCAD HH 1027 A

512 France / 1830–1840 / Matt ground. Block-print 33 col. / 153 × 53 / BF 2130

513 France / 1840–1845 / Matt ground. Block-print 29 col. / 170 × 54 / BF 473

514 Martin POLISCH / Manufacture DESFOSSE et KARTH / 1840–1845 / Matt ground. Block-print 23 col. / 201 × 66 / BF 715

515 Martin POLISCH / Manufacture DESFOSSE et KARTH / 1840–1845 / Matt ground. Block-print 33 col. / 204 × 66 / BF 716

516 Martin POLISCH / Manufacture DESFOSSE et KARTH / 1840–1845 / Matt ground. Block-print 24 col. / 195 × 63 / BF 714

510 Manufaktur Amable LEROY / 1833 / Satinierter, gekämmter Grund. Handdruck, 2 Farben / 227 × 56 / UCAD HH 116 / Paris, 1900, S. 34 Nr. 141 – Paris, 1967, Nr. 137

511 Manufaktur JACQUEMART et BENARD / 1834 / Satinierter Grund. Handdruck, 4 Farben / 160 × 56 / Rückseitig beschriftet: »6460. Décor et coins imprimés chez JACQUEMART en 1834« / UCAD HH 1027 A

512 Frankreich / 1830–1840 / Matter Grund. Handdruck, 33 Farben / 153 × 53 / BF 2130

513 Frankreich / 1840–1845 / Matter Grund. Handdruck, 29 Farben / 170 × 54 / BF 473

514 Martin POLISCH / Manufaktur DESFOSSE et KARTH / 1840–1845 / Matter Grund. Handdruck, 23 Farben / 201 × 66 / BF 715

515 Martin POLISCH / Manufaktur DESFOSSE et KARTH / 1840–1845 / Matter Grund. Handdruck, 33 Farben / 204 × 66 / BF 716

516 Martin POLISCH / Manufaktur DESFOSSE et KARTH / 1840–1845 / Matter Grund. Handdruck, 24 Farben / 195 × 63 / BF 714

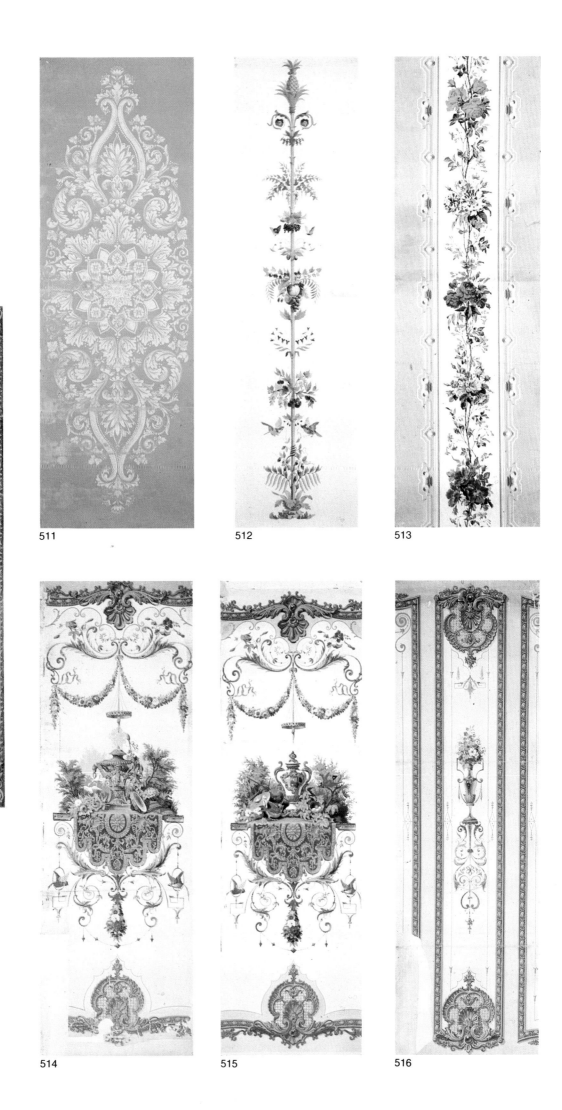

510

511

512

513

514

515

516

517 WAGNER / 1840–1845 / Fond mat. Imp. pl. 25 coul. Irisé / 70 × 48 / UCAD 29615

518 WAGNER / 1849 / Fond mat. Imp. pl. 25 coul. / 103 × 55 / UCAD 29674

519 Martin POLISCH / 1849 / Fond mat. Imp. pl. 34 coul. / 269 × 57 / Verso, manuscrit: «Polisch 1849» / BF 477

520 Martin POLISCH / 1850 env. / Fond mat. Imp. pl. 35 coul. / 209 × 57 / Verso, manuscrit: «Polisch» / BF 498

521 Jean BROC / 1850 env. / Fond mat. Imp. pl. 33 coul. / 161 × 52 / Verso, manuscrit: «Broc» / BF 551

522 WAGNER / 1850 env. / Fond mat irisé. Imp. pl. 18 coul. / 246 × 57 / BF 647

Vasques et coupes

523 France / 1805 env. / Fond mat. Dessin original 8 coul. / 52 × 48 / UCAD HH 2769

524 MADER ? / Manufacture DUFOUR / 1805 env. / Fond mat. Imp. pl. 15 coul. / 77 × 55 / BF 1458

525 France / 1805–1810 / Fond mat. Imp. pl. 7 coul. / 66 × 48 / UCAD 2766

526 France / 1805 env. / Fond mat. Imp. pl. 11 coul. / 71 × 103 / MISE 980 PP 800–1

---

517 WAGNER / 1840–1845 / Matt ground. Block-print 25 col. *Irisé* / 70 × 48 / UCAD 29615

518 WAGNER / 1849 / Matt ground. Block-print 25 col. / 103 × 55 / UCAD 29674

519 Martin POLISCH / 1849 / Matt ground. Block-print 34 col. / 269 × 57 / Verso, inscribed: 'Polisch 1849' / BF 477

520 Martin POLISCH / 1850 env. / Matt ground. Block-print 35 col. / 209 × 57 / Verso, inscribed: 'Polisch' / BF 498

521 Jean BROC / 1850 env. / Matt ground. Block-print 33 col. / 161 × 52 / Verso, inscribed: 'Broc' / BF 551

522 WAGNER / 1850 env. / Matt *irisé* ground. Block-print 18 col. / 246 × 57 / BF 647

Basins and Bowls

523 France / 1805 env. / Matt ground. Original design 8 col. / 52 × 48 / UCAD HH 2769

524 MADER? / Manufacture DUFOUR / 1805 env. / Matt ground. Block-print 15 col. / 77 × 55 / BF 1458

525 France / 1805–1810 / Matt ground. Block-print 7 col. / 66 × 48 / UCAD 2766

526 France / 1805 env. / Matt ground. Block-print 11 col. / 71 × 103 / MISE 980 PP 800–1

---

517 WAGNER / 1840–1845 / Matter Grund. Handdruck, 25 Farben. Irisiert / 70 × 48 / UCAD 29615

518 WAGNER / 1849 / Matter Grund. Handdruck, 25 Farben / 103 × 55 / UCAD 29674

519 Martin POLISCH / 1849 / Matter Grund. Handdruck, 34 Farben / 269 × 57 / Rückseitig beschriftet: »Polisch 1849« / BF 477

520 Martin POLISCH / Um 1850 / Matter Grund. Handdruck, 35 Farben / 209 × 57 / Rückseitig beschriftet: »Polisch« / BF 498

521 Jean BROC / Um 1850 / Matter Grund. Handdruck, 33 Farben / 161 × 52 / Rückseitig beschriftet: »Broc« / BF 551

522 WAGNER / Um 1850 / Matter, irisierter Grund. Handdruck, 18 Farben / 246 × 57 / BF 647

Schalen und Vasen

523 Frankreich / Um 1805 / Matter Grund. Originalentwurf, 8 Farben / 52 × 48 / UCAD HH 2769

524 MADER ? / Manufaktur DUFOUR / Um 1805 / Matter Grund. Handdruck, 15 Farben / 77 × 55 / BF 1458

525 Frankreich / 1805–1810 / Matter Grund. Handdruck, 7 Farben / 66 × 48 / UCAD 2766

526 Frankreich / Um 1805 / Matter Grund. Handdruck, 11 Farben / 71 × 103 / MISE 980 PP 800-1

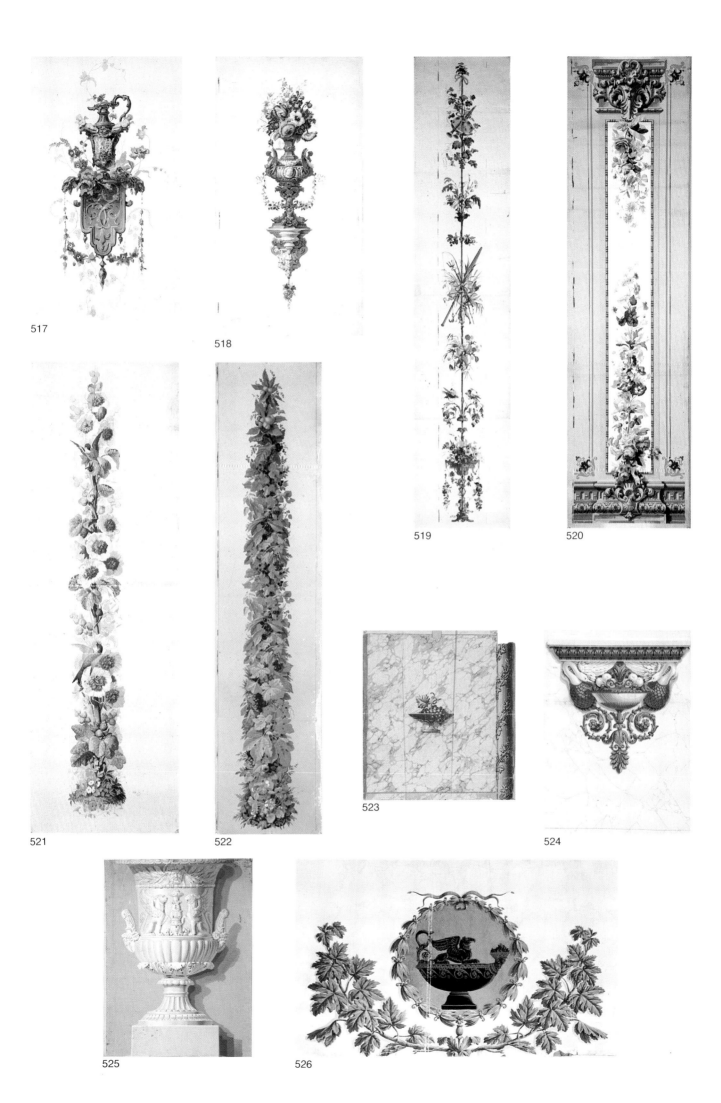

517

518

519

520

521

522

523

524

525

526

Trophées musicaux et militaires

527 France / 1805–1810 / Fond mat. Imp. pl. 6 coul. / 70 × 51 / MISE 980 PP 805–1

528 France / 1805–1810 / Fond mat. Imp. pl. 8 coul. / 140 × 56 / UCAD HH 469 A / Paris, 1967 / n° 85

529 France / 1805–1810 / Fond mat. Imp. pl. 8 coul. / 136 × 50 / UCAD HH 469 B / Paris, 1967, n° 85

530 France / 1810–1815 / Fond mat. Imp. pl. 11 coul. / 57 × 42 / UCAD HH 2750

531 France / 1815 env. / Fond mat. Imp. pl. 10 coul. / 145 × 57 / BF 1473

Candélabres

532 France / 1810–1815 / Fond mat. Imp. pl. 6 coul. / 127 × 54 / BF 1419

533 France / 1820–1825 / Fond mat. Imp. pl. 7 coul. / 176 × 45 / UCAD 29805 A / FOURNY, 1967, p. 63

534 France / 1815–1820 / Fond satin. Imp. pl. 8 coul. / 80 × 52 / UCAD HH 2132 B

Colonnes

535 Manufacture ZUBER / 1800 / Fond mat. Imp. pl. 12 coul. / 107 × 26 / BF 1421 / n° 404 et 616 de la Manufacture ZUBER

536 France/ 1800–1810 / Fond mat. Imp. pl. 6 coul. / 76 × 28 / BF 1422

537 France / 1815–1820 / Fond mat. Imp. pl. 13 coul. / 160 × 40 / UCAD HH 2767 A

538 France / 1815–1820 / Fond mat. Imp. pl. 13 coul. / 146 × 41 / UCAD HH 2767 B

539 France / 1815–1820 / Fond mat. Imp. pl. 13 coul. / 198 × 54 / Recto, manuscrit: «3454. Corniche. ft. d'or 14, bronze doré 24 rehaussé d'or 30. 3452 Rinceau ft d'or 14 bronze doré 24 rehaussé d'or 30. 3453 architrave. ft d'or 8 bronze doré 16 rehaussé d'or 20. 4525 fd ordinaire grise et ft d'or 12 bronze doré 20 rehaussé d'or 24» / UCAD HH 2775 A

540 France / 1815–1820 / Fond mat. Imp. pl. 13 coul. 210 × 54 / UCAD HH 2775 B

541 France / 1840 env. / Fond mat. Imp. pl. 22 coul. / 190 × 57 / UCAD 29672

Musical and Military Trophies

527 France / 1805–1810 / Matt ground. Block-print 6 col. / 70 × 51 / MISE 980 PP 805–1

528 France / 1805–1810 / Matt ground. Block-print 8 col. / 140 × 56 / UCAD HH 469 A / Paris, 1967: n° 85

529 France / 1805–1810 / Matt ground. Block-print 8 col. / 136 × 50 / UCAD HH 469 B / Paris, 1967, n° 85

530 France / 1810–1815 / Matt ground. Block-print 11 col. / 57 × 42 / UCAD HH 2750

531 France / 1815 env. / Matt ground. Block-print 10 col. / 145 × 57 / BF 1473

Candelabra

532 France / 1810–1815 / Matt ground. Block-print 6 col. / 127 × 54 / BF 1419

533 France / 1820–1825 / Matt ground. Block-print 7 col. / 176 × 45 / UCAD 29805 A / FOURNY, 1967, p. 63

534 France / 1815–1820 / Satin ground. Block-print 8 col. / 80 × 52 / UCAD HH 2132 B

Columns

535 Manufacture ZUBER / 1800 / Matt ground. Block-print 12 col. / 107 × 26 / BF 1421 / N° 404 and 616 of Manufacture ZUBER

536 France / 1800–1810 / Matt ground. Block-print 6 col. / 76 × 28 / BF 1422

537 France / 1815–1820 / Matt ground. Block-print 13 col. / 160 × 40 / UCAD HH 2767 A

538 France / 1815–1820 / Matt ground. Block-print 13 col. / 146 × 41 / UCAD HH 2767 B

539 France / 1815–1820 / Matt ground. Block-print 13 col. / 198 × 54 / Recto, inscribed: '3454. Corniche. ft d'or 14, bronze doré 24 rehaussé d'or 30. 3452 Rinceau ft d'or 14 bronze doré 24 rehaussé d'or 30. 3453 architrave. ft d'or 8 bronze doré 16 rehaussé d'or 20. 4525 fd ordinaire grise et ft d'or 12 bronze doré 20 rehaussé d'or 24' / UCAD HH 2775 A

540 France / 1815–1820 / Matt ground. Block-print 13 col. / 210 × 54 / UCAD HH 2775 B

541 France / 1840 env. / Matt ground. Block-print 22 col. / 190 × 57 / UCAD 29672

Musikalische und Waffentrophäen

527 Frankreich / 1805–1810 / Matter Grund. Handdruck, 6 Farben / 70 × 51 / MISE 980 PP 805-1

528 Frankreich / 1805–1810 / Matter Grund. Handdruck, 8 Farben / 140 × 56 / UCAD HH 469 A / Paris, 1967, Nr. 85

529 Frankreich / 1805–1810 / Matter Grund. Handdruck, 8 Farben / 136 × 50 / UCAD HH 469 B / Paris, 1967, Nr. 85

530 Frankreich / 1810–1815 / Matter Grund. Handdruck, 11 Farben / 57 × 42 / UCAD HH 2750

531 Frankreich / Um 1815 / Matter Grund. Handdruck, 10 Farben / 145 × 57 / BF 1473

Kandelaber

532 Frankreich / 1810–1815 / Matter Grund. Handdruck, 6 Farben / 127 × 54 / BF 1419

533 Frankreich / 1820–1825 / Matter Grund. Handdruck, 7 Farben / 176 × 45 / UCAD 29805 A / FOURNY, 1967, S. 63

534 Frankreich / 1815–1820 / Satinierter Grund. Handdruck, 8 Farben / 80 × 52 / UCAD HH 2132 B

Säulen

535 Manufaktur ZUBER / 1800 / Matter Grund. Handdruck, 12 Farben / 107 × 26 / BF 1421 / Nr. 404 und 616 der Manufaktur ZUBER

536 Frankreich / 1800–1810 / Matter Grund. Handdruck, 6 Farben / 76 × 28 / BF 1422

537 Frankreich / 1815–1820 / Matter Grund. Handdruck, 13 Farben / 160 × 40 / UCAD HH 2767 A

538 Frankreich / 1815–1820 / Matter Grund. Handdruck, 13 Farben / 146 × 41 / UCAD HH 2767 B

539 Frankreich / 1815–1820 / Matter Grund. Handdruck, 13 Farben / 198 × 54 / Vorderseite beschriftet: »3454. Corniche. ft d'or 14, bronze doré 24 rehaussé d'or 30. 3452 Rinceau ft d'or 14 bronze doré 24 rehaussé d'or 30. 3453 architrave. ft. d'or 8 bronze doré 16 rehaussé d'or 20. 4525 fd ordinaire grise et ft d'or 12 bronze doré 20 rehaussé d'or 24« / UCAD HH 2775 A

540 Frankreich / 1815–1820 / Matter Grund. Handdruck, 13 Farben / 210 × 54 / UCAD HH 2775 B

541 Frankreich / Um 1840 / Matter Grund. Handdruck, 22 Farben / 190 × 57 / UCAD 29672

527

530

528

529

531

534

532

533

535

536

537

538

539

540

541

Draperies

542 Manufacture DUFOUR / 1815–1820 / Fond mat. Imp. pl. 12 coul. / 219 × 71 / UCAD 29575 / RIOUX de MAILLOU, s. d., p. 348 / Paris, 1967, n° 123

543 Manufacture DUFOUR / 1810–1812 / Fond mat. Imp. pl. 11 coul. / 197 × 53,5 / UCAD 29576 / Paris, 1967, n° 117

544 Manufacture DUFOUR / 1810–1815 / Fond mat. Imp. pl. 19 coul. / 191,5 × 53 / UCAD 29577 / CLOUZOT et FOLLOT, 1935, p. 141 / Paris, 1967, n° 115

545 Manufacture DUFOUR / 1815–1820 / Fond mat. Imp. pl. 17 coul. / 203 × 53,5 / UCAD 29578 / CLOUZOT et FOLLOT, 1935, p. 169 / Paris, 1967, n° 120

546 Manufacture DUFOUR / 1815–1820 / Fond mat. Imp. pl. 12 coul. / 217 × 63 / UCAD 29579 / Paris, 1967, n° 122

547 Manufacture DUFOUR / 1808 / Fond mat. Imp. pl. 15 coul. / 104 × 54 / UCAD 29582 / RIOUX et MAILLOU, s. d. p. 352, repr. / Paris, 1967, n° 113

548 Manufacture DUFOUR / 1810–1815 / Fond mat. Imp. pl. 14 coul. / 164 × 58 / 54 × 54 / BF 610

549 Manufacture DUFOUR / 1820–1825 / Fond mat. Imp. pl. 27 coul. / 255 × 57 / BF 645

550 Manufacture DUFOUR / 1820–1825 / Fond mat. Imp. pl. 17 coul. / 224 × 67 / BF 1437

Maquettes

551 France / 1815–1820 / Dessin original, aquarelle 28 coul. env. / 53 × 38 / UCAD HH 1907 / Paris, 1967, n° 360

552 France / 1815–1820 / Dessin original, aquarelle 17 coul. env. / 29 × 27 / UCAD HH 1911 / Paris, 1967, n° 364 a

Draperies

542 Manufacture DUFOUR / 1815–1820 / Matt ground. Block-print 12 col. / 219 × 71 / UCAD 29575 / RIOUX de MAILLOU, n. d., p. 348 / Paris, 1967, N° 123

543 Manufacture DUFOUR / 1810–1812 / Matt ground. Block-print 11 col. / 197 × 53,5 / UCAD 29576 / Paris, 1967, N° 117

544 Manufacture DUFOUR / 1810–1815 / Matt ground. Block-print 19 col. / 191,5 × 53 / UCAD 29577 / CLOUZOT et FOLLOT, 1935, p. 141 / Paris, 1967, N° 115

545 Manufacture DUFOUR / 1815–1820 / Matt ground. Block-print 17 col. / 203 × 53,5 / UCAD 29578 / CLOUZOT et FOLLOT, 1935, p. 169 / Paris, 1967, N° 120

546 Manufacture DUFOUR / 1815–1820 / Matt ground. Block-print 12 col. / 217 × 63 / UCAD 29579 / Paris, 1967, N° 122

547 Manufacture DUFOUR / 1808 / Matt ground. Block-print 15 col. / 104 × 54 / UCAD 29582 / RIOUX de MAILLOU, n. d., p. 352, repr. / Paris, 1967, N° 113

548 Manufacture DUFOUR / 1810–1815 / Matt ground. Block-print 14 col. / 164 × 58 / 54 × 54 / BF 610

549 Manufacture DUFOUR / 1820 × 1825 / Matt ground. Block-print 27 col. / 255 × 57 / BF 645

550 Manufacture DUFOUR / 1820–1825 / Matt ground. Block-print 17 col. / 224 × 67 / BF 1437

Maquettes

551 France / 1815–1820 / Original design, water-colour approx. 28 col. / 53 × 38 / UCAD HH 1907 / Paris, 1967, N° 360

552 France / 1815–1820 / Original design, water-colour approx. 17 col. / 29 × 27 / UCAD HH 1911 / Paris, 1967, N° 364 a

Draperien

542 Manufaktur DUFOUR / 1815–1820 / Matter Grund. Handdruck, 12 Farben / 219 × 71 / UCAD 29575 / RIOUX de MAILLON, o. J., S. 348 / Paris, 1967, Nr. 123

543 Manufaktur DUFOUR / 1810–1812 / Matter Grund. Handdruck, 11 Farben / 197 × 53,5 / UCAD 29576 / Paris, 1967, Nr. 117

544 Manufaktur DUFOUR / 1810–1815 / Matter Grund. Handdruck, 19 Farben / 191,5 × 53 / UCAD 29577 / CLOUZOT und FOLLOT, 1935, S. 141 / Paris, 1967, Nr. 115

545 Manufaktur DUFOUR / 1815–1820 / Matter Grund. Handdruck, 17 Farben / 203 × 53,5 / UCAD 29578 / CLOUZOT und FOLLOT, 1935, S. 169 / Paris, 1967, Nr. 120

546 Manufaktur DUFOUR / 1815–1820 / Matter Grund. Handdruck, 12 Farben / 217 × 63 / UCAD 29579 / Paris, 1967, Nr. 122

547 Manufaktur DUFOUR / 1808 / Matter Grund. Handdruck, 15 Farben / 104 × 54 / UCAD 29582 / RIOUX de MAILLON, o. J., S. 352, repr. / Paris, 1967, Nr. 113

548 Manufaktur DUFOUR / 1810–1815 / Matter Grund. Handdruck, 14 Farben / 164 × 58 / 54 × 54 / BF 610

549 Manufaktur DUFOUR / 1820–1825 / Matter Grund. Handdruck, 27 Farben / 255 × 57 / BF 645

550 Manufaktur DUFOUR / 1820–1825 / Matter Grund. Handdruck, 17 Farben / 224 × 67 / BF 1437

Entwürfe

551 Frankreich / 1815–1820 / Originalentwurf, Aquarell, ungef. 28 Farben / 53 × 38 / UCAD HH 1907 / Paris, 1967, Nr. 360

552 Frankreich / 1815–1820 / Originalentwurf, Aquarell, ungef. 17 Farben / 29 × 27 / UCAD HH 1911 / Paris, 1967, Nr. 364 a

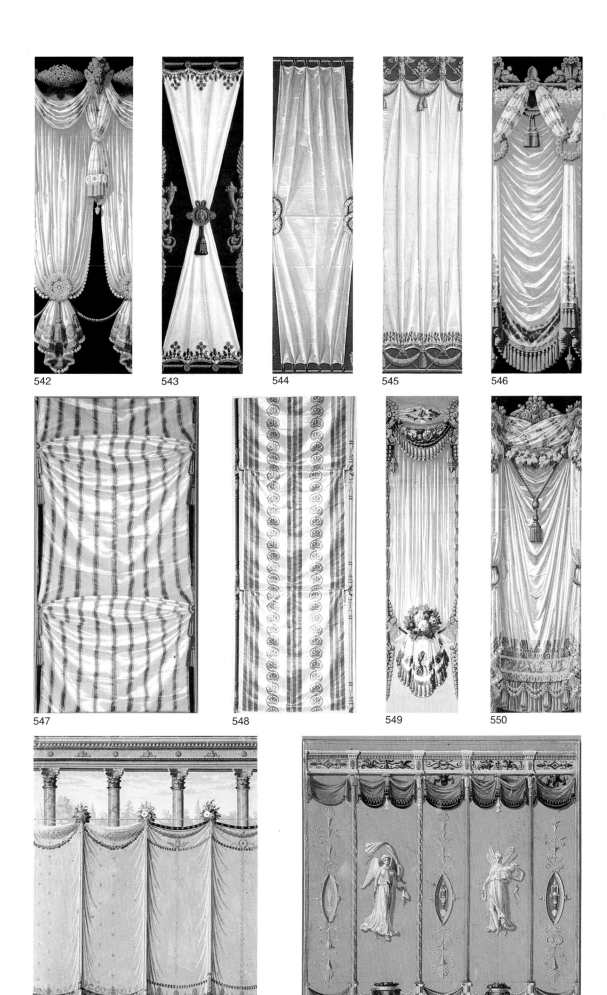

542   543   544   545   546

547   548   549   550

551   552

553 France / 1815–1820 / Dessin original, aquarelle 25 coul. env. / 45 × 45 / UCAD HH 1908 / Paris, 1967, n° 361

554 France / 1815–1820 / Dessin original, aquarelle 21 coul. env. / 38 × 26,5 / UCAD HH 1909 / Paris, 1967, n° 364 c

555 France / 1815–1820 / Dessin original, aquarelle 17 coul. env. / 32 × 50 / UCAD HH 1910 / Paris, 1967, N° 364 b

553 France / 1815–1820 / Original design, water-colour approx. 25 col. / 45 × 45 / UCAD HH 1908 / Paris, 1967, N° 361

554 France / 1815–1820 / Original design, water-colour approx. 21 col. / 38 × 26,5 / UCAD HH 1909 / Paris, 1967, N° 364 c

555 France / 1815–1820 / Original design, water-colour approx. 17 col. / 32 × 50 / UCAD HH 1910 / Paris, 1967, N° 364 b

553 Frankreich / 1815–1820 / Originalentwurf, Aquarell, ungef. 25 Farben / 45 × 45 / UCAD HH 1908 / Paris, 1967, Nr. 361

554 Frankreich / 1815–1820 / Originalentwurf, Aquarell, ungef. 21 Farben / 38 × 26,5 / UCAD HH 1909 / Paris, 1967, Nr. 364 c

555 Frankreich / 1815–1820 / Originalentwurf, Aquarell, ungef. 17 Farben / 32 × 50 / UCAD HH 1910 / Paris, 1967, Nr. 364 b

553

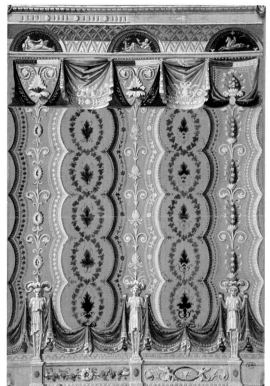

554

555

Médallons

556 France / 1840–1845 / Fond Satin. Impl. pl. 20 coul. Feuille d'or / 128 × 49 / UCAD 29671 / Paris, 1967, n° 285

557 WAGNER / 1840–1845 / Fond satin. Imp. pl. 32 coul. / 69 × 49 / UCAD 29687 B

558 France / 1840–1845 / Fond satin. Imp. pl. 41 coul. / 130 × 53 / UCAD 29676

559 WAGNER / 1845 env. / Fond mat. Imp. pl. 28 coul. Irisé / 148 × 51 / UCAD 29599 / Paris, 1967, n° 237

Figures

560 France / 1800–1810 / Fond mat. Imp. pl. 6 coul. / 56 × 33 / MISE 980 PP 806–1

561 France – Lyon ? / 1800–1810 / Fond mat. Imp. pl. 6 coul. / 142 × 65 / UCAD 12338 A / Paris, 1973, n° 337

562 France – Lyon ? / 1800–1810 / Fond mat. Imp. pl. 6 coul. / 142 × 65 / UCAD 12338 B / Paris, 1967, n° 170, Paris, 1973, n° 337

563 France – Lyon ? / 1800–1810 / Fond mat. Imp. pl. 6 coul. / 142 × 65 / UCAD 12338 C / Paris, 1973, n° 337

564 France – Lyon ? / 1800–1810 / Fond mat. Imp. pl. 6 coul. / 142 × 65 / UCAD 12338 D / Paris, 1967, n° 170, Paris, 1973, n° 337

565 Manufacture JACQUEMART et BENARD / Le Printemps / 1800–1810 / Fond mat. Imp. pl. 9 coul. / 120 × 56 / UCAD 29709 A / Paris, 1967, n° 155, Paris, 1973, n° 332

566 Manufacture JACQUEMART et BENARD / L'Eté / 1800–1810 / Fond mat. Imp. pl. 9 coul. / 120 × 56 / UCAD 29709 B / Paris, 1967, n° 155, Paris, 1973, n° 332

567 Manufacture JACQUEMART et BENARD / L'Automne / 1800–1810 / Fond mat. Imp. pl. 9 coul. / 120 × 56 / UCAD 29709 C / Paris, 1967, n° 155, Paris, 1973, n° 332

568 Manufacture JACQUEMART et BENARD / L'Hiver / 1800–1810 / Fond mat. Imp. pl. 9 coul. / 120 × 56 / UCAD 29709 D / Paris, 1967, n° 155, Paris, 1973, n° 332

Medallions

556 France / 1840–1845 / Satin ground. Block-print 20 col. Gold leaf / 128 × 49 / UCAD 29671 / Paris, 1967, N° 235

557 WAGNER / 1840–1845 / Satin ground. Block-print 32 col. / 69 × 49 / UCAD 29687 B

558 France / 1840–1845 / Satin ground. Block-print 41 col. / 130 × 53 / UCAD 29676

559 WAGNER / 1845 env. / Matt ground. Block-print 28 col. *Irisé* / 148 × 51 / UCAD 29599 / Paris, 1967, N° 237

Figures

560 France / 1800–1810 / Matt ground. Block-print 6 col. / 56 × 33 / MISE 980 PP 806–1

561 France – Lyon? / 1800–1810 / Matt ground. Block-print 6 col. / 142 × 65 / UCAD 12338 A / Paris, 1973, N° 337

562 France – Lyon? / 1800–1810 / Matt ground. Block-print 6 col. / 142 × 65 / UCAD 12338 B / Paris, 1967, N° 170, Paris, 1973, N°337

563 France – Lyon? / 1800–1810 / Matt ground. Block-print 6 col. / 142 × 65 / UCAD 12338 C / Paris, 1973, N° 337

564 France – Lyon? / 1800–1810 / Matt ground. Block-print 6 col. / 142 × 65 / UCAD 12338 D / Paris, 1967, N° 170, Paris, 1973, N°337

565 Manufacture JACQUEMART et BENARD / Le Printemps / 1800–1810 / Matt ground. Block-print 9 col. / 120 × 56 / UCAD 29709 A / Paris, 1967, N° 155, Paris, 1973, N° 332

566 Manufacture JACQUEMART et BENARD / L'Eté / 1800–1810 / Matt ground. Block-print 9 col. / 120 × 56 / UCAD 29709 B / Paris, 1967, N° 155, Paris, 1973, N° 332

567 Manufacture JACQUEMART et BENARD / L'Automne / 1800–1810 / Matt ground. Block-print 9 col. / 120 × 56 / UCAD 29709 C / Paris, 1967, N° 155, Paris, 1973, N° 332

568 Manufacture JACQUEMART et BENARD / L'Hiver / 1800–1810 / Matt ground. Block-print 9 col. / 120 × 56 / UCAD 29709 D / Paris, 1967, N° 155, Paris, 1973, N° 332

Medaillons

556 Frankreich / 1840–1845 / Satinierter Grund. Handdruck, 20 Farben. Blattgold / 128 × 49 / UCAD 29671 / Paris, 1967, Nr. 285

557 WAGNER / 1840–1845 / Satinierter Grund. Handdruck, 32 Farben / 69 × 49 / UCAD 29687 B

558 Frankreich / 1840–1845 / Satinierter Grund. Handdruck, 41 Farben / 130 × 53 / UCAD 29676

559 WAGNER / Um 1845 / Matter Grund. Handdruck, 28 Farben. Irisiert / 148 × 51 / UCAD 29599 / Paris, 1967, Nr. 237

Figuren

560 Frankreich / 1800–1810 / Matter Grund. Handdruck, 6 Farben / 56 × 33 / MISE 980 PP 806-1

561 Frankreich – Lyon ? / 1800–1810 / Matter Grund. Handdruck, 6 Farben / 142 × 65 / UCAD 12338 A / Paris, 1973, Nr. 337

562 Frankreich – Lyon ? / 1800–1810 / Matter Grund. Handdruck, 6 Farben / 142 × 65 / UCAD 12338 B / Paris, 1967, Nr. 170 – Paris, 1973, Nr. 337

563 Frankreich – Lyon ? / 1800–1810 / Matter Grund. Handdruck, 6 Farben / 142 × 65 / UCAD 12338 C / Paris, 1973, Nr. 337

564 Frankreich – Lyon ? / 1800–1810 / Matter Grund. Handdruck, 6 Farben / 142 × 65 / UCAD 12338 D / Paris, 1967, Nr. 170 – Paris, 1973, Nr. 337

565 Manufaktur JACQUEMART et BENARD / Le Printemps (Der Frühling) / 1800–1810 / Matter Grund. Handdruck, 9 Farben / 120 × 56 / UCAD 29709 A / Paris, 1967, Nr. 155 – Paris, 1973, Nr. 332

566 Manufaktur JACQUEMART et BENARD / L'Eté (Der Sommer) / 1800–1810 / Matter Grund. Handdruck, 9 Farben / 120 × 56 / UCAD 29709 B / Paris, 1967, Nr. 155 – Paris, 1973, Nr. 332

567 Manufaktur JACQUEMART et BENARD / L'Automne (Der Herbst) / 1800–1810 / Matter Grund. Handdruck, 9 Farben / 120 × 56 / UCAD 29709 C / Paris, 1967, Nr. 155 – Paris, 1973, Nr. 332

568 Manufaktur JACQUEMART et BENARD / L'Hiver (Der Winter) / 1800–1810 / Matter Grund. Handdruck, 9 Farben / 120 × 56 / UCAD 29709 D / Paris, 1967, Nr. 155 – Paris, 1973, Nr. 332

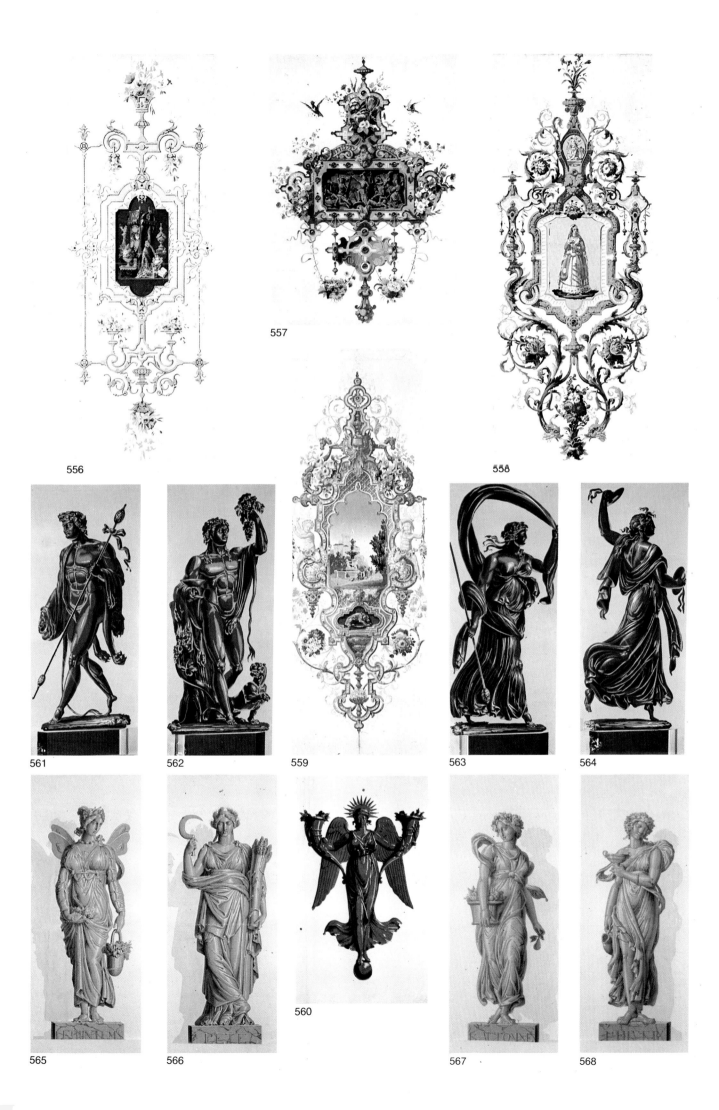

556

557

558

561 562 559 563 564

565 566 560 567 568

569 Manufacture DAUPTAIN? / 1810–1820 / Fond mat. Imp. pl. 11 coul. / 57 × 56 / UCAD HH 467 / Paris, 1967, n° 84

570 France / 1820–1830 / Fond mat. Imp. pl. 8 coul. / 54 × 90 / UCAD HH 2777

571 Manufacture MADER ? / 1825 env. / Fond mat. Imp. pl. 10 coul. / 98 × 56 / Recto manuscrit: «3451 fond gris 2, peint. d'or 4» / UCAD HH 136 / Paris, 1967, n° 172, Paris, 1973, n° 336

572 Manufacture MADER ? / 1825 env. / Fond mat. Imp. pl. 10 coul. / 93 × 56 / UCAD HH 138 / SEGUIN, 1968, p. 6 / Paris, 1967, n° 172, Paris, 1973, n° 336

573 Manufacture MADER ? / 1825 env. / Fond mat. Imp. pl. 10 coul. / 102 × 56 / UCAD HH 139 / Paris, 1967, n° 172, Paris, 1973, n° 336

574 Manufacture MADER ? / 1825 env. / Fond satin. Imp. pl. 12 coul. Poudre dorée / 100 × 56 / Recto, manuscrit: «3451 s/marbre et bronze doré 6» / UCAD HH 137 / Paris, 1967, n° 172, Paris, 1973, n° 336

575 Manufacture JACQUEMART et BENARD ? / 1820–1825 / Fond mat. Imp. pl. 9 coul. / 220 × 54 / Recto, manuscrit: «4118 les Arts. 4119 Le Commerce. 4120 L'Agriculture. 4121 L'Astronomie. Ord^re et grise 5.50 et fd d'or ou bronze ordinaire 5.50 et bronze doré 11,- et or 18,-.» «4123 gris ou ft d'or 2.50 bronze doré 4,- en or 5,- en argent 6,-» / UCAD HH 140

576 Manufacture JACQUEMART et BENARD / 1830 env. / Fond mat. Imp. pl. 7 coul. / 56 × 120 / Verso, tampon: R. J. B. / UCAD HH 132

577 France / 1830 env. / Fond mat. Imp. pl. 8 coul. / 110 × 54 / UCAD HH 133

578 France / 1830 env. / Fond mat. Imp. pl. 9 coul. Poudre dorée / 110 × 54 / UCAD HH 134

569 Manufacture DAUPTAIN? / 1810–1820 / Matt ground. Block-print 11 col. / 57 × 56 / UCAD HH 467 / Paris, 1967, N° 84

570 France / 1820–1830 / Matt ground. Block-print 8 col. / 54 × 90 / UCAD HH 2777

571 Manufacture MADER? / 1825 env. / Matt ground. Block-print 10 col. / 98 × 56 / Recto, inscribed: '3451 fond gris 2, peint. d'or 4' / UCAD HH 136 / Paris, 1967, N° 172, Paris, 1973, N° 336

572 Manufacture MADER? / 1825 env. / Matt ground. Block-print 10 col. / 93 × 56 / UCAD HH 138 / SEGUIN, 1968, p. 6 / Paris, 1967, N°172, Paris, 1973, N° 336

573 Manufacture MADER? / 1825 env. / Matt ground. Block-print 10 col. / 102 × 56 / UCAD HH 139 / Paris, 1967, N° 172, Paris, 1973, N°336

574 Manufacture MADER? / 1825 env. / Satin ground. Block-print 12 col. Gold dust / 100 × 56 / Recto, inscribed: '3451 s/marbre et bronze doré 6' / UCAD HH 137 / Paris 1967, N°172, Paris, 1973, N° 336

575 Manufacture JACQUEMART et BENARD? / 1820–1825 / Matt ground. Block-print 9 col. / 220 × 54 / Recto, inscribed: '4118 les Arts. 4119 Le Commerce. 4120 L'Agriculture. 4121 L'Astronomie. Ord^re et grise 5.50 et fd d'or ou bronze ordinaire 5.50 et bronze doré 11,– et or 18,–.' '4123 gris ou ft d'or 2.50 bronze doré 4,– en or 5,– en argent 6,–' / UCAD HH 140

576 Manufacture JACQUEMART et BENARD / 1830 env. / Matt ground. Block-print 7 col. / 56 × 120 / Verso, stamped: 'R. J. B.' / UCAD HH 132

577 France / 1830 env. / Matt ground. Block-print 8 col. / 110 × 54 / UCAD HH 133

578 France / 1830 env. / Matt ground. Block-print 9 col. Gold dust / 110 × 54 / UCAD HH 134

569 Manutaktur DAUPTAIN ? / 1810–1820 / Matter Grund. Handdruck, 11 Farben / 57 × 56 / UCAD HH 467 / Paris, 1967, Nr. 84

570 Frankreich / 1820–1830 / Matter Grund. Handdruck, 8 Farben / 54 × 90 / UCAD HH 2777

571 Manufaktur MADER ? / Um 1825 / Matter Grund. Handdruck, 10 Farben / 98 × 56 / Rückseitig beschriftet: »3451 fond gris 2, peint. d'or 4« / UCAD HH 136 / Paris, 1967, Nr. 172 – Paris, 1973, Nr. 336

572 Manufaktur MADER ? / Um 1825 / Matter Grund. Handdruck, 10 Farben / 93 × 56 / UCAD HH 138 / SEGUIN, 1968, S. 6 / Paris, 1967, Nr. 172 – Paris, 1973, Nr. 336

573 Manufaktur MADER ? / Um 1825 / Matter Grund. Handdruck, 10 Farben / 102 × 56 / UCAD HH 139 / Paris, 1967, Nr. 172 – Paris, 1973, Nr. 336

574 Manufaktur MADER ? / Um 1825 / Satinierter Grund. Handdruck, 12 Farben. Goldstaub / 100 × 56 / Vorderseite beschriftet: »3451 s/marbre et bronze doré 6« / UCAD HH 137 / Paris, 1967, Nr. 172 – Paris, 1973, Nr. 336

575 Manufaktur JACQUEMART et BENARD ? / 1820–1825 / Matter Grund. Handdruck, 9 Farben / 220 × 54 / Vorderseite beschriftet: »4118 les Arts. 4119 Le Commerce. 4120 L' Agriculture. 4121 L'Astronomie. Ord^re et grise 5.50 et fd d'or ou bronze ordinaire 5.50 et bronze doré 11,- et or 18,-« »4123 gris ou ft d'or 2.50 bronzedoré 4,- en or 5,- en argent 6,-« / UCAD HH 140

576 Manufaktur JACQUEMART et BENARD / Um 1830 / Matter Grund. Handdruck, 7 Farben / 56 × 120 / Rückseitig Stempel: »R.J.B.« / UCAD HH 132

577 Frankreich / Um 1830 / Matter Grund. Handdruck / 110 × 54 / UCAD HH 133

578 Frankreich / Um 1830 / Matter Grund. Handdruck, 9 Farben. Goldstaub / 110 × 54 / UCAD HH 134

570

571

572

569

573

574

575

576

577

578

579 Manufacture JACQUEMART et BENARD / 1830 env. / Fond mat. Imp. pl. 7 coul. / 108 × 56 / UCAD HH 135

580 Xavier MADER / Manufacture DUFOUR / Polymnie / 1830 env. / Fond mat. Imp. pl. 7 coul. / 106 × 56 / UCAD 29 712 / MAC CLEL- LAND, 1924, p. 193

581 France / 1820–1830 / Fond mat. Imp. pl. 8 coul. / 105 × 57 / UCAD 29 710 A

582 France / 1820–1830 / Fond mat. Imp. pl. 8 coul. / 105 × 57 / UCAD 29 710 B

584 France / 1820–1830 / Fond mat. Imp. pl. 8 coul. / 105 × 57 / UCAD 29 710 C

584 France / 1820–1830 / Fond mat. Imp. pl. 8 coul. / 205 × 57 / UCAD 29 710 D

585 France / «Esméralda»; Gypsy, person- nage de *Notre-Dame* de Victor Hugo / 1831 / Fond lissé. Imp. pl. 25 coul. / 200 × 54 / BF 712 / MAC CLELLAND, 1924, p. 248

586 France / 1830–1840 / Fond mat. Imp. pl. 10 coul. / 100 × 55 / UCAD HH 2778

587 France / 1830–1840 / Fond mat. Imp. pl. 10 coul. / 98 × 55 / UCAD HH 2779

588 France / 1840–1845 / Fond mat. Imp. pl. 11 coul. / 112 × 50 / BF 434

589 Jean BROC / Manufacture RIOTTOT et PACON / 1845–1850 / Fond mat. Imp. pl. 30 coul. / 177 × 54 / Recto, tampon: «Jules Riot- tot et Pacon». Verso, manuscrit «Broc» / BF 485

579 Manufacture JACQUEMART et BENARD / 1830 env. / Matt ground. Block-print 7 col. / 108 × 56 / UCAD HH 135

580 Xavier MADER / Manufacture DUFOUR / Polymnie / 1830 env. / Matt ground. Block- print 7 col. / 106 × 56 / UCAD 29 712 / MAC CLELLAND, 1924, p. 193

581 France / 1820 –1830 / Matt ground. Block-print 8 col. / 105 × 57 / UCAD 29 710 A

582 France / 1820–1830 / Matt ground. Block-print 8 col. / 105 × 57 / UCAD 29 710 B

583 France / 1820–1830 / Matt ground. Block-print 8 col. / 105 × 57 / UCAD 29 710 C

584 France / 1820–1830 / Matt ground. Block-print 8 col. / 205 × 57 / UCAD 29 710 D

585 France / 'Esméralda'; Gypsy, a character in *Notre-Dame* by Victor Hugo / 1831 / Smooth ground. Block-print 25 col. / 200 × 54 / BF 712 / MAC CLELLAND, 1924, p. 248

586 France / 1830–1840 / Matt ground. Block-print 10 col. / 100 × 55 / UCAD HH 2778

587 France / 1830–1840 / Matt ground. Block-print 10 col. / 98 × 55 / UCAD HH 2779

588 France / 1840–1845 / Matt ground. Block-print 11 col. / 112 × 50 / BF 434

589 Jean BROC / Manufacture RIOTTOT et PACON / 1845–1850 / Matt ground. Block- print 30 col. / 177 × 54 / Recto, stamped: 'Jules Riottot et Pacon'. / Verso, inscribed: 'Broc' / BF 485

579 Manufaktur JACQUEMART et BENARD / Um 1830 / Matter Grund. Handdruck, 7 Farben / 108 × 56 / UCAD HH 135

580 Xavier MADER / Manufaktur DUFOUR / Polymnie (Die Muse Polyhymnia) / Um 1830 / Matter Grund. Handdruck, 7 Farben / 106 × 56 / UCAD 29 712 / MAC CLELLAND, 1924, S. 193

581 Frankreich / 1820–1830 / Matter Grund. Handdruck, 8 Farben / 105 × 57 / UCAD 29710 A

582 Frankreich / 1820–1830 / Matter Grund. Handdruck, 8 Farben / 105 × 57 / UCAD 29710 B

583 Frankreich / 1820–1830 / Matter Grund. Handdruck, 8 Farben / 105 × 57 / UCAD 29710 C

584 Frankreich / 1820–1830 / Matter Grund. Handdruck, 8 Farben / 205 × 57 / UCAD 29710 D

585 Frankreich / »Esméralda« (Zigeunerin aus »Notre Dame« von Victor Hugo) / 1831 / Geglätteter Grund. Handdruck, 25 Farben / 200 × 54 / BF 712 / MAC CLELLAND, 1924, S. 248

586 Frankreich / 1830–1840 / Matter Grund. Handdruck, 10 Farben / 100 × 55 / UCAD HH 2778

587 Frankreich / 1830–1840 / Matter Grund. Handdruck, 10 Farben / 98 × 55 / UCAD HH 2779

588 Frankreich / 1840–1845 / Matter Grund. Handdruck, 11 Farben / 112 × 50 / BF 434

589 Jean BROC / Manufaktur RIOTTOT et PACON / 1845–1850 / Matter Grund. Hand- druck, 30 Farben / 117 × 54 / Vorderseite Stempel: »Jules Riottot et Pacon«. Rückseitig beschriftet: »Broc« / BF 485

585

579

580

581

582

583

584

588

586

589

587

Dessus de porte – devants de cheminée

590 Manufacture ZUBER / 1803 / Fond mat. Imp. pl. 24 coul. / 64 × 76 / Verso: «N° 609 Dessus de porte» MISE S. 547 P 1

591 France / 1800–1805 / Fond mat. Imp. pl. 22 coul. / 69 × 69 / MISE S. 547 P 2

592 France / 1805–1810 / Fond mat. Imp. pl. 15 coul. / 68 × 102 / UCAD 29766

593 France / 1805–1810 / Fond mat. Imp. pl. 12 coul. / 70 × 87 / UCAD 29765 A

594 France / 1805–1810 / Fond mat. Imp. pl. 12 coul. / 70 × 99 / UCAD 29765 B

595 France / 1800–1810 / Fond mat. Imp. pl. 18 coul. / 88 × 64 / MISE S. 547 P 8

596 France / 1810 env. / Fond mat. Imp. pl. 25 coul. / 72 × 98 / MISE S. 547 P 6

597 France / 1815–1830 / Fond mat. Imp. pl. 50 coul. / 70 × 95 / MISE S. 597 P 3

598 Manufacture Amable LEROY / 1827 / Fond satin. Imp. pl. 34 coul. / 68 × 96 / UCAD 29587 A / Paris, 1967, n° 134

599 Manufacture Amable LEROY / 1827 / Fond satin. Imp. pl. 34 coul. / 70 × 96 / UCAD 29587 B / Paris, 1967, n° 134

600 Manufacture ZUBER / Oiseau chinois / 1834 / Fond mat. Imp. pl. 20 coul. Irisés / 70 × 75 / MISE S 547 P 35

Over-doors and Chimney-screens

590 Manufacture ZUBER / 1803 / Matt ground. Block-print 24 col. / 64 × 76 / Verso: 'N° 609 Dessus de porte' / MISE S. 547 P 1

591 France / 1800–1805 / Matt ground. Block-print 22 col. / 69 × 69 / MISE S. 547 P 2

592 France / 1805–1810 / Matt ground. Block-print 15 col. / 68 × 102 / UCAD 29766

593 France / 1805–1810 / Matt ground. Block-print 12 col. / 70 × 87 / UCAD 29765 A

594 France / 1805–1810 / Matt ground. Block-print 12 col. / 70 × 99 / UCAD 29765 B

595 France / 1800–1810 / Matt ground. Block-print 18 col. / 88 × 64 / MISE S. 547 P 8

596 France / 1810 env. / Matt ground. Block-print 25 col. / 72 × 98 / MISE S. 547 P 6

597 France / 1815–1830 / Matt ground. Block-print 50 col. / 70 × 95 / MISE S. 597 P 3

598 Manufacture Amable LEROY / 1827 / Satin ground. Block-print 34 col. / 68 × 96 / UCAD 29587 A / Paris, 1967, N° 134

599 Manufacture Amable LEROY / 1827 / Satin ground. Block-print 34 col. / 70 × 96 / UCAD 29587 B / Paris, 1967, N° 134

600 Manufacture ZUBER / Chinese bird / 1834 / Matt ground. Block-print 20 col. *Irisé* / 70 × 75 / MISE S 547 P 35

Supraporten – Kaminschirme

590 Manufaktur ZUBER / 1803 / Matter Grund. Handdruck, 24 Farben / 64 × 76 / Rückseitig beschriftet: »N° 609 Dessus de porte« / MISE S. 547 P 1

591 Frankreich / 1800–1805 / Matter Grund. Handdruck, 22 Farben / 69 × 69 / MISE S. 547 P 2

592 Frankreich / 1805–1810 / Matter Grund. Handdruck, 15 Farben / 68 × 102 / UCAD 29766

593 Frankreich / 1805–1810 / Matter Grund. Handdruck, 12 Farben / 70 × 87 / UCAD 29765 A

594 Frankreich / 1805–1810 / Matter Grund. Handdruck, 12 Farben / 70 × 99 / UCAD 29765 B

595 Frankreich / 1800–1810 / Matter Grund. Handdruck, 18 Farben / 88 × 64 / MISE S. 547 P 8

596 Frankreich / Um 1810 / Matter Grund. Handdruck, 25 Farben / 72 × 98 / MISE S. 547 P 6

597 Frankreich / 1815–1830 / Matter Grund. Handdruck, 50 Farben / 70 × 95 / MISE S. 597 P 3

598 Manufaktur Amable LEROY / 1827 / Satinierter Grund. Handdruck, 34 Farben / 68 × 96 / UCAD 29587 A / Paris, 1967, Nr. 134

599 Manufaktur Amable LEROY / 1827 / Satinierter Grund. Handdruck, 34 Farben / 70 × 96 / UCAD 29587 B / Paris, 1967, Nr. 134

600 Manufaktur ZUBER / Oiseau chinois (Chinesischer Vogel) / 1834 / Matter Grund. Handdruck, 20 Farben. Irisiert / 70 × 75 / MISE S. 547 P 35

590

592

593

594

591

595

600

596

597

598

599

Index
Indexes
Register

Manufactures
Factories
Manufakturen

Dessinateurs ou graveurs
Designers or Engravers
Entwerfer und Gravierer

Impression et reliure / Printed and bound by / Gesamtherstellung	Druckerei Georg Appl, Wemding
Photolitho	eurocrom 4, Treviso
Maquette et fabrication / Design and production / Gestaltung und Produktion	Verlagsbüro Walter Lachenmann, Buchendorf
Conseiller artistique	Léon Larfillon

Printed and bound in the Federal Republic of Germany